MAYAN VOICES FOR HUMAN RIGHTS

BOOK NINE

Louann Atkins Temple Women & Culture Series

MAYAN VOICES FOR
Human Rights

Displaced Catholics
in Highland Chiapas

CHRISTINE KOVIC

University of Texas Press ⟡ Austin

Chapter 3 contains material from "Mayan Catholics in Chiapas, Mexico: Practicing Faith on Their Own Terms," by Christine Kovic, in *Resurgent Voices in Latin America: Indigenous Peoples, Political Mobilization, and Religious Change,* edited by Edward L. Cleary and Timothy J. Steigenga, copyright 2004. Printed with permission of Rutgers University Press.

The segment "Gender Relations and the Word of God" in Chapter 7 contains material from "Demanding Their Dignity as Daughters of God: Catholic Women and Human Rights," in *Women of Chiapas: Making History in Times of Struggle and Hope,* edited by Christine Eber and Christine Kovic, copyright 2003. Published with permission of Routledge Press.

Requests for permission to reproduce material from this work should be sent to Permissions, University of Texas Press, P.O. Box 7819, Austin, TX 78713-7819.

⊗ The paper used in this book meets the minimum requirements of ANSI/NISO Z39.48-1992 (R1997) (Permanence of Paper).

Library of Congress
Cataloging-in-Publication Data

Kovic, Christine Marie.
  Mayan voices for human rights : displaced Catholics in highland Chiapas / by Christine Kovic. — 1st ed.
    p.   cm. — (Louann Atkins Temple women & culture series ; bk. 9)
  Includes bibliographical references and index.
    ISBN 0-292-70620-0 ((cl.) : alk. paper) — ISBN 0-292-70640-5 ((pbk.) : alk. paper)

  1. Mayas—Mexico—Chiapas—Religion. 2. Mayas—Civil rights—Mexico—Chiapas. 3. Mayas—Mexico—Chiapas—Social conditions. 4. Indian Catholics—Mexico—Chiapas—Social conditions. 5. Human rights—Religious aspects—Catholic Church. 6. Church and social problems—Mexico—Chiapas—Catholic Church. 7. Catholics—Mexico—Chiapas—Political activity. I. Title. II. Series.

F1435.3.R3K68   2005
323.1197′4207275—dc22

2004013286

Contents

Acknowledgments

More people than I can name supported me in the ten years that I have researched and written this book. In Mexico and the United States, friends, family, and colleagues have shared their stories, knowledge, enthusiasm, and encouragement and made this book possible—many thanks to all.

My most profound debt is to the indigenous Catholics of a colonia of San Cristóbal de Las Casas, Chiapas, who shared their stories of struggle and hope. They gave hours of their time to talk with me, welcomed me into their homes, answered my questions, encouraged me to attend religious celebrations, and carefully explained their experiences, wanting to make sure I understood their lives. *Batzi colavalik* (Thank you very much).

In addition, many friends and colleagues in Chiapas supported this project in myriad ways. Thanks to the members of the Fray Bartolomé de Las Casas Center for Human Rights, especially to Bishop Samuel Ruiz García, Pablo Romo, and Patricia Gómez, and the many pastoral workers of the Diocese of San Cristóbal who generously shared their time and experience. Many friends shared conversation and support through the good and bad of living in Chiapas during a time of intense political conflict: thanks to the Castañeda Guthreau, Méndez Medina, and Ojeda Santana families. The libraries and librarians of the Instituto de Asesoría Antropológica para la Región Maya (INAREMAC) and the Instituto de Estudios Indígenas provided assistance with documents and reference materials. Xalik Guzmán translated and transcribed interviews from Tzotzil to Spanish.

Many thanks to those who read chapters or the entire manuscript and provided valuable feedback: Federico Anaya, Francisco Argüelles, Ruth Chojnacki, Jane Collier, Christine Eber, Douglas Holmes, Susan Fitzpatrick Behrens, Charlene Floyd, Frank Reynolds, Michael Rolland, Jan Rus, Diane Rus, and Jeanne Simonelli. Patricia Seed read the entire manuscript at a critical moment and offered encouragement and suggestions. Many thanks to June Nash for encouraging me to go to Chiapas in the first place and for all her support throughout the years. At the Graduate Center of the City University of New

York, I benefited from the advice and suggestions of Delmos Jones and Jane Schneider in the early stages of this project. A Rockefeller Fellowship on Religion in the Americas at the University of Florida, Gainesville, gave me the time and space to complete much of the manuscript. Thanks to Philip Williams, Manuel Vásquez, Anna Peterson, and Milagros Peña for creating a wonderful work environment.

I am grateful for the support of my colleagues at the University of Houston–Clear Lake and the University of Houston. Lori Nolen deserves special mention for her assistance with the maps in the book and much more. Christine Eber and Gary Gossen offered valuable suggestions for revision in their detailed reviews of the book. I have also benefited from the tireless assistance of Theresa May and Allison Faust at the University of Texas Press.

Thanks to my family for their support and to my husband, Francisco Argüelles, for his love and encouragement and for making me laugh.

The Chiapas Photography Project (Archivo Fotográfico Indígena, or AFI) generously granted permission to reprint the photos illustrating this book. The AFI was created in 1996 as "an artistic project by and for indigenous photographers in Chiapas" (http://chiapasphoto.org). The photography collection at AFI contains approximately 75,000 images created by more than 200 Mayan photographers who are documenting their lives and communities and expressing themselves on their own terms. The photos have been published in numerous books and exhibited in Mexico, the United States, and Europe. The AFI works in collaboration with the Centro de Investigaciones y Estudios Superiores en Antropología Social, CIESAS Sureste (Southeastern Center for Research and Advanced Studies in Social Anthropology) in San Cristóbal de Las Casas, and was initiated by Carlota Duarte.

Nine photos from the AFI illustrate this book. Together, the photos provide a wonderful visual essay on the lives of Chamulas living in San Cristóbal. Some of the photos are linked to events described in the chapters that follow them. Xunka' López Díaz and Juana López López, two women from Chamula, are photographers of eight photos originally produced in color. Their photos document life in San Cristóbal de Las Casas, such as those of a girl selling belts in the streets, a rainbow above homes in a colonia on the edge of the city, and a Presbyterian church. Genaro Sántiz Gómez is the photographer of Figure 4.1, a traditional fiesta in front of a church in Chamula. All photo captions were written by the photographers and appear in English, Spanish, and Tzotzil.

MAYAN VOICES FOR HUMAN RIGHTS

Photo and caption by Xunka' López Díaz, 2000
My little sister Cristina is selling belts on the streets of San Cristóbal.
Mi hermanita Cristina está vendiendo cinturones en las calles de San Cristóbal.
Li jmuk Ristinae tey ta sye' chukiletik ta soral be yu'un Jobel.

1

Introduction

CONSIDER TWO SCENES:

March 26, 1995, San Cristóbal de Las Casas, Chiapas, Mexico. Thousands of indigenous people and mestizos walked in a pilgrimage to announce their commitment to building peace with justice and dignity in Chiapas. Walking through the narrow streets of the colonial city, the pilgrims carried white lilies, clay bowls of incense, banners bearing the image of the Virgin of Guadalupe, and signs in support of Catholic Bishop Samuel Ruiz García. Several groups of musicians played traditional wooden instruments, and the pilgrims shouted "Viva la Virgen de Guadalupe" at the end of each song. Some 20,000 people from hundreds of villages had traveled to this mestizo-dominated city to walk together in the pilgrimage. Most of the indigenous women and many of the men wore the traditional dress of their communities, with the sharp contrast in the colors of their clothing separating one group from the next.

Pueblo Creyente (People of Faith) organized the pilgrimage. This grass-roots organization started by Catholics has been successful in uniting peasants from diverse ethnic groups, political organizations, and regions of Chiapas. The vast majority of the pilgrims were Catholic, although some Protestants also participated.

The pilgrims walked to demand that their human rights be respected, to show their support for the work of Bishop Ruiz, and to demonstrate their strength in numbers. They denounced the dramatic militarization of their communities and human rights violations such as arbitrary arrest, interrogation, and torture that accompanied the military presence. The pilgrims also demanded respect for economic and social rights, in their words, the right to a dignified life. As explained in a Pueblo Creyente press release: "As children of Mary, we continue working so that peace with justice and dignity comes to our pueblos today. We do not want this dirty war. We want to live as the words of Jesus say, 'To have life, and have it abundantly' (John 10:10)."[1]

July 2, 1994. San Juan Chamula. A very different demonstration took place in the town center of this indigenous municipality just six weeks before the state and national elections.[2] Some 5,000 Tzotzil (Maya) men and women in traditional dress gathered in the plaza to welcome Eduardo Robledo Rincón, the gubernatorial candidate of the Institutional Revolutionary Party, or PRI, Mexico's ruling party from 1929 to 2000. Robledo, a mestizo dressed in a *chuj,* the wool poncho used by Chamulan men, began his speech with a few words in Tzotzil and presented his plan for economic development in the municipality. Images of Robledo and the PRI's presidential candidate, Ernesto Zedillo, adorned the town's light posts.

San Juan Chamula, located a few miles north of San Cristóbal, is often used as a showcase of indigenous culture. Two of the most elaborate festivals in the highlands are Chamula's Carnival and Day of San Juan (St. John). PRI politicians commonly visit Chamula during election campaigns, put on traditional indigenous clothing, and are handed a walking stick that symbolizes traditional power. During Robledo's visit, a group of Chamulan women succinctly expressed the corporate politics of the PRI in declaring that "All those of San Juan Chamula will vote for the PRI" and that they needed mills, markets, and support for agrarian production (*La Jornada,* July 3, 1994). In late August 1994, amid widespread charges of electoral fraud, Robledo was declared governor of Chiapas.

A group of pilgrims supporting the work of Bishop Ruiz and denouncing human rights abuses committed by the government, and a group of Chamulas supporting the PRI—both groups struggle for access to political and economic resources, although they have chosen distinct paths of action. The Pueblo Creyente pilgrims criticize the government's human rights violations and its "dirty war," while the Chamulas welcoming Eduardo Robledo have allied themselves with the PRI to receive benefits. The pilgrims view Catholicism and their alliance with the Diocese of San Cristóbal as central to their struggle for human rights, broadly defined as the right to a dignified life. The Chamulas who support the PRI do so as a means to simultaneously gain material resources and to limit outside intervention in their local affairs.

The events are two of many forms of indigenous political activism in contemporary Chiapas. The most visible form of rebellion is the Ejército Zapatista de Liberación Nacional, EZLN (Zapatista Army of National Liberation), composed primarily of Tzeltal, Tzotzil, Ch'ol, and Tojolabal Mayas. Yet indigenous people have participated in many other types of political groups, including peasant organizations, women's groups, and faith-based movements such as Pueblo Creyente through which they work to defend and promote their human rights.

This book examines the ways Mayan Catholics of highland Chiapas define and defend their human rights. It focuses on Tzotzil-speaking Mayas who live in "Guadalupe," the name I have given to a *colonia* (a neighborhood or unregulated urban settlement) on the edge of the city of San Cristóbal de Las Casas. The Catholic residents of Guadalupe have been exiled, in many cases violently, from their native municipality of San Juan Chamula. Through their stories of exile and conversion to Catholicism, I explore how they conceptualize human rights and how they have struggled to create a new community in a semi-urban area.

The text examines the defense of human rights alongside their abuse. It describes structural constraints such as poverty and racism that affect indigenous peoples as well as the ways Mayan Catholics, even in extraordinarily difficult situations, work to improve their own lives and their communities. Indigenous people's efforts to defend human rights are at once a political struggle—carried out in marches, sit-ins, and other forms of protest—and an everyday struggle to live a dignified life. The story of the Catholics of Guadalupe is placed within the broader context of the pastoral project of the progressive Catholic Diocese of San Cristóbal de Las Casas. I explore the impacts the diocesan project has had on indigenous awareness of human rights and, in turn, how indigenous views forced the Church to reconsider its mission.

The book differs from most scholarship on human rights in that it explores how ordinary people—in this case impoverished Mayas, as opposed to lawyers, intellectuals, and nongovernmental organizations, among others—define and defend their rights. Human rights, a global concept codified by the United Nations and other groups, takes on new significance in the hands of Mayan Catholics. Most notable are (a) the emphasis on economic and social rights, rights often considered secondary in the West; (b) a critique of national and global inequalities and a demand for structural change; (c) a demand for dignity and equality that is justified in religious terms; and (d) the inclusion of community obligations or reciprocal responsibilities as rights. In this ethnography I attempt to humanize the concept of rights by exploring how indigenous peoples conceptualize rights and how rights are mediated by economics, religion, politics, and indigenous traditions.

Political and Economic Transformations in Highland Chiapas

The Mayan Catholics of Guadalupe are a small group of the thousands of indigenous people who have been exiled from highland communities, primarily San Juan Chamula, in the past three decades. The term *los expulsados* (the expelled) refers to those who have been forced to leave their communities of origin. Expulsion began in the 1970s, when traditional Chamulan authorities led the move against those who challenged their power, expelling dissidents from their homes and land. Although the expulsion of 20,000 indigenous people during the past thirty years constitutes one of the most significant social and political problems in Chiapas, the consistent response of state and federal authorities has been to minimize it as a religious and cultural conflict. Yet the reasons behind expulsion are linked to the dramatic economic and political changes in highland Chiapas in past decades, which resulted in accelerated pressure for emigration from Chamula. This section presents an overview of these changes as a means to contextualize expulsion.[3]

Although highland communities never were isolated from outside political and economic influences, in the 1960s scholars depicted them as self-contained units with their own civil and religious governments. Describing his work in the highlands, Frank Cancian (1992:1) states, "When I first went to Zinacantán in 1960, I found a tight-knit community of peasant corn farmers. Zinacanteco men dressed in a distinctive costume that set them apart from their neighbors, and almost all of them were dedicated to the ceremonial life that defined the boundaries of their community. For the most part, they shut out the world around them and concentrated on each other."

In spite of their seeming isolation, indigenous communities were inextricably linked to broader political and economic structures well before the 1960s. Indigenous people began participating in migratory wage labor outside their own communities by the late 1800s. Indeed, the state government imposed several types of taxes on indigenous peoples in order ensure a steady supply of labor for nonindigenous Ladino-run commercial agriculture (Rus and Collier 2003:36). Many indigenous migrants worked as seasonal contract laborers on *fincas,* or plantations, that produced coffee, bananas, and other crops. Yet these seasonal migrants remained tied to their communities of origin, the center of cultural and social life, where they cultivated cornfields.

Unequal land distribution, historic land dispossession, and demographic pressure in the highlands forced significant numbers of families to work for wages to supplement what they produced on their own land. By the 1970s in Chamula, the highland municipality with the highest population density, most

Map of highland Chiapas
Adapted from Eber (1995)

men worked part of the year outside their community to survive. A demographic study of several Chamulan hamlets in the 1970s revealed that 77 percent of heads of household relied on wage labor or sharecropping outside of the municipality, since the size or quality of their land was insufficient to meet family consumption needs (Wasserstrom 1977).

Chiapas's agrarian sector entered a period of crisis in the late 1970s and 1980s, challenging the already precarious survival strategies of highland families. In response to the oil boom, inflation, and peso devaluation of 1976, the federal government cut its guaranteed price for corn (Rus and Collier 2003: 40–41). To keep their land profitable, large landowners of Chiapas's Grijalva Valley began to move from agriculture to cattle production. This displaced large numbers of agricultural sharecroppers and day laborers, as cattle ranching required minimum labor input.[4]

Many of these displaced agricultural workers found employment in a number of new government projects in the 1970s and early 1980s. With the oil boom, Mexico financed oil refineries, dams, roads, bridges, and other projects. Zinacantecos and residents of other highland municipalities found work as masons, construction laborers, and merchants from 1976 to 1982 due to the dramatic increase in government spending in the region (Cancian 1992).

The boom in government projects and corresponding jobs that were created ended with the economic crisis of 1982. Soon after the crash in world petroleum prices, Mexico declared that it could no longer pay its large foreign debt. The International Monetary Fund and the United States provided bailout loans on the condition that Mexico would adopt structural adjustment measures. These measures, begun under the presidency of Miguel de la Madrid (1982–1988), included dramatically cutting public spending, devaluing the currency, privatizing state enterprises, abolishing barriers to foreign investment, and setting salary caps. The economic changes had severe impacts on highland communities of Chiapas (Collier 1994; Harvey 1994). Cuts in credits and subsidies for rural producers made it increasingly difficult for poor campesinos to continue farming.[5] Analyzing census data from the Chamulan hamlet of K'at'ixtik, anthropologist Diane Rus (1990) found that just 5 percent of families were able to make a living from their own cornfields in 1977, and the percentage had declined even further by 1988.

As highland residents searched for work on fincas as they had done for decades, they found themselves competing with thousands of Guatemalan refugees fleeing the violence of the civil war. To make matters worse, in 1989 world coffee prices collapsed, causing many fincas to stop production altogether. Peasants who had cultivated coffee in small quantities as a cash crop experienced a drop in income.

Land scarcity in the highlands exacerbated the economic crisis. The population of highland communities increased significantly and in some cases more than doubled between 1970 and 1990, placing tremendous pressure on land. This growth took place even as thousands of people were emigrating from the highlands to the federally owned land in the Lacandon jungle under the encouragement of President Echeverría's administration (1970–1976). Some 5,000 Chamulas migrated to the Lacandon jungle and formed new communities such as Nuevo San Juan Chamula (Rus and Collier 2003). The increased use of rainforest for cattle ranching and oil exploration made migration a less viable option in the 1980s and 1990s (Ascencio Franco and Leyva Solano 1992).

In 1992, continuing with the structural adjustment policies of his predecessor, President Carlos Salinas de Gortari reformed Article 27 of the Mexican Constitution, declaring an end to agrarian reform and allowing the once-inalienable *ejidos* (communal lands) to be bought and sold. The reform made it possible to privatize ejidal lands and set the stage for the 1994 North American Free Trade Agreement between Mexico, the United States, and Canada. The continued implementation of structural adjustment policies hurt peasant farmers and favored large-scale agribusiness (Collier 1994; Harvey 1998; Nash and Kovic 1996).

With the economic crisis in Chiapas, the traditional way of organizing politics began to collapse. From the 1930s to the 1960s, communities were linked to the state and federal government through the corporate model put in place during the postrevolutionary presidency of Lázaro Cárdenas (1934–1940). In exchange for land (or even the promise of land), credit, subsidies, and other government benefits, peasants in Chiapas and other regions of Mexico were expected to ally themselves with the state party and support it in elections. At the municipal level, small groups of indigenous leaders called *caciques* monopolized political power and served as mediators between the government and their communities (Rus 1994). These leaders were supported by the state. Municipal leaders ensured that communities delivered votes to the state party, and the leaders controlled access to government resources.

Although there was always resistance to this corporatist model, overall the system held together in highland Chiapas as long as the state and federal government continued to provide material resources. With significant decline in government support for the agrarian sector beginning in the mid-1970s, the power of the PRI, which for decades had been the ruling party in the highlands, began to crumble, although many would continue to affiliate with the PRI to gain access to resources as well as political benefits.

In the context of this crisis, highland residents searched for new ways to survive, some forming cooperatives and some entering into political alliances with opposition parties, peasant organizations, and religious groups. Economic crisis and political dissent went hand in hand. For example, in many communities indigenous women intensified production of artisan goods for sale and engaged in other income-generating activities to help support their families (Eber and Rosenbaum 1993; Nash 1993; Rus 1990). Women joined artisan cooperatives in order to improve access to markets and credits for their goods. Through participation in independent cooperatives many indigenous women became involved in political organizing (Castro Apreza 2003; Eber and Kovic 2003:5–6; Gómez Monte and Rus 1990).

Opposition to political and economic oppression grew throughout Chiapas in the 1970s and especially in the 1980s. A number of new organizations emerged with demands for land, wage increases for rural day laborers, higher prices for crops, and respect for human rights. Even as they were met with government repression, these groups offered an alternative to the PRI politics that had dominated the state for decades. Particularly important to the formation of these independent organizations was the work of the Catholic Diocese of San Cristóbal de Las Casas. Beginning in the 1970s, Samuel Ruiz García (bishop of the diocese from 1960 to 2000) and pastoral workers committed themselves to constructing a church that would defend the dignity of the poor. The training of indigenous catechists who took on social and political roles in their communities that extended well beyond preparing people to receive sacraments was an imperative move in respecting communities' ability to create their own path to liberation. By 1985 there were more than 6,000 catechists in the diocese (Floyd 1997). In their alliance with the Catholic Church, indigenous people gained concrete skills (from literacy to organizing), a language that justified their ongoing struggle for liberation, and a base for the development of regional networks. These Catholics describe themselves as followers of the Word of God and differentiate themselves from Protestants and from Traditionalists (those following a folk Catholicism that incorporates Mayan beliefs). The term "Word of God" refers to reading and discussion of the Bible, as well as to participation in diocesan activities such as meetings, workshops, and other events. Word of God Catholics form part of the organizational and decision-making structure of the diocese.

At the same time that many indigenous people affiliated with the Catholic Diocese of San Cristóbal, others converted to Protestantism, with the Presbyterian and Pentecostal denominations attracting the largest number of new converts. According to government census data, the percentage of Protestants in Chiapas increased dramatically from 1970 to 2000, from less than 5 percent to more than 21 percent. Like Word of God Catholics, many Protestants opposed traditional leadership in highland communities. Indigenous Catholics and Protestants commonly organized against alcohol abuse, and many women joined together to prohibit the sale of alcohol in their communities.

In order to make a living, thousands of indigenous people migrated to urban areas within and beyond Chiapas. Rus and Collier (2003:46) estimate that as many as 100,000 indigenous peoples of the highlands moved to Chiapas's cities in the 1980s and 1990s. In San Cristóbal indigenous people established dozens of colonias on the mountains surrounding the city. Traveling farther, some migrated to Mexico City, Cancún, and Villahermosa and even to the United States in search of temporary wage labor.[6]

In San Cristóbal indigenous people from the highlands began to identify with religious and political organizations oriented beyond the local community as they struggled to control geographic, political, and economic space. For example, the new urban residents drove taxis, ran for political office, controlled the street market, and attended small Catholic and Protestant churches where religious services were conducted in their native languages. These activities are evidence of the rise of a new indigenous leadership that is fighting for rights and opposes the power of traditional caciques (Cruz Burguete and Robledo 1998).

On January 1, 1994, the day the North American Free Trade Agreement (NAFTA) went into effect, the EZLN took over seven towns in Chiapas and demanded democracy, social justice, and an end to the hundreds of years of exploitation of indigenous peoples and peasants. The Zapatista rebellion followed previous protests in Chiapas in its opposition to the corporatist politics and corruption of PRI and in its critique of neoliberal reforms, especially NAFTA, which were described as a "death sentence" for Mexico's indigenous peoples. Zapatista sympathizers include Protestants, Word of God Catholics, and to a lesser extent, Traditionalists, demonstrating that political alliances can be formed across diverse religious groups.

In San Juan Chamula, community of origin for the Catholics of Guadalupe, political conflict intensified in the 1970s as a new group of young leaders challenged the power of traditional authorities or caciques. The political and religious aspects of the conflict were closely linked. Anthropologists have long recognized that the politics of indigenous communities have traditionally been contained within local civil-religious hierarchies and that political-economic life is necessarily linked with religious practice among the Maya. Caciques commonly define themselves as Traditionalists, that is, they combine Mayan beliefs and customs with Catholicism, and their religious life revolves around prayer, saints' fiestas, and pilgrimages to sacred sites. The new leaders joined opposition parties or independent organizations and unsuccessfully ran their own candidates against the caciques in local elections of the 1970s. Many of these new leaders affiliated with Protestant or Catholic churches for support in challenging the political and economic power of traditional leaders. The converts further challenged the caciques' authority by denouncing their wealth and refusing to purchase alcohol sold for profit by the leaders themselves.

Beginning in the 1970s, caciques began to expel these dissidents for challenging their political, economic, and religious power. In some cases, especially in the early years, expulsion was accompanied by violence. Dissidents were beaten or jailed, their homes burned, their crops destroyed. By the year 2000, more than 20,000 people had been expelled.[7] Yet state and federal authorities did not act to stop the expulsions. For the PRI, interference meant risking the loss of thousands of votes of support in state and federal elections. However, media and popular accounts of expulsion often fail to place the events in their historical context. Such accounts instead describe indigenous peoples as inherently violent and intolerant and blame them for expulsion.

From the time the expulsions began, Protestants, Catholics, and even Traditionalists have been forced to leave their native communities, demonstrating that political and economic factors underlie expulsion. My research focuses on Word of God Catholics because they have often been overlooked by scholars, journalists, and government officials who emphasize Protestant conversion as a key cause of expulsion. Time and again expulsion has been described exclusively as a religious conflict between Catholics and evangelical Protestants. The emphasis on religious conflict understates the connection between religious and political power. This explanation fails to recognize the political and economic roots of expulsion and fails to distinguish between the Traditionalists of Chamula and the Word of God Catholics who affiliate with the Diocese of San Cristóbal de Las Casas. The focus on Mayan Catholics also allows for examination of the ways Mayas are appropriating two global institutions—human rights and Catholicism—to use as tools of resistance.

Progressive Catholicism in Chiapas

Mayan Catholics of Guadalupe along with other Word of God Catholics in Chiapas link their struggle for human rights to their faith. The Catholics of Guadalupe constantly made biblical references in explaining their struggle for a dignified life. Many explained, "We are all children of God, and we are all equal." They further noted that mestizos and indigenous peoples, men and women, and rich and poor are all equal in the eyes of God. This seemingly simple statement affirms the rightful equality of all humans and carries a critique of the status quo in Chiapas, where a small group of mestizos have held political and economic power for decades. In the same vein, members of Pueblo Creyente proclaim that the evengelization of the Catholic Diocese of San Cristóbal has been instrumental to their struggle for a dignified life. During the pilgrimage of March 1995 described at the beginning of this chapter, members of Pueblo Creyente noted that "in this long diocesan process, the Word of God has taught us and helped us to understand that the God of the poor walks at our side daily."

The present study of Mayan Catholics in Chiapas is a small chapter in a larger story of religious change taking place in recent decades in Latin America. Key to these changes were the historic meetings of the Second Vatican Council (1962–1965) and the Second General Conference of Latin American Bishops, in

Medellin, Colombia (1968). One of the most important themes of Vatican II was "the opening of the Church to the world" or the recognition that the Church must be involved in the realities and problems faced by the people, particularly by the poor. The Latin American bishops at Medellin strongly denounced the structural injustice of Latin America, affirmed the Church's responsibility to work in solidarity with the poor, and called for the *concientización*, the promotion of political awareness and empowerment, of popular sectors. The meetings along with dramatic political and economic upheaval in Latin America in the 1960s and 1970s led to the development of liberation theology, a rereading of the Bible from the perspective of the oppressed. Liberation theology recognizes the poor not only as subjects of their own history but as the preferred subjects for the revelation of the Word of God and the history of salvation. All of these events shaped a progressive Catholicism in which church leaders and laypeople worked to promote social justice and democracy in many regions of Latin America.

Progressive Catholicism of the Diocese of San Cristóbal de Las Casas was linked to and influenced by this larger movement in Latin America, yet it developed its unique path in response to historic conditions of Chiapas. Retired in 2000,[8] Bishop Samuel Ruiz García arrived in Chiapas in 1960, and in his early visits to rural communities he noted the stark contrast between Chiapas's wealth of natural resources and the impoverishment of most of the indigenous peoples and peasants. Bishop Ruiz is a storyteller whose homilies are punctuated by tales of what he learned from his experiences in Chiapas. He tells one about visiting a finca, a coffee plantation, in the 1960s where he celebrated mass and then stayed the night in the home of the landowner. The next morning the peasants who worked on the finca asked the bishop what type of banquet had been awaiting him in the owner's home. He said that he had been offered nothing more than a cup of coffee. The peasants told him that each one of them had been asked for a monetary donation to support his visit, and all realized what had happened to the money. The bishop reflects, "That was the most expensive cup of coffee I've ever had."

Moved by this and other visits to rural communities, Ruiz slowly underwent a process he calls "conversion"—not a change of religion, but a change of heart. It was a growing awareness of the oppression around him and eventually a commitment to walk with the poor in their struggles for a dignified life. Profoundly influenced by the meetings of Vatican II and Medellin, members of the diocese formally committed themselves to work "with and for the poor" at their 1975 assembly.

The conversions of Ruiz and pastoral workers involved a move from paternalism to accompaniment in the 1970s and 1980s. Church workers began to recognize indigenous people as the subjects of their own history; that is, church workers respected indigenous peoples' own paths to liberation rather than imposing Westernization as the only means to end poverty and exploitation. The liberationist Church is placed in a difficult, if not contradictory position, of promoting indigenous rights while allowing the poor to remain subjects of their own history. As promoters of indigenous rights, Bishop Ruiz and pastoral workers risk the paternalism of speaking *for* the Indians rather than allowing them to speak *for themselves*. As Catholic missionaries, they risk bringing Westernization through conversion. Yet, church workers are aware of and struggle with these contradictions. This book details some their difficulties in working with indigenous communities as well as their desire to listen to rather than speak for the poor. It departs from most writing on the progressive Catholic Church in its focus on indigenous people's understandings and practices of Catholicism. In Chiapas, thousands of indigenous people have affiliated with the Catholic Church in their struggle for human rights. Because of his work to promote human rights, Bishop Ruiz is profoundly popular among indigenous people of Chiapas. His popularity extends beyond indigenous Catholics to include Protestants and even Traditionalist supporters. Letters from Protestant organizations arrived at the Fray Bartolomé de Las Casas Center for Human Rights addressed to "our Bishop Samuel Ruiz García."

In many parts of Latin America, progressive Catholicism with its emphasis on justice and equality provided resources for oppressed groups to confront repressive governments (see for example Berryman 1987, Cleary 1990, Levine 1992, Mainwaring and Wilde 1989, and Peterson 1997). Over the past thirty years, the Church has created and supported informal transnational networks through publications, centers, and grassroots movements to facilitate democracy (Levine and Stoll 1997:69). This is certainly the case in Chiapas, where the Church has established human rights centers; provided material assistance following political crises; trained thousands of catechists in religious instruction, leadership, and literacy; and denounced the ongoing repression of indigenous peoples. Cleary and Steigenga (2004) observe that few researchers have examined the link between religion and indigenous activism. They note that the topic merits further study, given the importance of religion in indigenous life, its role in motivating political action, and its facilitation of transnational networks of people who may support indigenous causes.

Yet, this book not only examines the Church as an institution, it also explores faith, that is, the way that indigenous peoples understand religion and how it influences their day-to-day lives. As such, the study follows those who focus on religion as practice, the "everyday thinking and doing of lay men and women" (Hall 1997: vii; see also de Certeau 1988 and Orsi 1997). I hope to contribute to understandings of the ways that "ordinary people, and not just professional theologians, construct, adapt, and seek to live by theological and ethical systems" (Peterson 1997: 11). Hence, this study examines how the pastoral work of the Catholic diocese has affected indigenous understandings and awareness of human rights and in turn, how indigenous views have affected the bishop and pastoral workers.

In many ways, the indigenous people are Catholics on their own terms; they understand and live their religion in their own context. Yet, as Talal Asad states, religion cannot be separated from power and history, for "it is not simply worship but social, political, and economic institutions in general, within which individual biographies are lived out, that lend a stable character to the flow of a Christian's activity and to the quality of her experience" (1993:33). The Catholic Church's relationship with the state conditions what it means to be Catholic in Chiapas. For the most part the Church has opposed the government's repressive policies, and as a result Catholics have been targets for further repression. Understanding the "thinking and doing" of the indigenous Catholics necessarily includes exploration of the political and economic processes in which Catholicism is embedded at a state, national, and international level.

Research Site and Methods
I first traveled to San Cristóbal de Las Casas in January 1993, a year before the Zapatista uprising. Like other visitors to the city of San Cristóbal, I encountered many indigenous women and children selling friendship bracelets and other items in the streets of the city (Figure 1.1). The vendors described themselves as *expulsados* who had been expelled from Chamula because of their religious affiliation. Wanting to know more, I visited the nongovernmental organization Fray Bartolomé de Las Casas Center for Human Rights, where the director explained the political, economic, and religious motives behind expulsion. The center had been founded in 1989 by Bishop Samuel Ruiz García to attend to the increasing number of human rights abuses reported by the indigenous and poor peasants of the Diocese of San Cristóbal de Las Casas.

In August 1993, I began a two-year collaboration with the Center for Human Rights. The center was the logical place to start examining records of expulsion because, since its foundation, it has documented and denounced cases of expulsion. Collaborating with the center allowed me to explore the context in which human rights abuses take place and to examine abuses at the state level before beginning work in a single community. Reading through the many human rights case files at the center, I learned that violations are not isolated incidents carried out by a few corrupt authorities but are part of a repressive power structure within Chiapas. By condoning human rights abuses by police, militia, and local representatives, the state government attempted to repress political mobilization that opposed the PRI and to maintain the concentration of political and economic resources in the hands of the few. In cases such as expulsion, peasants were pitted against one another, making conflicts appear to be internal, when in reality they are a result of competition for scarce resources and of government negligence and corruption.

The Center for Human Rights was located in the chancery of the diocese at the time, and it was there that I first met Bishop Ruiz García, priests, nuns, and other pastoral workers. In our early conversations I learned about the history of the diocese and its recent pastoral plans. In time, I was able to conduct interviews with the bishop and pastoral workers on their work with indigenous people. These interviews, along with observations of diocesan events and meetings, shed light on the Church's complex relationship with indigenous peoples.

I conducted more than eighteen months of fieldwork from September 1994 to August 1995 and in the summers of 1996 to 2001 in Guadalupe, a community I selected because of the population of expelled Tzotzils with a concentrated Catholic population of twenty-six families. Working in one community allowed me to observe how people define human rights, how they act to protect their rights, and what impact these violations have on daily life.

Initially, participant observation was important for getting to know the Catholic members of the community and gaining their trust. I attended Catholic celebrations in the local chapel to get to know church leaders, and at the suggestion of community members, I began to teach a literacy class. Between eight and twelve students attended the literacy class two days a week for a six-month period. I taught the class mostly in Tzotzil, since the students spoke very little Spanish. The class served to establish trust with the people of Guadalupe and helped establish some mutuality in my work, as I was able to assist a group of people in a small way.

When I began visiting the homes of the Catholic families of Guadalupe, I was eager to hear their stories of how they were exiled from Chamula and wanted to know how they talked about the human rights abuses involved, but I worried that people would be reluctant to open up to a *caxlan,* a non-Indian, and therefore an outsider.[9] To the contrary, I found that they were eager to talk and were pleased that I had an interest in their history. They saw me as someone who did not know about their lives, suffering, and customs, but they wanted me to understand what had happened. They told me over and over about the Word of God, the authorities in Chamula, their arrival in Guadalupe, and the role of God in their lives. Talking served to denounce what had happened to them, and they told me in hopes that I would continue to denounce their suffering in Mexico as well as in my own country. People were well aware that the problem of expulsion had been presented as a conflict between Protestants and Roman Catholics, and they wanted me understand the "true" story. They also told of expulsion as a testimony to their faith. In spite of what they had suffered, they never gave up their religion. Women spent hours talking to me as they sat weaving, spinning wool, making bracelets, or combing their children's hair. I spoke to men in the evenings and weekends, since they commonly walked to San Cristóbal to work during the day.

As I listened to and recorded stories of conversion, expulsion, and resettlement in Guadalupe, I realized that while the experience of exile (which involved jailings, beatings, and threats) was difficult, exile's most painful aspect was starting a new life separated from their land, houses, and families. Rather than describing their cultural rights as indigenous people, Guadalupe residents focused on their poverty and the need for access to land and basic services.

Conducting fieldwork during a time of intense political conflict in Chiapas presented numerous challenges. Following the 1994 Zapatista uprising, the local and state government accused many pastoral agents and human rights workers of being Zapatistas or subversives. Mayan Catholics throughout the diocese, especially catechists and deacons, were also targets of repression. In this context, any conversation about human rights or the work of the Catholic Church carried significant political relevance and could be considered dangerous. In spite of this risk, human rights workers and indigenous peoples wished to make their voices heard and to express their side of the story. In addition, they hoped to publicize the human rights abuses in Chiapas and establish national and international support networks. In this context of repression and conflict, it was important to the Catholics in Guadalupe that I was linked to the human rights center and the Catholic diocese. This link was crucial in establishing trust and was emphasized whenever I visited new communities with Guadalupe catechists.

Although I was raised Catholic, I had not been active in the church (or even attended mass) in the ten years before I went to Chiapas. In the field, I was an active participant in the church, and this was perhaps the most important factor in building trust with the people of Guadalupe. Religion is a central reference point in their lives, and I was constantly asked, "What is your religion?" It was important that I attend religious celebrations in the local chapel as well as baptisms, first communions, and weddings. My religious affiliation provided an important link, for otherwise I was extraordinarily different—separated from my parents, living in Chiapas without a husband, and a female adult without children, my life did not make any sense to Guadalupe residents. In addition, my work involved writing at a desk rather than physical labor, and I did not know how to make tortillas (although I tried to learn) or to weave and embroider, all-important tasks for women. Our shared faith provided a link, albeit a fragile one, in spite of our obvious ethnic and class differences.

In order to place the community of Guadalupe within the wider context of the phenomenon of expulsion and human rights, I conducted interviews with leaders outside the community and analyzed documentation of the history of the issue. I consulted primary and secondary sources in San Cristóbal at the Instituto de Asesoría Antropológica para la Región Maya Asociación Civil, INAREMAC (the Anthropological Consultancy for the Maya Region) that document the history of the Diocese of San Cristóbal. The local press—primarily the newspaper El Tiempo, which has an important history in documenting the plight of the indigenous of Chiapas—provided information on the twenty-year history of expulsion, the response of government officials to the problem, and the mobilization of the indigenous population of exiles. Interviews in the community were complemented by interviews of political leaders of the expelled and pastoral workers of the Diocese of San Cristóbal de Las Casas.

Structure of the Book

Given the subjects of this book—displaced indigenous Catholics—it necessarily travels through a number of sites from the colonia of Guadalupe to San Juan Chamula to other highland communities. The book also examines the Catholic Diocese of San Cristóbal de Las Casas not only as a region, but also as a religious and political project. Maps and a chronology of key events are presented to assist the reader in locating these sites. This book is organized into eight chapters following this introduction that examine how indigenous notions of human rights have developed in the national, regional, and local context, above all in the Diocese of San Cristóbal de Las Casas. Chapter 2 introduces the colonia of Guadalupe, its inhabitants, and its history. Taking this community as a unit of analysis allows for in-depth exploration of Mayan Catholics' understandings of rights, religion, and community as well as their struggle to live a dignified life. Chapter 3 presents a history of the diocese's mission under the leadership of Bishop Ruiz (1960–2000) and its attempt to work with the marginalized and excluded and to promote indigenous rights. Chapter 4 turns to San Juan Chamula, the place of origin of the Catholics of Guadalupe. It explores the diocese's attempt to establish a mission in this municipality and the events leading up to the first massive expulsion.

Chapters 5 through 7 examine indigenous concepts of human rights, both in theoretical terms and in definitions given by Word of God Catholics of Guadalupe. Chapter 5 analyzes the diverse understandings of and theoretical debates surrounding human rights as related to the issue of expulsion. It explores anthropological debates, Mexican legislation, Catholicism, and the work of the Fray Bartolomé de Las Casas Center for Human Rights as related to indigenous rights. Chapters 6 and 7 describe the ways the expelled Catholics of Guadalupe define and practice human rights and traditions. Chapter 6 details how the indigenous Catholics mix doctrine emanating from the Catholic Church, legal codes, and traditional indigenous views in defining human rights, and Chapter 7 explores the ways these Catholics have re-created traditions in their search for a new life. Finally, Chapter 8 explores concrete actions and mobilizations by diocesan Catholics to defend their rights. The local networks of Guadalupe as well as the diocesan-wide networks built through Pueblo Creyente form a community of faith that can lead to a shared path of resistance. The larger question of what the case of Guadalupe and the work of the Diocese of San Cristóbal contribute to understandings of indigenous rights is addressed in Chapter 9.

When I asked the people in Guadalupe if I could write a book about their community, religion, and expulsion, they responded with great enthusiasm. They felt that it was important to document their history and wanted others to know what they had experienced. In fact, when I first explained my research plans, they asked me to write a booklet for them in Tzotzil telling how they had left Chamula and established a new community. They taught me about their lives so that I would understand what they had experienced and what they were living. A central theme in our conversations was suffering. Over and over, they repeated to me, "Cristina, here we are suffering a lot." They took me into their homes to show me how they lived, told me of their illnesses, described the difficulty of finding work, and expressed sadness in having to leave their land, houses, and community in Chamula.[10] They wanted me to understand the poverty they encounter in the city, the discrimination from mestizos, and the refusal of state and federal authorities to address their situation. Theirs is not only a history of suffering, but also of hope expressed in their faith and their ongoing struggle for a dignified life.

Photo and caption by Juana López López, 1998
The rainbow is near my house.

El arco iris está cerca de mi casa.

Li vaknobale tey nopol ta sts'el jna.

2

Exodus and Genesis
Leaving Chamula, Creating Community in Guadalupe

To reach Guadalupe, one has to climb a steep path that winds up a mountain, passes trees and rocks, and during the rainy season is covered with mud. A *combi,* or Volkswagen bus, provides service from the market in San Cristóbal to the top of hill, but most of Guadalupe's residents walk forty minutes to their homes, unable to spare the twenty cents for combi fare. When I walked up the hill, I would pass women going down carrying infants on their backs and accompanied by other children as they took their sheep to graze in the fields. Women walked home from the city's market with fruits and vegetables wrapped in their shawls. Even barefoot and with their bundles, the women and children walked faster than I. As people passed me going up the hill, we exchanged greetings in Tzotzil and sometimes stopped to talk. When I finally reached the community, out of breath, children ran to greet me shouting in Tzotzil, "Cristina, Cristina, *bu xa bat*" (Where are you going?). Then they started to giggle; they weren't used to seeing *caxlanes* in their community.

As I passed the small stream that runs through Guadalupe, I greeted women bent over the rocks washing clothes. Walking through the community during the day, I passed women and girls carrying plastic containers that they filled with water from one of two tanks. No one had running water, so it had to be carried to each home for cooking, drinking, and cleaning. On sunny days, I greeted women who sat in the front of their homes working. Most often they were making clothing. It takes a woman a full week to make a wool skirt, first cleaning the wool, then spinning it, and weaving it on a backstrap loom. They also sewed and embroidered blouses. Some worked drying, cleaning, or sorting beans and corn.

For years government officials have defended expulsion by arguing that the exiled refuse to participate in community life and hence threaten the social fabric that has held indigenous communities together for centuries. In Guadalupe I found, to the contrary, that community serves to organize life. Guadalupe's Catholics have worked for years to create a space where members know one another, where people meet for worship in a chapel several times a week, and where each member carries out obligations toward other members.

I spent hours with each of the Catholic families of Guadalupe listening to their stories of conversion to Catholicism, of expulsion from Chamula, and finally, of their struggle to build a new community. In this chapter, I explain the significance of conversion and exile in the social history of the Catholics of Guadalupe and present a socioeconomic portrait of their community and its history.

Don Lucas and Micaela: The Search for a Dignified Life

I begin with the story of Don Lucas and Micaela,[1] one of the oldest couples living in the community and two of the most enthusiastic participants in the Catholic church. Their story denounces what they suffered in being expelled from Chamula at the same time that it announces their hope of living a dignified life. Don Lucas is in his seventies. He does not know his exact age but said he grew up when there were no cars or planes in Chiapas. He and Micaela jointly held the position of sacristan, which required them to "take care of the church," that is, to see that there are candles and flowers for the altar, pine boughs on the floor for special celebrations, and coffee and bread or chicken soup for religious holidays and special visitors. They described their position as a *cargo*—a duty or responsibility carried out for the benefit of their community. Both Micaela and Lucas were widowed by their first spouses, and they had a total of eleven children between them, nine from their previous marriages. I spent hours sitting in this couple's home listening to their stories. As we talked, Micaela's hands were always busy. She prepared food for her family or wove intricate friendship bracelets that she sold to earn small amounts of cash. On warm days we sat outside in the sun as Micaela wove woolen cloth for skirts and ponchos on her backstrap loom. If it was rainy or cold we sat in the kitchen around the open fire used for cooking, shifting our chairs on the dirt floor to avoid the smoke. The walls of their home are made of boards, and plastic and cardboard boxes cover the space between the slats as protection from the wind and water.

Until they were expelled ten years earlier, Micaela and Lucas lived in Chamula working their land and selling *pox*, a locally produced rum. They told me about the problems that began after they heard the Word of God and converted to Catholicism. They were jailed by Chamulan authorities and upon release were told that they could either give up their new religion or leave the community. Micaela and Lucas decided to attempt to make a living elsewhere, and they eventually moved to Guadalupe.

The first time we met, Lucas and Micaela talked of their plans to be confirmed in the Catholic Church. Having already received the sacraments of baptism and first communion, they viewed confirmation as an important demonstration of their commitment to the Word of God and as a necessary step so that they, as elders, could set an example for the community. They told me that I would have to buy the chickens that would be eaten in the celebration following the religious service. Then they laughed—the joke was on me. Asking a young caxlan whom they had only just met to buy food for the confirmation was almost ridiculous. This was the expected role of the godparent, and how could I be godparent to a couple old enough to be my grandparents? But there was some seriousness to the demand. In spite of my youth and gender, my status as a caxlan marked me as someone with access to resources. It was clear that if I were to have any role in the community, I also would have to contribute, and in time I did through money for a concrete floor of a new chapel, medicine for some who were ill, literacy classes, or chickens. In April 1997, coadjutor Bishop Raul Vera visited Guadalupe to confirm Don Lucas and Micaela as well as twelve other residents of the community. Their confirmation symbolized the continual importance of religion in their daily lives.

The stories they told me—of their childhood, their work in the fincas, their conversion and subsequent expulsion from Chamula, their lives in Guadalupe—were full of contrasts that referred to the changes they experienced after hearing the Word of God. Some of the changes were welcome—for example, living in peace in Guadalupe as compared to the violence of Chamula—while others were described as difficult and painful. Micaela stated that life was easier in Chamula because she and her husband owned a significant amount of land. She lamented that in Guadalupe "there isn't any land, there isn't anything. When I left Chamula, I cried a lot."

In explaining the significance of their conversion and the transformations it unleashed, Lucas and Micaela told me about their childhood in Chamula. Micaela's mother died when she was a young child, so her grandmother raised her. Her father drank a lot and regularly traveled to work in the fincas. Don Lucas's mother was shot, "killed with a bullet," when Lucas was eight years old. He told me, "People said that she was a witch and for this they killed her. They said that they would get sick after visiting her. I don't know if this was true or not. I was very sad when my mother died, and I cried a lot." Of his father Lucas recalls, "He drank a lot because it is *costumbre* [custom or tradition]. If I didn't work hard enough, my father would beat me."

Lucas continued, "We didn't go to school, and because of this we are very foolish," referring to the disadvantages he and his wife experienced because of illiteracy. They had limited options for work and could not read the Bible. Poverty prevented him from going to school:

> There is a school in my hamlet, but my parents didn't want to send me to school, they didn't have any money. They were worried that we would be sent far away to study. When the teachers came to take our names [to register the children for school] we hid in the mountain. We couldn't play in the street because the teacher would see us there. It is because of this that I don't know anything about reading and writing . . . The teachers would come to the fiestas, they would write down the names of the children. We worried that they would send us far away, so we would run to hide in the mountain, "Here come the teachers to look for children!" Some children would hide in the large pots used to make *pozol* [a drink made from ground corn]. Some parents would dress their sons as girls [the teachers insisted that all boys, but not girls, attend school]. Our parents were very foolish. Those who entered school before are now teachers. But now it's the same, we're all very poor. I don't know where I'm going. I don't know where I am going to look for work. I'm almost half-blind.

As adults living in Chamula, Micaela and Lucas were able to make a living for themselves by selling rum and cultivating their land. Micaela recalled:

> We had two hectares of land in Chamula. We worked well there growing potatoes. We used to sell rum in Jovel [San Cristóbal] for 2,000 pesos a liter. That's how we bought our food. With the money I earned, I could eat. We didn't plant the land ourselves but looked for workers who planted for us. We paid them with corn, beans, and potatoes, two baskets of potatoes for a day's work.

However, this changed once Micaela heard the Word of God; she gave up drinking and stopped producing rum. Without the money she earned through sales of pox and her land, she and Don Lucas had no way to support themselves. She described how she felt after she was forced to leave Chamula:

I wanted to die. I asked that God give me an illness that would kill me, better that I die once and for all. Where could I eat? I suffered a lot, my God Father, I was going to die. But I didn't get sick, God didn't send me an illness. I suffered a lot because I didn't have a house, I didn't have anywhere to sleep. My children said to me, "You are to blame, woman, you didn't leave the Word of God, now we don't have a house."

The couple's conversion to Word of God Catholicism embodied a break with their past and a search for a way of life different from that of their parents. Their story of conversion, like the stories shared with me by other Roman Catholics of Guadalupe, began with the time they first "heard the Word of God." In Tzotzil the verb "to hear"—a'iel—also translates as to listen, feel, or understand. At first, people began "to hear" the Word of God but in time began to understand it and "change their hearts."

In spite of the Catholic Church's violent history in Latin America, especially its repression of indigenous peoples and cultures, Mayas of Guadalupe describe their affiliation with the Catholic Church as a liberating act. In "changing their hearts" the Guadalupe Catholics reject alcohol, construct new gender roles, and make use of the institutional support provided by the Church as they struggle to make a living in an urban area. In writing about the shift to Protestantism among Maya-Kaqchikel widows in Guatemala, Linda Green distinguishes between religious conversion, "a transformation in ideology or worldview," and affiliation, or membership (1999:151). She argues that affiliation describes the ways indigenous widows join Protestant and other religious groups as subjects "deeply involved in the shaping of their lives within the context of profound social upheaval" (Green 1999:151). Further, this shifting religious affiliation is not at odds with Mayan worldview, as the women draw on past and present influences to reconstruct their lives. The residents of Guadalupe similarly "affiliate" with the Catholic Church as subjects who shape their lives in the urban context and resist the political power of caciques. They are Catholics on their own terms with their own understandings of the Word of God, shaped by their everyday experience as indigenous people. In this sense, Micaela and others describe "hearing the Word of God" as religious affiliation. I also use the terms affiliation and conversion interchangeably because the Guadalupe Catholics talked about belonging to (or their membership in) the Catholic Church and the dramatic changes embodied in their religious conversion.

Some residents of Guadalupe first heard the Word of God when they walked to the Catholic church of Chenalhó, a municipality that shares a border with Chamula. Others heard the Word of God from Catholic catechists (men and women selected by the community to serve as lay preachers) who work in Chamula or from friends who already converted. Some converted while they were working in fincas or on lands in the Lacandon jungle. In most cases, people walked great distances to attend mass and religious meetings. Micaela recalled how she and Lucas became acquainted with the Word of God:

> We were already old when we first heard the Word of God. I heard the Word of God seven years ago from a man who lives in Candelaria, three hours' walking distance from our hamlet in Chamula and another three hours to return. I first heard the Word of God because I was sick. It healed my illness. Before we heard the Word of God, we got sick a lot.

For Micaela, the reason for conversion is simple: she was ill and cured through prayer. Others repeated similar stories of illness and conversion. When afflicted with a serious or long-term illness, people traditionally visited a *curandero,* a traditional healer in Chamula who asked for money, alcohol, soft drinks, candles, chickens, and other items. Many women told me that when they or their children were ill they became frustrated with the curanderos, either because they did not have the money to pay them and to buy the necessary offerings or because the curanderos did not cure the illness. Instead, these women were cured by praying to God or by using medicine along with prayer. Micaela later discovered that the Word of God heals much more than illness. Her heart began to change, as did her relationship with her husband. However, once Micaela and Lucas began to follow the Word of God, "the problems started." The authorities of Chamula were angered by their decision to convert to Catholicism. Although Micaela attempted to worship in private, spies who watched the churches of Caridad (a chapel in San Cristóbal where indigenous Roman Catholics meet to celebrate the Word of God in Tzotzil) and Chenalhó would report back to the authorities in Chamula. Micaela explained:

> The *agentes* [local authorities who report to the municipal president] said that they wanted us to go to the school to meet with them; they asked to meet with us four times. Don Lucas decided to give up his religion. He abandoned it for four weeks because he was afraid, there were so many problems. But I didn't. I said that I was going to continue with

the Word of God. I continued to go to the Church of Caridad in Jovel [San Cristóbal].

Women commonly converted first and then attempted to convince their husbands to do the same. The Guadalupe residents' interpretation of Catholicism offers particular benefits for women, namely the emphasis placed on respect between husband and wife as well as the rejection of drinking and domestic violence. Men have more to lose in conversion. Don Lucas noted that he lost the status he had gained in Chamula through his age and gender. In fact, he was ridiculed by the authorities who were annoyed that someone so old, and therefore presumably wise, had converted. Don Lucas recounted:

> When they first threatened to kick me out of Chamula, they said to me, "You don't have any shame. Why don't you give up your religion? Your hair is already very white, you are teaching people. Who knows what you are learning, who is teaching you bad things, your eyes are shut, your hair is very white. You're going to get what you deserve."

Younger people more commonly converted to Catholicism or Protestantism, leading to generational conflicts between those who follow traditional ways and those who reject or re-create tradition. Lucas was accused of being blind, of not understanding the importance of traditional values. As an elder (with white hair), he is accused of setting a bad example. Because of the couple's refusal to give up their religion, they were thrown into jail for a day, a common punishment in Chamula.[2] Micaela described her experience:

> I told the *agente* that I wasn't going to give up my religion. He told me that I had to go to talk to the [municipal] president of Chamula. I was thrown into jail with many others. I was taken to the town center of Chamula in a truck. There was so much suffering. In jail were nine men and eighteen women, many women. All were Catholic. Four people agreed to give up their religion, and they left the jail. The rest stayed. Many people learn the Word of God, but when the problems start, they renounce their religion. I entered the jail at eight in the morning and left at six in the evening.
>
> After leaving jail, I went back to my land. They gave me a period of fifteen days to leave Chamula. When the fifteen days were up, the *agentes* met and plotted against us since we still hadn't left. Don Lucas left our

home in the night; he was very sad. He didn't have a house. He looked for a place to live in the central valleys [of Chiapas]. He was very sad without his house, without his land. He thought that he wouldn't be able to return to Chamula; he thought the people would beat him. There was a lot of sadness. When we left Chamula, there was a lot of illness. We didn't have land. We were afraid. The people wanted to kill us.

Don Lucas and Micaela, like others, described the involvement of the authorities of Chamula, for the most part local authorities. Because of the participation of government authorities, these acts are human rights violations, not personal conflicts between families. Lucas and Micaela do not separate religious motives for expulsion from political-economic motives. Caciques view the act of religious conversion as an overt threat to their political and economic authority. As will be described in Chapter 4, the history of the corporate state in Chamula and of the first expulsions has much to do with the ways political, economic, and religious power overlap in Chamula. In short, the act of affiliating with the Catholic Church undermines the absolute civil and religious control of caciques.

Lucas and Micaela eventually moved to Guadalupe, where they purchased land and built a home. Don Lucas rented land in Betania (a community of Mayan immigrants in the municipality of Teopisca), where he plants corn for household consumption and makes and sells charcoal. Micaela makes and sells bracelets to earn small amounts of cash. In stark contrast to their position in Chamula, the couple is by far one of the poorest of the Catholic families in Guadalupe. Given the violence and suffering they experience as a result of conversion, why did Micaela and Lucas, along with many others, decide to reject the traditional religion of Chamula to convert to Catholicism? The couple told me that they had found the true way to worship God. Micaela noted that religion healed her illness, and Lucas stated, "We saw that Our Lord God is very powerful." Contained within these seemingly simple statements is a series of dramatic and powerful transformations in their lives, changes that began before conversion but correspond to a vision of a new way of life.

One of the most important changes is the rejection of alcohol. While Catholic doctrine does not prohibit drinking, many indigenous Catholics in Chiapas reject the use of alcohol. Residents of Guadalupe described drinking as problematic because it leads to violence and illness and because men spend precious money on alcohol rather than on food and other necessities for their families. Don Lucas told me of his drinking:

I drank a lot when I lived in Chamula. I was going to die from alcohol. So, they were pissed off when I threw down my cup . . . My cup remained there in my hamlet and so did my land. I left a lot of land. I used to sell corn, I used to sell squash. I left three houses, four counting my kitchen. But little by little, these things left my heart [I forgot them]. Here in Guadalupe I don't have any land.

Micaela recalled matter-of-factly that Lucas used to beat her when he was intoxicated, but when he accepted the Word of God, he stopped beating her and began to treat her with respect. Many other women in Guadalupe reported that their husbands had beaten them before they accepted the Word of God. For them, their husbands' giving up drinking was synonymous with conversion, and they felt that they lived much better lives without alcohol. Some women in Guadalupe had accepted the Word of God in Chamula and then decided to leave their husbands because they refused to give up drinking.

Another important factor in conversion was the rejection of the "custom" of taking two or more wives. Women complained not of polygamy, but of men who abandoned their wives and children to take a "second wife." Women told me that according to the Word of God, a husband must "respect his family," which means working in cooperation with his wife, providing food and other necessities, and not fighting with or beating his wife.

Many of the changes that came with conversion to Catholicism are reported as being positive: people gave up alcohol, men reportedly treated their wives with more respect, and one could freely worship in Guadalupe. However, stories of expulsion also contain the pain of loss. In exile, people left behind their homes, families, land, crops, and animals. Juana, a widow who was expelled with her three young children and left with nothing but the clothes on her back, summed up her experience with this simple statement: "I left everything I had in Chamula."

Living in Guadalupe: "Here we are poor"
Like Lucas and Micaela, other Guadalupe residents emphasized the separation from their land in Chamula as one of the most difficult aspects of exile. They noted that in Guadalupe there is not enough land to cultivate subsistence crops or to allow animals to graze. However, land scarcity is not a problem that began with exile but rather is a continuation of a problem that existed in Chamula. A few families (like Micaela and Lucas) had owned as many as four hectares of land in Chamula, but most had less than one hectare and were forced to par-

ticipate in other strategies to supplement their small harvests. Many males and some females had labored seasonally on fincas, working long hours with very low pay. A few families had migrated to the Lacandon jungle in eastern Chiapas to settle lands in a colonization process encouraged by the federal government, and others had worked as sharecroppers on lands in the Grijalva Valley. For example, Don Lucas regularly traveled to work on the finca. Anthropologists studying highland Maya municipalities have documented these and other survival strategies (see for example Collier 1975, Rus 1994, and Wasserstrom 1977, 1983).[3] Guadalupe residents combined subsistence production, the sale of artisan goods, and wage labor when they lived in Chamula. They challenged the common stereotype of Chamula and other highland communities as being self-contained, isolated from the regional and national economies. Indigenous people of Chamula and the urban colonias do not fit neatly in the category of peasant or proletarian. Like rural households throughout Mexico and Latin America, Guadalupe households depend on diverse survival strategies, combining a number of economic activities to survive.[4]

A lack of land increasingly separates the economic activities of the residents of Guadalupe from subsistence production. Nonetheless, the tie to land continues to have economic and symbolic significance. No matter how small their plots of land, many families plant corn and raise chickens or sheep. For the majority of the families, the yield is not significant. They harvest at best a few tender ears of corn, which are roasted and eaten. However, planting serves as a reminder of the land lost and that they are peasants.

Most of the men of Guadalupe directly sell their labor, working for wages in town. They do not, however, refer to themselves as proletariat but rather describe themselves as poor or as peasants. Displaced from land that once provided part of their means of production, they lack regular employment, commonly work in the informal sector, and make up a reserve army of labor that serves the mestizo merchants of San Cristóbal. As Fernando the sandal maker observed, he is a peasant out of place, no longer able to do the work he knows best, and struggling to make a living in the city.

Eight of twenty-two male heads of household in Guadalupe are *peones,* or day laborers who perform menial work in the construction of homes and public works. The work is physically exhausting. Men carry concrete blocks and bags of cement, pour concrete, clear roads, and shovel gravel. The pay was around three U.S. dollars a day. All of the day laborers in Guadalupe work irregularly. They are hired for a few days or weeks at a time to complete a specific project.

During this time, they work nine hours a day. When the work is completed, they search for another project but can go for weeks or months without work. A few men in Guadalupe rent small plots of land in highland townships or in the central valleys of Chiapas where they cultivate corn and beans for family consumption. However, rent, which is commonly paid as a share of the harvest, plus the cost of transportation, fertilizer, and seeds make it difficult to earn much. A few men sell *paletas* (Popsicles) from small, insulated carts that they rent and push around the city; others sell produce or goods in the market. Those who work as *albañiles* (masons or construction workers) are better off. These men work on the same projects as the day laborers, but their pay is higher since they have been trained in construction and give orders to the day laborers. However, like the day laborers, the work of the albañil is irregular and depends on finding an available project. Some families have small stores where they sell soft drinks, pasta, rice, and other items. All of these projects provide an irregular source of income. Workers cannot count on earning money from one day to the next.

Women and children earn money for their families by making artisan objects, most commonly handwoven bracelets and belts. Bracelets are sold to vendors for the price of about a dollar a dozen, and the vendors (also expelled Chamulas) sell them in the city to tourists. Women also weave wool ponchos, vests, jackets, and purses and embroider blouses. These items commonly are sold to "middlemen" who then sell them in tourist shops or in the city streets. Although this method of sale pays less, it is more secure and the women do not have to spend time in the streets attempting to sell.[5] Women's contribution to the household income through the sale of artisan products is small but stable. It is important in making ends meet since men's income is often irregular.

The Genesis of Guadalupe

Community is a central dynamic in the lives of the expelled—they re-create their churches and neighborhoods in urban areas outside their municipalities of origin. Guadalupe was founded by and for Catholics who had been exiled from Chamula. It is just one of the many colonias on the edge of San Cristóbal de Las Casas. Indigenous people from Chamula and other highland communities founded numerous colonias surrounding San Cristóbal with names such as Palestina, Nueva Esperanza, and Paraíso. The families of Guadalupe are but a small group of thousands of "urban Indians" who search for ways to make a living in the city, leaving the countryside either because they did not have

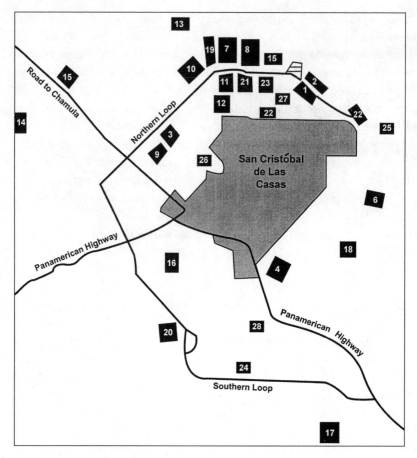

Map of San Cristóbal de Las Casas and colonias *Adapted from Jan Rus (n.d.)*

Sources: Gutiérrez Gutiérrez (1996:40–41) and Calvo Sánchez (1990:56–57)

KEY

Colonias founded in the 1970s
1. Nueva Esperanza
2. Benito Juárez
3. Palestina
4. Cascajal

Colonias founded in the 1980s
5. La Frontera
6. Fracción La Garita
7. La Hormiga
8. Getsemaní
9. Erasto Urbina

10. Prudencio Moscoso
11. Paraíso
12. Ampliación Tlaxcala
13. San Antonio del Monte
14. La Selva
15. Mazariegos
16. Explanada del Carmen
17. Aserradero
18. Santa Cruz

Colonias founded in the 1990s
19. San Juan del Bosque

20. Caridad
21. Fracción La Hormiga
22. 4 de Marzo
23. Patria Nueva

Recent colonias
24. Molino de la Albarrada
25. Molino de Utrilla
26. Molina La Isla
27. Molino de Los Arcos
28. Salsipuedes

enough land to cultivate or were no longer able to supplement the cultivation of cornfields with part-time work as sharecroppers or contract workers. The population of San Cristóbal has grown dramatically in recent decades, jumping from 60,000 in 1980 to 130,000 in 2000, with indigenous migrants making up more than half the population growth (Rus and Collier 2003:46).

Mateo, a Catholic catechist who was expelled from Chamula in 1983, founded the community of Guadalupe. At that time, he recalls, he was one of three catechists in the Church of Caridad in San Cristóbal de Las Casas where indigenous Catholics met to celebrate the Word of God in Tzotzil:

> I arrived in the Church of Caridad to prepare for my baptism. But because I went to Caridad, I was accused of being an evangelical and was expelled.[6]

Word of God Catholics who needed a place to live began to approach Mateo. He worked to purchase land to found a community for these exiles:

> In 1983 I began to go to the Church of Caridad to hear the Word of God. Later, some people from the community of San José Buenavista had a course for catechists, and I attended the course, which lasted five days. I returned to the Church of Caridad, and together with another catechist, we held a general meeting for the catechists there in May 1983. When I began attending the Church of Caridad, there were about fifteen or twenty believers. We began to work hard, and little by little we gathered more people, believers from San Cristóbal, from Corazón de María, and other communities. In two or three years the church was full. The people were asking us, "Where are we going to live?" Together with another catechist, I began to look for land. We found the land in Guadalupe, which belongs to my mother-in-law. She sold us the land for a good price. She said that it was good that Catholics were going to live there.

Perhaps Mateo's mother-in-law thought that Chamula-style Catholics (i.e., Traditionalists) would live on the land, or perhaps she preferred to sell the land to diocesan Catholics rather than Protestants. In any case, Mateo purchased the land at a very low price:

> We bought twelve hectares at the price of 25,000 pesos per hectare. We found the money little by little. On December 12, 1983, we bought the

land and also obtained the papers for it. We made announcements in Caridad that we had land; we told the people that they could build their homes and live there. At first, only three to five families went to live in Guadalupe, no more. It was only mountain and brush.[7]

I lived in Guadalupe for six years, from 1983 to 1989. It had only Catholic families then, about 120 Catholic families in all. Some of the other colonias of expelled weren't established yet. I worked for three years as representative of the expelled.

Mateo directly helped many people to acquire land and establish themselves in their new home, and many families spent their first months in Guadalupe living with him or on land that he lent them. Antonia, a widow, remembered his help:

The catechist [Mateo] looked for and bought the land here in Guadalupe. At first, I lived with Mateo because I had no home. He gave me land to live on. I didn't have any money because I came here from Chamula without anything. Later, I was able to sell my house and land in Chamula and give Mateo 5,000 pesos. He had a good heart. He shared his coffee, corn, and beans with others. He didn't get sad when he didn't have his food, his corn.

Initially, people walked to the Church of Caridad in the city of San Cristóbal to attend celebrations of the Word of God. Little by little the community grew, and by 1988 there were thirty-five Catholic families and a provisional chapel in the house of Mateo. As more and more families moved to Guadalupe, it grew beyond the initial twelve hectares. People built homes near the original settlement without acquiring legal title to the land. They told me with pride that the bishop of San Cristóbal de Las Casas, Samuel Ruiz García, had visited the community in 1988 to celebrate mass. They met in Mateo's home for the mass. The floor was covered in pine needles, as is traditional in Chamula during festivals and other important events, and there was much music and singing. Later they built a simple chapel in the center of the community.

In 1990, there was a split in the community, and gradually most of the people left the Catholic Church. Several related reasons were given for the split. One factor, which everyone seemed in agreement about, was that Mateo began to drink and more importantly "took a second wife." Disapproval of his actions was not based on personal conflicts with Mateo. Drinking alcohol and taking more than one wife are said to be two of the primary practices of the Traditionalists that the Catholic converts rejected in Chamula. Hence, the people of Guadalupe felt betrayed by Mateo, who was the founder of the community and above all a catechist who was expected to provide moral and spiritual leadership. In taking a second wife and drinking, he represented what they had left behind. They demanded that Mateo leave the community, and he moved to another colonia inhabited by exiles from Chamula. The Catholics noted that since then Mateo gave up drinking and lived with only one woman, whom he married.

The legal quagmire of acquiring the titles to the community's land contributed to the division. Guadalupe's residents decided that everyone would contribute fifty pesos to carry out the necessary legal procedures. Mateo said it would cost twelve million pesos to legalize the title to the land, and people started to give him money. Then another Catholic, Salvador, said that he had inquired among several lawyers who said it would only cost two and a half million pesos. The people began to wonder what Mateo was doing with their money and decided to give it to Salvador instead. They asked Mateo to give back what they had already invested, but he said that he did not have it because he had already started the legal procedure. People were angry. Meanwhile, Salvador kept asking for more money, ultimately claiming that he needed a total of thirty-six million pesos to legally buy the land. People asked what was happening to their money and why they still lacked the titles to the land. Mateo said it was not his fault, that he was working hard but that "the lawyers don't want to work. They are lazy, and one had cheated me of my money." Salvador still needed more money and still did not have the papers. The people were angry. Since both Mateo and Salvador had been active Catholics, the fraud was associated with the Church. People were disenchanted, and many left the Church.

A third reason for the split was that Mateo was accused of being "too political." The complaint is not simply that he was involved in politics but that he was shifty or untrustworthy. People came to see Mateo's leadership as deceptive. After all, Chamulan and mestizo authorities had deceived them in the process of expulsion, and they were alarmed by his growing power. Mateo had been involved in founding the Consejo de Representantes Indígenas de los Altos de Chiapas, CRIACH (Council of Indigenous Representatives of the Highlands of Chiapas), an organization dedicated to the defense of indigenous rights that has worked toward the end of expulsion as one of its fundamental goals. As a leader of the group, he visited government officials demanding that something be done about the problem of expulsion. He also asked for concessions to help the people of the community. The state government, through the office of Asuntos Indígenas (Indigenous Affairs), had given twenty-five homes each to several communities of exiles. Mateo was able to obtain forty homes for Guadalupe instead of twenty-five. Other members of CRIACH were angered by this, as were many residents of Guadalupe. They felt that Mateo should not accept the government offer. Their demand was and had always been for the government to help them return to Chamula, not settle in San Cristóbal. With the concession of the forty homes, suspicion toward Mateo grew, and people felt that he had betrayed their cause.

At the same time that sentiment against Mateo was increasing, an indigenous Pentecostal pastor began to evangelize in the community. Soon a Pentecostal church was built, and people began leaving the Catholic church to join the Pentecostal one. A second Pentecostal pastor began to assist in preaching, but soon a personal conflict developed between the two pastors, and a second Pentecostal church was built. The majority of the inhabitants of Guadalupe attend one of the Pentecostal churches in the community, and many others walk to one of several Protestant churches in the nearby colonias. In 1992, almost a decade after Guadalupe was founded, with the assistance of lawyers, papers to the community were finalized as *copropriedad* (property with joint ownership), with a total of twenty hectares. This means that the entire community owns the land and that each family has rights to its specific lot. Having the papers that recognize the families of Guadalupe as legitimate owners of the land is critical in a state with permanent conflicts regarding the access to and tenure of land. However, Mateo remains owner of the land he has not sold.

The community members disapproved of Mateo's taking on certain behaviors associated with caciques of Chamula. Guadalupe was predicated on some shared behaviors for its members: all were Tzotzil Catholics who had been expelled from Chamula, and it was expected that all would abide by new norms. Perhaps more important than Mateo's drinking and taking a second wife was his growing economic success. This made him a traitor to the community, especially since he was earning money from the sale of land at the expense of the exiled. While Chamulan caciques profited from the sale of alcohol and charged high interest from loans, many Chamulan families lived in extreme poverty. Although the residents of Guadalupe did not force Mateo to leave, he was excluded from the community. In the end, he chose to leave on his own rather than being further marginalized.

Mateo is not the only person who was excluded from the community of Guadalupe. Others left voluntarily, feeling ostracized for their failure to comply with community norms. One man recalled that he moved to another colonia because people of Guadalupe were constantly scolding him for drinking. Although residents of Guadalupe embrace a religious and political diversity that was not possible in Chamula, they work to maintain a limited sense of unity through certain behaviors such as the rejection of alcohol and domestic violence. In Guadalupe, unity is not maintained through violence as it is in Chamula. Without romanticizing Guadalupe, one can see the community itself as a form of resistance to the violence and exclusion in Chamula.

Don Lucas told me that when he and Micaela arrived in Guadalupe, they stayed on Mateo's land, as had other newcomers. He recounted his growing sense of deception:

> I didn't have any corn, I didn't have my house, and we slept under a tree. Mateo said to us, "Don't suffer because we are going to buy more land. I am going to live here as your neighbor. We're not going to suffer any more because each of us is going to receive a hectare of land."
>
> That was a lie. We weren't going to have a hectare, just one small lot [of 10 by 20 meters] for each of us. It cost me plenty to pay for the land. I went to work in the finca to get the money. Here in Jovel there is no work. So after I built my house, Mateo told me that some help would come.
>
> I am content now because I have my house. I don't sleep under a tree any more. I built my house four years ago.

Lucas's success at buying land and building a home came through his own hard work, not through assistance from Mateo. Lucas was frustrated with Mateo's unfulfilled promises.

The residents of Guadalupe had ambivalent feelings toward Mateo. While he was still remembered as the founder of the community and someone who helped others when they first left Chamula, his later actions were criticized. With much apprehension, I decided to visit Mateo to hear his own story. I worried that he would not want to speak with me since I had been talking to the people of Guadalupe. When I arrived at his home on the edge of the road in the north of the city, his wife answered the door, invited me to sit down, and served lemonade. Mateo sat with me and spent hours telling about his conversion, exile, and founding of Guadalupe. His own story was almost identical to that repeated to me by others. Mateo was sad that his relationship with Guadalupe had turned out badly. He had since stopped drinking and was again active in the Catholic Church. Toward the end of the interview, he expressed concern about his health. He told me that he had diabetes for four years and that it was harder to work then than it once was. He was worried that he might soon die from the disease. I insisted that he seek medical help and later arranged for a visit to a doctor. When I told him that many people live for years with diabetes, he was not convinced, and I wondered if he saw the disease as punishment for his actions.

I have reflected on the complexity of Mateo's life and what it revealed about the difficulty of defending human rights in indigenous communities. Before I met Mateo, I knew that he had been expelled from his home in 1983. However, in our conversation, he told me that years before he left Chamula he had participated in expelling a large group of Catholics and Protestants from Chamula:

> The first large expulsion took place in 1974. I participated in this event. A cacique controlled the problem. He directed the people and deceived the community. He said that these people [those threatened with expulsion] were no longer using candles, that they no longer respected the saints. I was around fifteen years old at the time, and I joined the crowd that demanded that they leave.

Perhaps Mateo felt that it was necessary to tell me this story to demonstrate how easy it was to be convinced and deceived by caciques. Indeed, criticizing the abuses of caciques was extremely dangerous. Some critics were labeled political dissidents, and some were expelled.

In March 1994, Mateo was detained by federal soldiers at a military checkpoint on the road outside San Cristóbal and accused of carrying several boxes of bullets. According to his testimony, the police blindfolded him and then planted the boxes in his car. It turned out to be irrelevant how the bullets got there. An investigation by several lawyers at the Fray Bartolomé de Las Casas Center for Human Rights revealed that the type of bullets in question could be legally transported according to Mexican law. When this was brought to the attention of the authorities, Mateo was released from jail, but only after paying a fine. Even though he has more economic resources than many people in his community, Mateo is still indigenous and therefore subject to intimidation by soldiers and discrimination in the judicial system. Without the assistance of the human rights center, he could have spent a long time in jail, even though he did not break the law.

Four months after his arrest, Mateo was detained again, this time by Chamulan caciques who stopped him on the road between Chenalhó and San Cristóbal. He and four other Tzotzil men were kidnapped and brought to jail in Chamula. The caciques stated that they would release the five men when the state authorities released five Chamulan men who had been detained by police. Mateo and the four others were held for five days, and during this time they feared for their lives.

The contradictions in Mateo's life story show the futility of dividing people into innocent victims and powerful victimizers. He participated in expelling people from Chamula and later worked to defend the human rights of the expelled while making a profit off selling land to them. He was arbitrarily detained and kidnapped and later struggled to find adequate medical care. People in Guadalupe were reluctant to judge Mateo as a "bad guy." Their awareness of the complexities of human life serves to humanize Mateo's motives for his behavior, although they do not excuse it. Their insistence on hearing the whole story underscores the need for an ethics based not only on abstract values, but related to concrete experience. Mateo's story demands an understanding of indigenous people as subjects with human agency rather than as mere objects of abuses. Further, his relationship with the community of Guadalupe emphasizes a shared understanding of each person's right to be heard, that is, to tell his or her own story in all its complexity. Stripping his story of its complexity masks the historical power relationships between indigenous peoples and mestizos. For, even though Mateo earned money from the sale of land to expelled Catholics, he lived in a racist society where he was detained and denied due process of law because he is an indigenous man.

Religion: Celebrating the Word of God

Currently, some 220 families, more than a thousand people, live in Guadalupe. The community has an elementary school, a road, several small stores, and numerous churches. In 1995, there were twenty-six Catholic families, and the remaining families were Protestant. There are great differences among the Protestant groups, although Catholics of Guadalupe commonly refer to all as *evangélicos*. Several Pentecostal churches in the community are full on Sundays and weeknights, and other residents walk to worship with Presbyterians, Seventh Day Adventists, or Jehovah's Witnesses in temples located in nearby colonias. The residents of Guadalupe emphasize that their hearts are now "content" because they live together in peace. In fact, it was only from 1984 to 1990 that most of the inhabitants were Catholic and that the community seemed united in religious terms. However, it is significant that there is no violence in Guadalupe. Catholics, Protestants, and Traditionalists live side by side. People constantly told me that according to the Bible, Catholics and Protestants worship the same God and must work together. At times, the members of various churches in Guadalupe unite to build roads and schools and to give money for burials.

Nonetheless, most socializing ties and networks exist among people of the same religion. When one Catholic man's father fell ill, two catechists, the sacristan, and several other men walked up the hill to his house to pray for him. They carried food and stayed several hours into the night praying for his health and offering spiritual support. When a Catholic child died at birth, two catechists gave up a day's wages to bury the child and comfort the grieving family. Through such religious events, assistance is ritualized. Giving to others is not an individual event but a communal act of support, demonstrating the individual's dependence on others and the work of serving God. The small chapel in Guadalupe is a central meeting place where Catholics unite four times a week to celebrate or listen to the Word of God. Several prayer leaders explained to me that since many Guadalupe residents cannot read or write, they regularly meet in the chapel to read the Word of God together. After the celebration, information is shared about current political events and other issues important to the community.

Catechists, or lay preachers, make a commitment to promote reflection of the Word of God, and they play an important leadership role in religious and civil matters, and they are central to maintaining a sense of community in Guadalupe. They commonly receive orientation in the study of the Bible, Catholic doctrine, and sacraments through courses from the San Cristóbal diocese. Since catechists are expected to set an example in following the Word of God in their daily lives, they have moral authority in their communities and are often sought out for advice and to mediate conflicts. There are currently some 8,000 catechists in the Diocese of San Cristóbal de Las Casas. Given the shortage of priests, the catechists are the most important spiritual leaders in their communities. While conducting fieldwork in Guadalupe, I met the three catechists of the community—Juan, Agustín, and Salvador. Juan, the oldest of the three, had been a catechist for more than twenty-five years and received his first religious training in the 1960s during a four-month course organized by the Marist brothers. Agustín and Salvador are younger men who did not complete formal training but became catechists because they were elected by the community and demonstrated initiative and interest in serving others.

The ritualized support and sharing among the Catholic families of Guadalupe was evident in a wedding I attended one rainy Saturday in late August 1995. Preparation for the wedding began weeks before the event. Emiliano and Pascuala, the couple to be married, borrowed money from other Catholics to buy rings, clothing, food, and other items. Rosa and Juan, the godparents, spent hours with the couple reading and discussing several biblical texts and also made a financial contribution to the event. Juan and his wife expressed their pride at being chosen godparents. The two couples came from the same hamlet in Chamula but were not related through kinship. I was invited to play a role in the wedding as a "pseudo-godparent." A young, unmarried woman and a caxlan, I was not expected to offer advice to Emiliano and Pascuala. Instead I was asked to help pay for the food for the celebration that would follow the religious service. Although I never bought the chickens for Lucas and Micaela's confirmation, I helped purchase the chickens along with vegetables, soft drinks, and other items for Emiliano and Pascuala's wedding.

On the day of the ceremony, two Catholic priests and several pastoral workers who serve the community visited Guadalupe. They entered the chapel where just a few days earlier a group of men had worked for two days to pour the concrete on the dirt floor so that it would be ready for the event. This was to be a special mass: aside from the wedding, seven children would be baptized and four people would receive first communion. As people gathered in the chapel, the priests wrote down the names and birth dates of everyone who would receive sacraments and then listened to the confessions of several men and women. The catechists selected passages from the Bible to be read during mass.

Emiliano and Pascuala sat in chairs in the front of the chapel dressed in their best clothes. Pascuala had a new white blouse, a traditional garment of Chamula, for the wedding. The godparents sat on either side of the couple. The children who would be baptized and celebrate their first communion sat with their godparents in the front row of benches. Mass was celebrated, mostly in Spanish, with parts translated to Tzotzil by the catechists. Of particular interest were the selected readings, both of them focused on love: "If I have all faith, so as to remove mountains, but do not have love, I am nothing" (from

I Corinthians 13:1–8), and "You shall love your neighbor as yourself" (from Matthew 22:35–40). During the homily, the congregation was asked to comment on the meaning of the readings in their lives.[8] Micaela spoke up—she commonly made comments during homilies, as one of the oldest women in the community and not shy about being heard—emphasizing the importance of demonstrating love through helping others.

After the mass, most of the congregation walked up a steep hill to the house of Don Emiliano and Pascuala to celebrate their recent marriage. It had started to rain, and we struggled not to slip in the mud. At the time, Don Emiliano's house had walls built of wooden slats, a roof of corrugated metal, and a dirt floor. The walls did not reach the roof of the house, nor did they cover its four sides, so it was cold and damp. Several tables had been set up in the home, and we ate in shifts. Each person was served chicken soup, tortillas, and a soft drink. A group of women of the chapel had gathered the day before to help make the tortillas for the wedding.

The wedding had been a community effort in many respects. The families had cooperated to give the money to buy concrete for the floor of the chapel; godparents had been selected, forming new kinship relations and strengthening networks of support; and the women had worked together to prepare the meal that followed the wedding. Above all, most of the Catholics of the community had participated in the mass and the meal.

Contrary to the claim of Chamulan caciques that Roman Catholic converts threaten community, the residents of Guadalupe have established a new community where their indigenous identity as Tzotzils continues to be important. The shared experience of being expelled from Chamula is one that unites the Catholics of Guadalupe. The memory of the suffering entailed in being jailed, of losing one's home and belongings, and of starting a new life in the colonia was repeated time and again in interviews. Their shared Catholicism was fundamental to establishing a new community. Faith takes on powerful meaning in their daily lives, especially since they claim that religion is the reason they were forced to leave their homelands.

In expressing their hope that people can work together to find strength and change their situation, catechists and prayer leaders repeated to me that they were attempting "to walk with one united heart." Puzzled, I would mention the many divisions and conflicts within Guadalupe and ask if it was possible to walk in unity. One catechist answered that while it is true that many do not want to walk together, unity continues to be valued and is a motive in his religious work. Others explained that it is only when people work together that they have the strength to fight poverty and injustice. While the people of Guadalupe recognize the difficulty of walking with one heart in the face of diversity, they told me that one must be strong in faith and never give up the struggle.

Photo and caption by Xunka' López Díaz, 2000
The bishops and Bishop Samuel Ruiz García [center] walking with Raúl Vera.
Los obispos y Don Samuel Ruiz García caminando junto con Raúl Vera.
Li mol obixpoetike, li Samuel Ruise ko'ol ta xanavik batel xchi'uk Raúl Vera.

3

Opting for the Poor
The Catholic Diocese of San Cristóbal and Human Rights

[T]he oppressed are not "marginals," are not people living "outside" society. They have always been "inside"—inside the structure that made them "beings for others." The solution is not to "integrate" them into the structure of oppression, but to transform that structure so that they can become "beings for themselves."

—PAULO FREIRE (1970:55)

As children of God, humans, in all their expanse and dignity, deserve to be respected, for the simple fact that they exist. Human beings are created in the image and likeness of God, and have a dignity that has to be recognized, and overall, respected by all. All violation or abuse of human dignity is also committed against God.

—FIRST ENCOUNTER OF LATIN AMERICAN
PASTORAL WORKERS ON HUMAN RIGHTS (1994:20)

In their conversion stories, the Catholics of Guadalupe narrate the profound changes embodied in following the Word of God: from the rejection of alcohol and domestic violence to exile and the search for a new community. This chapter turns to another conversion—Bishop Samuel Ruiz García's conversion to the poor. Samuel Ruiz was consecrated Bishop of the diocese of San Cristóbal de Las Casas in January 1960. He arrived in Chiapas at age thirty-five, an ardent anticommunist who hoped to modernize and Christianize the Indians. However, as he spent time in rural communities witnessing the poverty and humiliation of daily life along with the faith and hope evident in the day-to-day struggles for survival, Bishop Ruiz began to undergo a process of transformation that he calls a conversion. His conversion was a slow awakening, in this case a growing awareness of the oppression around him and eventually a commitment to walk with "the poor" in their struggles for a dignified life.[1] Bishop Ruiz found that the very structure of the Church and its project would be necessarily transformed when its clergy listened to the voices of the poor. Like many other pastoral workers in Latin America, those of the Diocese of San Cristóbal began to "accompany" (*acompañar*, to stand by) the poor. To accompany the poor was to walk with them—not in front of them—to learn from them, witness their needs and faith, share their material conditions, and join them in the struggle for justice.[2] Over time the bishop would earn the nickname "El Caminante" (The One Who Walks) because he had to physically walk at least a short distance to reach many of the rural communities in the diocese. He symbolically walked with the poor in their path to liberation. At the same time, the bishop hoped to encourage the poor to *tomar consciencia*, that is, to wake up, question oppression, and become the "subjects of their own lives."[3]

In many ways the diocese's work under Bishop Ruiz's leadership (1960–2000) was revolutionary. Its pastoral project seriously attempted to incorporate the excluded into the diocesan structure by sharing with them ecclesial responsibility and accompanying them in their process of liberation. At its best the relationship between the poor and the bishop was one of dialogue rather than domination, of speaking *with* the poor rather than speaking *for* them.[4] And just as the pastoral project of the Catholic diocese has affected indigenous understandings and awareness of justice and rights, indigenous views have forced the Church to rethink its mission. However, the bishop's conversion to the poor and the diocesan commitment to walk with the poor were not without contradictions and ambiguities. One persistent question was "Who is the subject?" For if the poor are to be the subjects of their own history, what is the role of the Catholic Church in working with the poor to promote liberation? In other words, is it possible for the Church to assist the poor to become conscious of their oppression without being the actor that transforms them into subjects? This is a particularly difficult question for the Catholic Church with its long history of repression in Latin America, especially in working with indigenous peoples.

Another difficulty was in defining the Church's relationship with the indigenous people of the diocese. In many ways, the bishop encountered indigenous people as "an other," a group different from and exterior to himself.[5] Just as missionaries who had worked before him in Chiapas and throughout Latin America, Bishop Ruiz had difficulty accepting indigenous people as humans on their own terms with all their strengths and weaknesses. Born in Irapuato, Guanajuato, in central Mexico and trained in the seminary in León, Guanajuato, and in Rome, the "backwardness" of Chiapas, particularly of its rural communities, troubled Bishop Ruiz. He thought indigenous people needed to be assimilated to modern Mexican society. In time, Bishop Ruiz's views changed dramatically. He recognized a need to incorporate indigenous traditions as part of the Church. Yet a distance remained between indigenous people and pastoral workers—the Indians were romanticized. This romantic image of Indians contrasted with the prevailing racist stereotypes of Indians as lazy, dirty, violent, and backwards. As I argue in the following, in their attempt to promote justice, pastoral workers constructed an abstract and romantic image of indigenous culture that failed to address the heterogeneity within and between communities. The terms *los pobres* (the poor) or *los hermanos* (the brothers) were used to describe an essentialized and undifferentiated group. This would later cause conflict within the diocese. Not all Mayas of Chiapas supported the Church's project. Traditionalists (such as the caciques of Chamula) had political differences with the diocese and accused it of being an external institution that brought the destruction of indigenous culture.

This chapter presents a description of the conditions in which pastoral agents of the Diocese of San Cristóbal de Las Casas committed themselves to working with and for the poor. Bishop Samuel Ruiz's leadership, the historic meetings of the Second Vatican Council and the Latin American Bishops Conference in Medellin, and the specific historical context of the indigenous and peasant poor of Chiapas all played roles in the diocese's option for the poor.

A Sleeping Bishop Awakens: The Bishop and the Catholic Church in the 1960s

I was like the fish that sleep with their eyes open. For a long time, I didn't see. I passed through communities where people were being beaten because they didn't want to work more than eight hours [a day]. But I saw old churches and a popular religiosity in process, and I said, "what good people." I didn't see the tremendous oppression of which they were victims.

—SAMUEL RUIZ GARCÍA (CITED IN FAZIO 1994:106)

Sleeping with his eyes open, looking but not seeing. So Samuel Ruiz remembers his early years in Chiapas, traveling through the indigenous communities without noticing poverty and injustice. In one of the bishop's many stories, he tells about visiting an indigenous community in the early 1960s where he encountered an atmosphere of tremendous grief—a number of children in the community had recently died of measles and diarrhea. He asked what had happened and people told him:

> When the children got sick, we went to the closest place to ask that a doctor or nurse come to give us some medicine. And they told us, "Tomorrow the doctor will come. Wait there at the crossroads." We waited all day and he did not come. We went to see what had happened, and they told us they had been sent away on another task. The second time they said, "He will come the day after tomorrow." Well, we waited and he still didn't arrive . . . The third time: "The nurse will go there." The nurse never arrived. The fourth time we no longer needed anyone; all of the children had died (quoted in Fazio 1994:57).

One man in the community stated that there was nothing the people could do; it had been the will of God. Bishop Ruiz expressed his strong disagreement. He told the indigenous Catholics that this had not been the will of God—that God desires that all his children have life in abundance. Bishop Ruiz told them that poverty itself goes against God's will.

Nonetheless, at that time Bishop Ruiz concerned himself with converting and modernizing the poor. He did not see the need, in Freire's words, to "transform the structure" of society; rather he followed the development and modernization theories of the 1960s that emphasized economic and technological change as the best way to solve the indigenous "problem." In short, he believed the situation of indigenous people could be improved by making them more like mestizos. In the early 1960s Bishop Ruiz elaborated a preliminary pastoral plan with three fundamental goals: first, to teach indigenous peoples Spanish; second, to give them shoes since the majority were barefoot or wore sandals; and third, to teach them catechism. Rather than evangelize in native indigenous languages, Bishop Ruiz felt that indigenous people should speak Spanish since they were Mexicans (Fazio 1994). Decades later, after becoming known as one of the most progressive bishops of Latin American, Ruiz criticized his early goals, joking that perhaps he had desired to see people wear shoes because he was from the state of Guanajuato, a region dedicated to the production of shoes (Álvarez Icaza 1998:120).

To use the words of the bishop, the early pastoral project viewed the Indians as "objects" in need of evangelization rather than as "subjects" with their own ways of understanding and interacting with the world. At best the missionary philosophy and work of the diocese in the early 1960s viewed indigenous culture as irrelevant to evangelization and at worst as an impediment to pastoral work. In 1962 the diocese opened two schools for catechists in the city of San Cristóbal de Las Casas, and seven hundred catechists studied at these schools in the six years that followed. The schools, like Ruiz's preliminary pastoral plan, taught Western values along with catechism in order to Christianize indigenous people, and they treated students as passive receptors of evangelization. Lessons emphasized salvation through prayer, ignoring the poverty and marginalization common in rural communities. In 1968, a group of catechists expressed their dissatisfaction with this top-down approach to evangelization: "The church has taught us about the salvation of the soul, but not the body. We have worked for salvation and at the same time we experience hunger, sickness, pain, poverty, and death."[6] The indigenous Catholics demanded an evangelization that addressed their reality, their concerns of daily life.

Bishop Ruiz's pastoral work was influenced by broader changes in the Catholic Church, particularly by the Second Vatican Council (Vatican II, 1962–1965) and the Second General Conference of Latin American Bishops (1968), which underscored the structural roots of poverty and called on the Church to take concrete actions to end injustice. He rejects the idea that he created his own theological and pastoral line for the diocese but emphasizes the influence of these meetings, particularly Vatican II. "With some preoccupation I hear said many times: 'We are in the line of Don Samuel' and this worries me because I do not have *my* line; I have one: the Conciliar line."[7]

From 1962 to 1965, bishops from all over the world gathered in Rome for the meetings of Vatican II. Bishop Ruiz was one of the youngest bishops in attendance, and the event began to alter his view of the Church's mission. Pope John XXIII had convened these meetings to discuss theological and pastoral issues internal to the Church, such as faith and style of public worship. Issues "external" to the Church were also addressed, most notably social justice. Some of the most commonly remembered changes emanating from Vatican II are those in the mass. Liturgies were translated to local languages rather than being read in Latin, and priests faced their congregations rather than celebrating mass with their backs to the people. The Catholic Church was symbolically turned around—the people were to be the focus. One of the most important themes of Vatican II was "the opening of the Church to the world," or the recognition that the Church must be involved in the realities and problems faced by the people, particularly by the poor. Hence, evangelization of the spirit was no longer seen as being separate from daily material reality, and the ways the Church could contribute to a just society were explored.

Gaudium et Spes (the Pastoral Constitution on the Church in the Modern World), one of the documents produced as a result of Vatican II, denounces poverty and proclaims the right of all people to have what is necessary to live. "God destined the earth and all that it contains for the use of all people . . . Furthermore, the right to have a share of earthly goods sufficient for oneself and one's family belongs to everyone."[8] In addition, *Gaudium et Spes* underscores the relationship between human rights and human dignity, as it affirms that the Church should play a role in fostering human rights.[9]

At Vatican II, Pope John XXIII urged the Church to read the "signs of the times," that is, to explore and respond to the political, economic, and social context in which the Church worked. For most Latin American participants, the signs were clear—poverty, marginalization, and political repression.

Bishop Ruiz began to formulate his response to these "signs" upon his return to the diocese, initially by attempting to fashion an organizational structure better suited to the reality of Chiapas. In 1965 he created the Diocesan Pastoral Council and organized the diocese into six zones according to cultural-linguistic divisions (Iribarren 1985:4). This reorganization would allow for more communication at the local level and was intended to make pastoral work congruent with local needs. Pastoral workers of each zone would meet periodically to share their experiences and coordinate their work. Bishop Ruiz, influenced by these events, began to change his approach to indigenous communities, but the bishop's conversion had just begun.

In April 1968, Samuel Ruiz attended the international meeting of the Department of Missions of the Conference of Latin American Bishops (CELAM) in Melgar, Colombia. There, anthropologist Gerardo Reichel-Dolmatoff explained that evangelization, as carried out on the continent of Latin America, is a dominating action that is destructive of indigenous culture. The bishop struggled with the relationship between evangelization and culture and asked himself, "What thing is evangelization? Is it the destruction of culture? Should I sit down to contemplate cultures or revive them to their pre-Columbian splendor? Why did God permit the existence of so many cultures?" (quoted in Fazio 1994:87). Shaken by his own questions, Bishop Ruiz slowly began to reconsider the meaning of evangelization, asking about his own relation to indigenous culture. This questioning about culture continued for years and slowly led to changes in the style of evangelization implemented in the diocese.

The 1968 meetings of the Second General Conference of Latin American Bishops in Medellin, Colombia, were a turning point for the Latin American church.

In the preparatory meetings for the conference, Bishop Ruiz was asked to give a formal presentation on evangelization and catechism in Latin America. The strength of his address lies in the contention that evangelization is not only about celebrating the sacraments, but also about changing the way the Church acts in relation to the poor. He stated, "We cannot evangelize the poor if we are the owners of large estates. The weak and oppressed will alienate themselves from Christ if we appear to be allies of the powerful; we cannot evangelize the illiterate if our religious institutions continue seeking the comforts of large cities and ignore the small towns and suburbs" (quoted in Fazio 1994:93). The presentation was well received, and the bishop became known as an expert on the topic of evangelization in Latin America. He was elected president of the bishops of the Department of Missions of CELAM and led the Committee for Indigenous Peoples of the Mexican Bishops Conference (CEM).

The documents produced at the Medellin meetings, like Ruiz's presentation, stressed that the Church must play a role in denouncing poverty in Latin America. The meetings emphasized the importance of an awakening of the masses in order to achieve social justice. Peace, defined as social justice rather than only the absence of war, was to be achieved "by means of a dynamic action of awakening (conscientización) and organisation of the popular sectors which are capable of pressing public officials who are often impotent in their social projects without popular support" (Second General Conference of Latin American Bishops 1979:176, quoted in Dorr 1983:160).

The meetings of Vatican II and Medellin demanded that Bishops and priests explore the social implications of their work and reformulate their role as pastors to respond to poverty and other forms of oppression. Ironically, as pastoral workers interacted with poor people and consequently began to denounce repression, racism, and marginalization, the Catholic hierarchy increasingly opposed liberation theology, critiquing the use of Marxist categories, and fearing that faith was becoming politicized. Members of the Church hierarchy could not accept the profound criticism of capitalism and social changes posited by the theology (Boff and Boff 1986:75).

Liberation theology, one of several pastoral lines that emerged from Vatican II and Medellin, had an important impact on the Diocese of San Cristóbal, particularly in its path to accompany the poor. At its center, liberation theology "contends that the Christian gospel, the 'good news,' is that God is working— and that God's people should therefore be working—in history to combat and eradicate all forms of oppression and domination, whether social, cultural, political, economic, or spiritual" (Smith 1991:27). Not only does liberation theology proclaim that oppression and domination are wrong, but that the Church (God's people) should be working to protect human rights, especially in the defense of a dignified life for all human beings.[10]

Liberation theology describes a God who takes the side of the poor and oppressed against the rich and powerful. Leonardo and Clodovis Boff, two of Latin America's leading theologians, state, "God is especially close to those who are oppressed: God hears their cry and resolves to set them free. God is father of all, but most particularly father and defender of those who are oppressed and treated unjustly. Out of love for them, God takes sides, takes *their* side against the repressive measures of all the pharaohs" (Boff and Boff 1987:50–51). Liberation theologians criticize the Catholic Church for its traditional links to the established order and the ruling classes and call on the church to change its stance, to act with and be evangelized by the poor. Indeed, liberation theology involves reading scripture from the perspective of the oppressed. As Peruvian Gustavo Gutiérrez, one of the most important liberation theologians, wrote: "We will have an authentic theology of liberation only when the oppressed themselves can freely raise their voice and express themselves directly and creatively in society and in the heart of the people of God, when they themselves 'account for the hope' which they bear, when they are protagonists of their own liberation" (Gutiérrez 1973:307).

Liberation theology describes sin as a collective or structural act, not only as an individual one. Suffering results from sin—the root cause of evil in the world and in history. Poverty, repression, and domination are all expressions of sin. Hence, the poor are not to be blamed for their poverty but are suffering due to "structural sin" or "institutionalized violence."

Many of the basic principals of liberation theology influenced the direction of the work of the Diocese of San Cristóbal. Most important is the commitment to work *with* the poor to assist in constructing the reign of God on earth. However, Bishop Ruiz has recently attempted to distance himself from this theological line. To give just one example, in a 1998 interview with Carlos Monsiváis, Bishop Ruiz stated, "They always ask me about liberation theology, and I always respond that a theology without liberation does not deserve the name theology. There is no theology of slavery, because Christ came to liberate humanity."[11] On one level, his distancing from liberation theology seems to have much to do with its falling out of favor with the Church hierarchy. In 1993, Papal Nuncio Girolamo Prigione harshly criticized the work of the Diocese of San Cristóbal and sought Bishop Ruiz's removal from Chiapas. Were the diocesan project to be affiliated with liberation theology, it could be labeled as radical and Marxist, and subsequently it could be further discredited. On another level, Bishop Ruiz is correct to give a wider context for his work. In that the call to work with the poor comes out of Vatican II and a number of papal encyclicals, it is not limited to liberation theology.

Searching for Liberation

The reality of poverty, racism, land scarcity, political repression, and a lack of social services in Chiapas in the 1960s demanded a pastoral line centered in liberation. In some regions, indigenous people worked as indentured laborers on their ancestral lands. They were called *peones acasillados* (literally, housed peons) because they lived on the lands where they worked. Estate owners could evict the acasillados if they stopped working (Rus and Collier 2003). Land poverty in the highlands forced indigenous people to search for work outside their municipalities. Many seasonally migrated to the fincas where they harvested coffee, tropical fruit, or sugarcane, working long hours for extremely low pay (Rus, Hernández Castillo, and Mattiace 2003). Throughout rural communities, malnutrition, tuberculosis, and death from gastrointestinal and respiratory infections were, and continue to be, common.

Beginning in the 1930s, peasants who worked on plantations near Ocosingo, Altamirano, Comitán, Las Margaritas, and other towns began to migrate east to the Lacandon jungle in search of arable land to cultivate (Ascencio Franco and Leyva Solano 1992). The colonization continued through the 1970s. In the jungle, the peasants encountered tremendous hardships—disease and a lack of potable water, social services, and schools—but also the hope of freedom from the oppressive conditions of working for others. In the early 1970s, the pastoral workers of Ocosingo and Altimirano saw the colonization as a search for liberation and decided to respond to it. The pastoral team would no longer plan and disseminate catechism but would work in coordination with the peasants to plan themes responding to their lived experiences. Indigenous people were to be the subjects, not objects, of catechism. In Ocosingo, the Dominican missionaries along with Marist Brother Javier Vargas saw the similarity between the peasants' search for land and the Bible's second book, Exodus. The misery and oppression of the Catholics and their search for a "promised land," dignity, and liberty was described as an exodus, and the book became a central theme of the catechism (Coello Castro 1991).

The following sections of this chapter focus on key events in the diocese's involvement in promoting and defending human rights: the Indigenous Congress of 1974, the formation and repression of peasant organizations, the

Map of Diocese of San Cristóbal de Las Casas and its pastoral zones

arrival of Guatemalan refugees, the founding of the Fray Bartolomé de Las Casas Center for Human Rights, and the 1994 Zapatista uprising. In all these events, Bishop Ruiz and pastoral agents did not, for the most part, impose their own ideology about human rights on the poor. Diocesan projects developed from historical circumstance, most importantly their contact with the indigenous and peasant communities.

"Speaking for Ourselves": Indigenous Voices in the 1970s

The First Indigenous Congress, held in San Cristóbal de Las Casas in October 1974, marked a watershed in the political mobilization of peasants in Chiapas as well as in the diocese's commitment to working with the poor. The importance of this congress cannot be overemphasized; it was the first opportunity in five hundred years for the four ethnic groups to unite and speak about their situation in public spaces that had been dominated by mestizos. The congress was conceived by then-governor of Chiapas Manuel Velasco Suárez to commemorate the five hundredth anniversary of the birth of the first bishop of Chiapas, Fray Bartolomé de Las Casas (1474–1566), remembered as Defender of Indigenous People.[12]

Recognizing the weakness of the PRI's networks in indigenous communities, the governor asked Bishop Samuel Ruiz to assist in convening the congress. Given the historical separation between church and state in Mexico, the governor's request for assistance from the Church was one of many paradoxes of the congress. Perhaps Governor Velasco Suárez recognized the Church's influence in the region and encouraged its participation in an attempt to control the Church's power and to identify local opposition organizations that could later be co-opted (Floyd 1997:130). In any case, Bishop Ruiz agreed to help coordinate the congress on the condition that it would not be a touristic or folkloric event, but rather that indigenous participants would be permitted to give their word in public after being ignored for so many years.

Preparations for the congress began a year prior to the event and lay the groundwork for much of the organizing that would follow. Between October 1973 and September 1974, local, regional, and municipal meetings were held in indigenous communities to discuss the upcoming event. Initially, people met to "know our reality," that is, to talk about the situation of indigenous communities, and to discuss Fray Bartolomé de Las Casas's work in relation to indigenous rights. Hopes, desires, and future goals were also addressed, and the four major ethnic groups of the diocese—Tzeltals, Tzotzils, Ch'ols, and Tojolabals—prepared their presentations on the themes of the congress: land, commerce, education, and health. In the course of these meetings, representatives were democratically selected to attend the congress. The social conditions of the early 1970s favored the beginning of an organizational process. Although the catechist movement within the Catholic Church had opened local-level discussion on such issues as land scarcity and the inequity of land distribution, few institutional political structures representing indigenous people existed. Day laborers who worked on plantations challenged their oppression and took over land. People called for an end to commercial exploitation (Morales Bermúdez 1992:248).

More than 1,230 indigenous delegates from the state of Chiapas attended the congress: 587 Tzeltals, 330 Tzotzils, 152 Tojolabals, and 161 Ch'ols. They represented 327 communities with a combined population of 250,000. During the congress, agreements were reached on each of the four themes discussed. The issue of land distribution was of special importance, given the prevalence of large estates and plantations (many of them illegal under Mexican law). The critical agreements reached on the issue of land were that *la tierra es de quien la trabaja* (the land belongs to those who work it)[13] and that "the communal lands which were taken from our fathers be returned to us" (Indigenous Congress of 1974, quoted in Morales Bermúdez 1992:349).

The indigenous participants in the congress recognized that they shared similar problems and could unite in their political struggles. For example, in one of the agreements on land: "We all want to resolve the problems of land, but we are divided, each one on his own. Because of this we do not have strength. We are looking for the organization of each group in order to have strength because unity gives us strength" (Indigenous Congress of 1974, quoted in Morales Bermúdez 1992:349).

The importance of the event in uniting indigenous peoples from various regions and in initiating organization beyond local communities is worth noting. Juan, a catechist from Guadalupe, attended the conference and was most impressed by the presence of so many indigenous peoples from throughout the diocese. In 1994, twenty years after the congress, he proudly recalled the enormous number of Tzotzils, Tzeltals, Ch'ols, and Tojolabals who united to exchange ideas, to reach agreements, and even to dance and play traditional music.

But the notion of "unity" described in the Indigenous Congress was, in 1974, a goal to strive for rather than the reality. There was not—and is not—unity within or among indigenous communities, and different groups within communities chose distinct political options. Some affiliated with the PRI in order to receive benefits, however small, in the form of land or credit. In the 1970s, increasing numbers joined one of several Protestant churches. There were also inequalities within communities based on age, gender, and, to a limited extent, economic status. During the very days of the Indigenous Congress, a group of Chamulas opposed to the hegemony of the PRI and the established leaders had attempted to take control of their local government. As will be detailed in the next chapter, the Chamulan leaders, with the assistance of the state government, prevented the dissidents from taking power. This early failure to adequately address (or in some cases even to recognize) the divisions within and among communities would lead to numerous conflicts in the diocesan project.

Father Iribarren, a Dominican priest who carefully recorded much of the diocese's history in published and unpublished manuscripts, remarked on the importance of the congress, noting that one of its key achievements for the poor was "the discovery that the plan of God was not their actual situation of misery and marginalization. God had other more just and kind projects for them. But in their action, the projects were impeded by the ambition of the powerful and the lack of adequate channels for their voices to be heard" (Iribarren 1985:6). Here it is worth pointing out that the poor did not suddenly wake up to "discover" their oppression; it was obvious enough. Perhaps they realized that their suffering contradicted the will of God; perhaps they were already aware of this. I view the Catholic Church's new role as an interlocutor (albeit a mestizo one) willing to engage in a dialogue with indigenous people and support their struggle for dignity as the congress's most important outcome. It is not that the Church spoke *for* the poor, as they already could speak for themselves. The Church listened to the poor and, as Pablo Iribarren states, provided a channel for their voices to be heard.

The congress was also important in establishing logistic and symbolic ties among the four ethnic groups. Indigenous representatives—*hombres de buena palabra* (men of good word), those who were consistent in what they said and what they did—were elected to take the proposals of the congress to their communities. It provided the space for the formation of independent peasant organizations.[14] Pastoral workers assisted with the founding of an organization named after Fray Bartolomé de Las Casas to continue the congress's work. A Marist brother from the Tojolabal zone served as its president, and other pastoral agents served as its advisors. In 1977, an advisor to this group asked, "Who will be the new Fray Bartolomé de Las Casas?" Indigenous people answered, "We will. We are Bartolomé. We needed one before because everything was decided in Spain, where we couldn't go and where we didn't have a voice; then they spoke for us. Now we are beginning to speak for ourselves" (Ruiz García 1999:17–18).[15]

The congress also had an important impact on the consciousness of the pastoral workers of the Diocese of San Cristóbal. They recognized indigenous people's ability to organize, the values that can and must come from evangelization, and the evidence of a liberating process supported by the Gospel. Furthermore, they decided to revise all pastoral work (Iribarren 1985). Decades later Bishop Ruiz reflected on the importance of the 1974 congress:

When the pastoral agents of the diocese saw and heard what indigenous people were saying about their own situation, it was very clear that our Pastoral Plan had been elaborated without taking into account the aspirations, necessities, and hopes of the communities. In response to this appeal we made a Plan that tried to respond in some way to the faith of the necessities described. (Ruiz García 1993:26)

In a November 1975 diocesan meeting (which later became known as the First Diocesan Assembly), priests, nuns, and lay workers began to plan the new direction of their pastoral work.[16] In this historic meeting two key lines of work emerged: first, a commitment to "work with and for the poor," and second, support for the formation of an autochthonous church (Iribarren 1985:7). Linking the work to the meetings of Vatican II and Medellín as well as liberation theology, the diocese chose at this 1975 meeting "the preferential option for the poor" as the path of all future work.

The second line of work, the autochthonous church, was more fully developed in the 1980s and 1990s and would include a series of changes in the diocese. The process involved an attempt to "inculturate" pastoral practices by recognizing and respecting the connection between faith and culture and taking culture into account in evangelization. In supporting the formation of an autochthonous church, Bishop Ruiz and the pastoral workers began to educate themselves about indigenous customs and beliefs. "Traditional" Mayan customs were incorporated in liturgy; ancient stories, symbols, and myths were reexamined; and some pastoral workers learned native languages. However, a romantic and reified view of culture prevailed. Questions of who would define culture and the ways tradition is linked to power were left unexplored. Another element of the project of building an autochthonous church was an attempt to change the very structures of the church to make it more relevant to indigenous and rural communities. In the 1980s and 1990s, this project led to the ordination of indigenous deacons who, along with catechists, were responsible for religious matters on a local level.[17]

In 1979, the third assembly of the Latin American Bishops Conference was held in Puebla, Mexico. Bishop Ruiz was not invited to these meetings, apparently due to Vatican attempts to limit progressive bishops' influence in the context of growing opposition to liberation theology. Having recently been appointed pope, John Paul II attended these meetings, visiting Mexico for the first time. He traveled to the southern state of Oaxaca, where he spoke to an audience primarily composed of indigenous peoples. He presented himself to indigenous people as someone who "wishes to be your voice, the voice of those who cannot speak or who are silenced" (quoted in Dorr 1983:212–213). Pope John Paul II affirmed his wish to be the voice of the indigenous peoples rather than to listen to and engage in dialogue with them. In this way the Catholic Church remained an advocate for the poor, "a voice for the voiceless," and hence, a voice of colonialism steeped in paternalism and power. This context gives even more importance to the alternative project of the Diocese of San Cristóbal and its attempt to walk with the poor.

Accompanying Peasant Organizations and Guatemalan Refugees

If we are to be the humble servants [of the people], we will accompany them. The need expressed by the people will tell us our level of political participation.

—FATHER IRIBARREN (1985:74)

As members of the diocese searched for effective, concrete solutions to the poverty of the indigenous peoples in Chiapas, they began to take a more direct role in accompanying peasant political organizations. Following the Indigenous Congress, pastoral workers played a key role in the formation of *Quiptic ta Lecubtesel*, a productive cooperative run by catechists in the region of Ocosingo. The name Quiptic ta Lecubtesel is a Tzeltal phrase meaning "Our Strength is Our Unity for Progress," and catechists called the organization "the little sister of the Word of God." Some 150 communities participated in cooperatives that took up the defense of their human rights and the struggles for access to land. In time, the group acquired more autonomy from the Church, and in 1980, members of Quiptic, together with five other organizations, formed the productive cooperative and political organization Unión de Uniones (Union of Unions). In addition, a number of nonreligious groups, including the Alianza Campesina (Peasant Alliance), CIOAC (Independent Confederation of Agricultural Workers and Peasants), and OCEZ (Peasant Organization of Emiliano Zapata), emerged during this period to demand the return of lands that had been illegally appropriated.[18]

As peasant organizations expanded in size and number, government repression against them increased. In 1980, this repression culminated in what is remembered as the massacre of Golochán.[19] In the region of Sitalá in north central Chiapas, peasants had been attempting to gain legal access to the land from the Secretary of Agrarian Reform for nineteen years but had not received a positive response. Following the Indigenous Congress of 1974, a peasant organization of the same name developed in the region. In 1980, pastoral workers realized that they could not offer a viable political solution to the problem and stopped advising peasants in the area. According to Pablo Iribarren (1985), the

Socialist Workers Party (PST, a left-of-center organization that was co-opted to be a satellite group of the PRI) was pushing for land invasions at a national level and took advantage of the Chiapas opening to become involved in the region. The PST advised the peasants to invade the plantation of Golochán. The invasion took place, and soon after, the police arrived accompanied by landowners of large holdings in the area. Hoping to prevent a violent conflict, Father Mardonio Morales, a Jesuit priest of the diocese, met with the state governor on June 2, 1980, and the next day the governor went to visit the plantation. Nonetheless, on June 15, 1980, police and soldiers arrived and fired at the 723 families who occupied the land. The firing lasted two and a half hours and left at least twelve people dead and countless others wounded. The government later offered to buy the land for the invaders, but only under the condition that the peasants would pay the government back within ten years and would affiliate with the PRI. The peasants refused.

The case of Golochán exemplifies the contradictions implicit in the Church's work to accompany the poor in their struggles for land and liberation. Ideally, the pastoral workers walk beside the poor, but this position is difficult given the privilege of pastoral workers in comparison to peasants. The vast majority of the pastoral workers are mestizos, and although many live modestly (having voluntarily renounced some of their economic privilege in order to walk with the poor), they have the backing of religious orders or other institutions. This is not to deny that pastoral workers sacrificed a great deal; because of their political commitments, some received threats and several were jailed in the 1990s. But in their desire to accompany the poor, the pastoral workers could never become "the other," just as the anthropologist engaged in participant observation cannot become a member of the society under study. Pastoral agents are aware of and struggle with this dilemma. The Church's role of accompaniment raises a number of difficult questions: If the Church is to play a role in raising awareness of injustice, what is the next step? Should the Church play a role in the political struggle for liberation that may follow? How far should the Church accompany people in their struggle for liberation?

Another dilemma faced by the diocese in accompanying peasant organizations is that catechists ran some of the organizations, making it difficult to separate religious and political affiliations. In some communities, two chapels were built, one for those supporting the government, another for those in opposition. In other communities Catholics followed one political option while Traditionalists or Protestants followed another. Father Iribarren notes that several catechists "were absorbed by the socio-political struggle, with the consequential weakening of the catechist cadres" (1985:75). Others used their religious position to pressure Catholics to follow a particular religious option, while another group rejected all political activity as going against the will of God (Iribarren 1985:72). The relationship between faith and politics is complex because the two cannot be completely separated. Catholic social teaching stresses the need to promote social justice and criticize structures that cause poverty and oppression, areas that are regarded as political.[20]

In response to the violent repression of land occupations, most notably the repression in Golochán, land was the central topic of the 1985 diocesan assembly. Pastoral workers began their meeting by examining what they had done to accompany the poor. In the area of economics, religious workers noted that they had assisted in the formation of productive and transport cooperatives, popular credit unions, and workshops and had offered technical assistance. In politics, they had supported people in filing claims to gain access to land, contributed to political formation through sponsoring courses and assemblies, and given critical support to organizations, regional catechists groups, refugees, and political prisoners, among other activities. In ideological work, they accompanied theological and biblical reflection groups, held mass for the successes and failures of land struggles, encouraged the participation of women, and informed people about Protestant "sects."[21] As important criteria for all of these projects, it was noted that they must not substitute actions that must be taken by the *pueblo* (the community) itself; the pueblo is the subject of its own history (Iribarren 1985:52).

At this 1985 assembly, concrete goals were established. First, a diocesan organization to assist the poor with land-related problems would be established to offer legal advice, provide a channel for denunciations, and defend human rights. Second, theology itself would be examined and used to illuminate the struggles related to land. Third, the relationship between politics and faith would be analyzed to see how the Church could act in conflicts. Finally, a diocesan plan was to be elaborated to explain and prioritize criteria for "accompanying the poor." The goal of this analysis was to reinforce the actions of the people, cause the Church to be present in their struggles and share their risks, relate the diocesan structure to the base, and assist in political formation (Iribarren 1985:52).

In 1986, the diocese elaborated a comprehensive Pastoral Plan that would guide its future work. The doctrinal framework begins, "We believe in God our Father who wills the lives of his children and a life of abundance," and it contains areas of evangelization, conscientization, accompaniment, culture, communications, and coordination. Overall the plan emphasized the value of recognizing the traditions and dignity of the people and the role of the Church in "inserting itself as Jesus did into the process of the liberation of the oppressed, in which they are the agents of their history, and together we build the new society in anticipation of the Kingdom" (quoted in Womack 1999:205). Of particular interest is recognition of the importance of culture in the process of evangelization. Pastoral agents are urged to study regional history and indigenous language and to promote cultural expressions. One of the goals is "to insert ourselves (as a Church) into the culture of our people and to take on the social utopia hidden there, accompanying them on their historic path and accepting the sacramental signs of the Indians and their ministries" (as reported in Iribarren 1991:32). In their recognition of the hidden social utopia, pastoral workers challenge development strategies that attempted to modernize and Westernize the supposedly backward peasants. The pastoral workers recognized the strong sense of community among peasants. But the view of rural communities as hidden utopias once again illustrates the diocese's romantic view of indigenous peoples.

The arrival of Guatemalan refugees beginning in the early 1980s forced the diocese as an institution to continue in its path of accompanying the poor. Thousands of indigenous people fled the repressive regimes of Guatemala's military leaders: Lucas García, Ríos Mott, and Mejía Víctores. The military counterinsurgency campaigns and "scorched earth" policies, which destroyed entire villages and their inhabitants, resulted in massive violations of human rights. During the civil war 440 villages were destroyed and some 200,000 people were killed. By 1984, the violence had displaced about a million people, and 150,000 of these refugees found their way to Chiapas (Verrillo and Earle 1993:227–228). Crossing into Mexico, the refugees first came in contact with the peasants of the border communities. The refugees told pastoral workers and peasants about the egregious human rights violations taking place in Guatemala. The pastoral workers in the Diocese of San Cristóbal were forced to decide how they would accompany the refugees. The Christian Solidarity Committee founded by the Diocese of San Cristóbal initially provided humanitarian relief but in time supported the organizing efforts of the refugees, cooperatives for the sale of artisan goods, the training of local health promoters and teachers, and other tasks. Numerous Mexican and international nongovernmental organizations as well as the United Nations set up health clinics and other types of support for the refugees (De Vos 2002; Hernández Castillo et al. 1993). The diocese's involvement with refugees also led to direct confrontations with the Mexican government, which considered the diocese's activities a political threat to Chiapas's stability. While the Mexican government "relocated" refugee camps (in some cases violently) and the Guatemalan army raided the camps, the diocese denounced these violations of human rights and continued to provide support for the refugees.[22]

The Legacy of Fray Bartolomé de Las Casas:
Defending Human Rights in the 1990s

In response to the countless human rights abuses reported to pastoral workers, Bishop Ruiz García established the Fray Bartolomé de Las Casas Center for Human Rights in 1989 to actively promote and defend the rights of the poor. As a nongovernmental, Christian organization, "the Center works to be loyal to the evangelical message of assisting, accompanying, and moving forward all humans in the revindication of their just demands, recognizing in them the presence of the Savior" (Fray Bartolomé de Las Casas Center for Human Rights 1994).

Established six months after Chiapas Governor Patrocinio González (1988–1993) took office, the center began to operate at a time when the state government punished dissent, whether in the form of a demonstration or written or spoken criticism of the government, with arrest. For example, in July 1991, a caravan of peasants from the region of Marqués de Comillas began a march to Mexico City to protest the corruption of government authorities. When the caravan reached the city of Palenque, it was met by 700 police officers with clubs and tear gas. A total of 303 male protestors were arrested and jailed for forty-eight hours.[23]

In the 1990s, as diocesan workers criticized the state and national governments, the government responded by attacking the diocese. On September 18, 1991, two state police arrested Father Joel Padrón, the parish priest of Simojovel de Allende since 1979. The police took Father Padrón to the jail in Tuxtla Gutiérrez. He was accused of robbery, conspiracy, damage to property, possession of illegal weapons, and inciting peasants to take land, among other crimes (Gómez Cruz and Kovic 1994:165–167). The government had fabricated these charges.[24] The arrest attacked the growing agrarian rights movement. Since the 1970s, Zoque and Tzotzil peasants who worked on coffee plantations in the region of Simojovel and Huitiupán had been organizing and demanding better working conditions and access to land (Harvey 1998). Simojovel was a strategic choice for the mobilization, as it represented one of the first regions to take on this struggle against plantations. Prior to the arrest, peasants had taken over several plots of land in Simojovel, and government officials accused Father Padrón of inciting peasants to take the land. However, Father Padrón's arrest served to punish the Diocese of San Cristóbal de Las Casas for its human rights work. Just four days before the arrest, Bishop Ruiz held a press conference in which he denounced the serious human rights abuses committed by state and federal officials in Chiapas.

On October 18, 1991, about five hundred peasants from Simojovel began a pilgrimage of 123 kilometers to Tuxtla Gutiérrez to protest the detention of Father Padrón. During the journey, many peasants—including Tzotzils, Tzeltals, Ch'ols, Tojolabals, Zoques, and mestizos—joined in, and a total of 18,000 united in Tuxtla Gutiérrez on October 21 (Gómez Cruz and Kovic 1994). There they attended a mass at the cathedral of San Marcos, then remained for three days of prayer and penitence. Some continued to the Basilica of Guadalupe in Mexico City, where Bishop Ruiz co-celebrated a mass with the participation of some fifty priests.

Why would the indigenous Catholics of Chiapas sacrifice so much for Father Padrón? For indigenous Catholics, the attack against Father Padrón was not an attack against an individual priest or an attack against Bishop Ruiz. It was an attack on indigenous rights, most explicitly the right to land.

Father Padrón was released from jail on November 6, 1991, largely as a result of the pilgrimage to Tuxtla Gutiérrez and Mexico City. Indeed, the pilgrimage and release represented a critical moment in the organizing of indigenous Catholics in Chiapas. As in the congress of 1974, the ethnic groups saw that they shared similar problems and goals and that in their unity they were more powerful.

The massive mobilization in response to Father Padrón's arrest led to the formation of Pueblo Creyente, an important diocesan-wide group that works to promote social justice in Chiapas.[25] Several other faith-based organizations were established in the early 1990s. Two such groups include Xi' Nich' (The Ant) and Las Abejas (The Bees), their names reflecting the collective base of their organizations.[26] Ch'ol, Tzeltal, and Zoque Indians formed Xi' Nich' in 1991 in the northeastern region of Chiapas, and Tzotzils formed Las Abejas in 1992 in the highland municipality of Chenalhó. In these groups indigenous Catholics and other indigenous people have united to defend their rights through nonviolent resistance. Participants of Pueblo Creyente, Xi' Nich', and Las Abejas organize local and regional sit-ins, fasts, marches, and other events and have publicized their demands in several pilgrimages from Chiapas to Mexico City.

Another important group created in the 1990s is CODIMUJ, the Diocesan Coordination of Women, which brings together Catholic women from throughout the diocese to participate in local discussion groups, regional workshops, cooperatives, and other activities. Although women religious have supported local women's groups since the 1970s, the commitment to women's rights was not formalized until 1992 with the creation of CODIMUJ.[27] Thousands of indigenous and mestiza women (primarily members of impoverished communities) take part in CODIMUJ. At the local level, women meet in community discussion groups to read the Bible "with the eyes, mind, and heart of a woman." At regional meetings and workshops, women share their experiences and recognize their common problems. Many CODIMUJ participants also take part in political organizations such as Xi' Nich'. Women of CODIMUJ have joined state, national, and international events such as marches for International Women's Day and the World March of Women 2000.

Bishop Ruiz as Mediator: Listening to Indigenous Voices

On January 1, 1994, the Zapatista Army of National Liberation (EZLN) took over seven towns in Chiapas and demanded basic human rights—land, housing, jobs, food, health care, democracy, and justice.[28] The Zapatistas declared "Enough is enough!" and denounced that indigenous people and peasants of Chiapas had been exploited and marginalized for hundreds of years. After twelve days of combat between the EZLN and the Mexican army, President Salinas de Gortari declared a unilateral cease-fire.

On January 1, bishops of Chiapas's three dioceses released a statement of their position: "We do not accept an armed uprising, nor the recourse to violence, but they both must serve as warnings of the danger of abandoning the marginalized groups."[29] Even though the bishops denounced violence, they called on society to recognize the injustice and inequality in Chiapas. Immediately after the Zapatistas appeared, government officials, the economic elite, and the media launched accusations at the Catholic Diocese of San Cristóbal, blaming it for instigating the uprising. The press claimed that priests Father Pablo Romo (a Dominican) and Jerónimo Hernández (a Jesuit), among others, were prominent Zapatista leaders. Critics labeled Bishop Ruiz "Comandante Sam," the supposed director of the uprising. Time and again, Bishop Ruiz has firmly responded that he does not support the use of violence. However, he added that if he had not helped to raise the consciousness of indigenous people about their rights in his many years as bishop, then he had not effectively carried out his work.

Attributing the struggles in Chiapas to "outside" actors like Bishop Ruiz fails to grant any agency to the indigenous poor. Some writers give the impression that diverse groups control indigenous people, who are unable to make decisions or take actions on their own.[30] The elusive Subcomandante Marcos, mestizo spokesman for the Zaptistas, became an international figure because of his charisma and media attention, but also because of the inability of many Mexicans to recognize an indigenous interlocutor.

In spite of the many accusations lodged against the diocese, Bishop Ruiz was asked to be the official mediator in the peace talks between the two parties in conflict, the EZLN and the federal government. The first round of peace talks began on February 21, 1994, in San Cristóbal's cathedral. In a country that spent a great part of the nineteenth century fighting over the separation of church and state, the political role of a religious figure was alarming and difficult for many Mexicans to accept. With the spectacular events of the Zapatista uprising, the Catholic Diocese of San Cristóbal received national and international attention. But the media, government officials, and public ignored the history of the diocesan process and came to know the diocese out of context, as if the Zapatistas themselves had brought it into existence.

Yet Bishop Ruiz could play the role of mediator only because he had worked for more than thirty years to build relationships with the indigenous communities of the diocese. He had undergone a significant transformation since the 1960s, when he hoped to give indigenous peoples shoes and teach them Spanish. In walking with poor people of the diocese, Bishop Ruiz learned to approach people with the desire to listen, to understand their point of view, and to dialogue with them. For a man of an institution that works to evangelize—an act of speaking to—it is paradoxical that Ruiz listened to and was converted by the poor.

Photo and caption by Genaro Sántiz Gómez, originally printed in Duarte (1998)
Celebration in Chamula
Fiesta de Chamula
K'in ta Chamula

4

The Sin of Westernization
Power, Religion, and Expulsion

The sin of Westernization occurs when we identify Christianity with Occidental Christian culture, demanding the resignation of culture, of the heart. It demands that in order for people to become Christians, they must renounce being human . . . In the work of the Church, we must decide if we are with Christ or against him, that is, if we are with the poor or above them.

— BISHOP SAMUEL RUIZ GARCÍA (1978)

Under Bishop Ruiz's leadership, the Diocese of San Cristóbal de Las Casas founded a mission in the highland municipality of San Juan Chamula in 1966. The mission was a well-meaning but poorly planned attempt to work with Tzotzil Mayas. After three years, the mission's priest, Father Leopoldo Hernández, left Chamula, having received numerous death threats from local Mayan authorities. The mission failed, in part, due to Father Hernández's racism but also due to his attempts to promote a new leadership in opposition to entrenched local leaders or caciques. To apply Ruiz's terms to the mission's work, it demanded that people renounce their culture in order to become Christian. This episode in the diocese's history is closely linked to the founding of the urban colonia of Guadalupe. Because of the Chamula mission, a number of Tzotzils decided to convert to Word of God Catholicism and to ally themselves with the Catholic Church. This religious alliance carried political significance, since the newly converted Catholics opposed the caciques, challenging their political and economic power. In time, Chamulan leaders expelled the Catholics, forcing them to leave their homes.

In many ways, the Chamula mission was out of step with the broader diocesan project described in the previous chapter. When members of the diocese evaluated their work in 1984, they divided their history into three periods.[1] They described the first period as the "civilizing missionary stage" (1952 to 1964), a time when pastoral workers set up missions along with schools, health clinics, and other developmentalist service-oriented projects. As the name suggests, rather than attempting to change the underlying structures that cause poverty, the goals followed the modernization approach of the time. Pastoral agents attempted to Christianize indigenous peoples and to assimilate them to mestizo customs. Pastoral workers labeled the second period, from 1965 to 1973, an *aggiornamento*, or an updating. During this period the catechist movement gained speed, and local peasants began to take up the work of announcing the Word of God. Finally, the third period, "the option for the poor," began in 1974, when the diocese formally committed itself to work with the poor and recognized the poor as the subjects of their own history.

The Chamula mission of 1966 to 1969 was behind the times, that is, it fits within the civilizing missionary stage because social services were provided, and above all, the project was carried out on the terms of the priest rather than on the terms of Chamulas. Years after the failure of the mission, a number of people from within the diocese harshly criticized the project for attacking indigenous identity and for promoting reformism rather than structural change. Nonetheless, the Chamula mission illustrates the complex political difficulties that pastoral agents had to address as they attempted to work in indigenous communities.[2]

To understand the failure of the mission, historical events within Chamula must be situated within the broader political and economic structures of highland Chiapas and Mexico, structures that excluded and exploited indigenous people. Anthropologist Gerald Sider writes that history is not just "'about' power, it *is* power" (1993:xxiii). He urges scholars to explore "how histories are, and have been, embedded in the way people have built their lives and their hopes" (Sider 1993:xxiii). Chamulas have built their lives and hopes in the context of a long history of exploitation (by Spanish colonists and later by mestizos), a forced and unequal incorporation in the colonial and contemporary state. Father Hernández could not see these structures and assumed that Chamulas would be liberated through internal change, that is, he felt that Chamulas needed to be "saved" and "civilized" through Christianity.

This chapter begins with a brief overview of Chamulan acts of resistance against Ladino dominance in the Cuscat Rebellion and Pajarito Movement, and then turns to the Chamula mission (1966–1969), the local elections of 1973, the first massive expulsion, and Protestant conversion. In each case political resistance was inextricably linked to religious faith and practice, and religious change corresponded to new forms of political resistance.

Of One Soul: Situating San Juan Chamula

San Juan Chamula has a reputation as the highland municipality most closed to mestizos, where indigenous tradition is most strongly preserved, in spite of, or more important, because of, political and economic pressures from the mestizo-dominated Mexican state. For decades Chamulan leaders have insisted on the unity of all community members and have placed extreme limits on dissent. Commenting on unity, Jan Rus (1994:294) notes, "The Tzotzil phrase for 'being of one soul' is jun ko'onton. Traditional Chamulas believe that even permitting a dissident to exist in their territory can destroy this 'oneness' and cause God and the saints to withdraw their protection from the entire community. Individual dissidence and nonconformity are therefore blamed for such collective calamities as drought, crop failure, and epidemics." This ideal of unity is a survival strategy. Chamulas, like residents of other highland municipalities, have resisted mestizo domination "by tenaciously defending the solidarity of local communities in the face of external authority" (Rus, Hernández Castillo, and Mattiace 2003:4).

During the colonial period, Chamulas continued to practice subsistence agriculture on their lands, but colonial administrators, priests, and Spanish entrepreneurs exploited indigenous peoples.[3] The colonial system of *repartimiento* granted Spanish settlers temporary access to indigenous labor. Given Chamula's proximity to the Spanish capital of San Cristóbal de Las Casas—at the time called Ciudad Real—Chamulas were particularly vulnerable to the extraction of tribute and forced labor. Yet during the colonial and post-independence periods, Chamulas actively resisted outside interference imposed by Spaniards and mestizos. The Cuscat Rebellion of 1867–1870 and the Pajarito Movement of 1910–1911 are two examples of the struggle of Chamulas to maintain even a small degree of autonomy in the face of exploitation, and they illustrate the central role that religion played in strategies of resistance.

The Cuscat Rebellion, 1867–1870

During the Cuscat Rebellion residents of Chamula adopted a new indigenous saint who was incorporated into the traditional fiesta cycle.[4] The economic roots of the Cuscat Rebellion are located both in mestizo exploitation of indigenous peoples in highland Chiapas and Tzotzil attempts to create autonomous social and economic communities in the post-independence period. During the mid-nineteenth century, mestizos seized native communal lands and forced indigenous peoples to pay rent to continue planting crops. At the same time, Creole priests (those of European descent born in Latin America) urged indigenous people to convert to Catholicism and exacted taxes for the church. Indigenous protest against this economic and religious domination began with the formation of a cult to an indigenous saint. On December 22, 1867, Agustina Gómez Checheb—a young Chamulan woman from the hamlet of Tzajalhemel—declared that she had seen three rocks fall from the sky while caring for sheep. She collected the rocks and built an altar. When Pedro Díaz Cuscat, a local Chamulan official, put the rocks in a box, he heard them speak. He stated that the talking rocks were sacred messengers and that Gómez Checheb was the mother of God who had given birth to the stones.

Tzajalhemel, located in a strategic area of the highlands because of its proximity to indigenous municipalities including San Andrés Larrainzar, Chenalhó, Tenejapa, and Mitontic, soon became an important pilgrimage site for Chamulas and other Tzotzils from neighboring municipalities. As Jan Rus (1983:145) states, "Having been mistreated by ladinos of all parties, especially during the preceding civil wars, many Indians seemed to find in the isolated shrine a kind of sanctuary, a place where they could not only pray in peace but could meet with their neighbors without fear of ladino interference." The shrine displaced the main church of Chamula and operated as an important mercantile center of the region. With indigenous peoples traveling to Tzajalhemel instead of San Cristóbal for trade and worship, Ladinos no longer had access to agricultural products Tzotzils sold, and indigenous people no longer purchased items in Ladino-owned stores. This threatened the exploitative economic relation between highland Tzotzils and urban Ladinos. To add to Ladino frustration, indigenous people paid neither alms to the Catholic Church nor fees for baptism and other sacraments, cutting into the Church's earnings (Rus 1983; Pérez López 1990).

As the cult to the talking stones continued to grow, the traditional San Cristóbal elite claimed they were threatened with a caste war. On December 2, 1868, they sent fifty men to Chamula who destroyed the temple at Tzajalhemel and took Agustina Gómez Checheb and Pedro Díaz Cuscat as prisoners. With the disappearance of these two leaders, the cult continued under new leadership.

In 1869, schoolteachers and secretaries began to collect a new head tax in the highlands, but some refused to pay. Interpreting the boycott as "an all-out attack on whites" (Rus 1983:149), Ladinos again claimed that Chamulas threatened San Cristóbal with violence. The Ladino priest Miguel Martínez traveled to Tzajalhemel to try to convince the Tzotzils to abandon their worship at the new shrine. He left with the shrine's possessions and, in the attempt to recover the sacred objects, indigenous people killed Father Martínez on his way to Chamula (Rus 1983:150). In June 1870, the San Cristóbal government sent more than a thousand troops to Chamula to crush the so-called rebellion. A small number of Ladinos died in the fighting, but the vast majority killed—perhaps as many as eight hundred—were indigenous people (De Vos 1979; Bricker 1981; Rus 1983).[5] By October 31, 1870, convinced that the indigenous resistance had been crushed, government troops abandoned Chamula.

From the late 1880s to the present, mestizos have mistakenly labeled the Cuscat Rebellion a "caste war" in which indigenous people suddenly and unexpectedly attacked and murdered mestizos. This myth conveniently absolves mestizos of any responsibility for the violence at the same time that it creates the fear that the highland Tzotzils are dangerous savages who must be controlled. In some stories of the rebellion, "the actual battles of the 'Caste War' itself were magnified until it seemed that the Indians had actually been on the point of overrunning San Cristóbal and slaughtering its inhabitants" (Rus 1983:158). To the present, *coletos* (mestizo residents of San Cristóbal) continue to express fear of Chamulas. While living in San Cristóbal, I heard a number of stories about the dangers of even stepping foot in the municipality of Chamula, especially at night. What is missing from this portrayal of "dangerous" Chamulas and the Cuscat Rebellion is that Chamulas rebelled to preserve their way of life—to farm their land, protect their economic interests, and worship in their chapel without outside intervention.

The Pajarito Movement, 1910–1911

The Pajarito Movement took place in the context of the end of the Porfiriato (the period of dictator Porfirio Díaz, 1872–1910) and the beginning of Mexico's civil war. In 1911, a group of Ladinos in San Cristóbal seized upon the confusion following the exile of Porfirio Díaz and formed an indigenous army—comprised principally of Chamulas—to overthrow the Porfirista state government in Tuxtla Gutiérrez (Rus 2004). Ladinos mobilized Chamulas to fight a Ladino battle, promising the Chamulas land grants and other benefits. Chamulas participated in hopes of overthrowing authorities who had extracted taxes and labor from them.

One of the agents recruited by Ladinos to organize indigenous troops was Chamulan Jacinto Pérez Chi'xtot, nicknamed "Pajarito" (Little Bird; *Chi'xtot* is Tzotzil for a species of bird). Pajarito claimed to have seen a new god, Saint

Matthew, who had arrived to teach Chamulas to defend themselves and promised victory (Hernández Lampoy 1994:34). The indigenous Brigada Las Casas led by Pajarito fought numerous battles in which more than three hundred indigenous people were killed. When the Chamulas met difficulties, the Ladino leaders abandoned them, and indigenous political and economic grievances were forgotten. Jan Rus points out, "What the cristobalenses had not counted on when they organized the 'Brigada Las Casas,' however, was that by legitimizing the Indians' opposition to the state government and established order, they would at the same time unleash all the resentments and hatred that had been building up within their own communities against the collaborationist ayuntamientos" (Rus 2004:70). That is, following the battles against the Porfirista state government, Chamulas directed their violence toward Pajarito and his followers for making them suffer the consequences of a Ladino conflict. Chamulas of the Brigada Las Casas attacked the indigenous people who had served Ladinos in carrying out local tax and labor recruitment policies during the preceding fifteen years. Within their own municipality, Chamulas killed previous municipal presidents and scribes and replaced them with "real Indians," men who had served in religious offices.

Through oral histories, the Pajarito Movement remains within Chamulan memory today. The experience of fighting for and subsequently being betrayed by Ladinos increased Chamulan suspicion and hostility toward outsiders. For example, in 1934 when a rumor circulated that anti-Catholics were coming from the state capital to burn the saints in Chamula, people hid images of saints and maintained an army for months on the road leading to the town center (Rus 1994). However, Chamulas directed much hostility toward Pajarito, who had been co-opted and then betrayed by Ladinos.

Anthropologist Gary Gossen (1999; 2002) finds similarities between the Pajarito Movement and the Cuscat Rebellion. Most important, in both events Chamulas mobilized to maintain control over their own affairs. In a context in which outsiders constantly exploited Chamulas by expropriating land, extracting labor, and enforcing taxes, Chamulas saw local control as paramount for survival. Chamulan Traditionalists use the pejorative term "prayer makers" to refer to those involved in both the Cuscat and Pajarito movements. Gossen notes, "The term is applied today to Protestant evangelical converts and, indeed, to practitioners of any 'new' religious movement. Those individuals in the Chamula traditional community who are opposed to 'new religions' use this very language, often citing the trouble that was provoked by the Cuscat and

Pajarito 'prayer makers' as good reason for avoiding any affiliation with 'new' cults and religious practices" (2002:1084). Given this history, when Father Hernández, a mestizo priest, initiated the Chamula mission in 1966, Chamulan authorities viewed him with great suspicion.

The Formation of Caciques

Another piece of the history of Chamula and expulsion is the project of the Mexican government to support local indigenous leaders who would ally themselves with the government at the same time they would defend local traditions. In the 1930s, the Mexican government intensified its attempts to co-opt indigenous leaders in order to consolidate the postrevolutionary state. This resulted in the formation of caciques, entrenched local leaders who control access to government resources at the same time that they use the resources for personal benefit.[6] In time the caciques became critical to preserving Chamula's partial autonomy from mestizo cultural, political, and economic control. In exchange for government resources, caciques had to ensure that residents of the municipality delivered votes to the PRI.

The formation of caciques is intimately linked to the violent expulsions from Chamula in the 1970s. Caciques maintain political control through violence, threats, arrests, or expulsion of those who challenge their authority. The roots of the *cacicazgo* phenomena were planted during the term of President Lázaro Cárdenas (1934–1940), who attempted to integrate indigenous peoples into the modern Mexican nation through *indigenismo* (Rus 1994). As early as 1935, President Cárdenas visited highland Chiapas, observed the poverty of the area, and created the Departamento de Acción Social y Cultural de Protección al Indígena, the Department of Social and Cultural Action for the Protection of the Indian (Pineda 1993). In 1936, Erasto Urbina (who by some accounts had Chamulan ancestry on his maternal side) was appointed as the state's director of this department. During his term, Urbina expropriated highland fincas, giving them to indigenous communities (Rus 1994). Urbina also provided for the education of some young Chamulan men in Spanish and in administrative skills to aid in the "development" of their communities. He appointed scribes in Chamula who were to serve as administrators in the town councils (Wasserstrom 1983).

In 1938, Urbina declared that only bilingual municipal presidents would be permitted to run in the local elections of 1939. The leaders of Chamula rejected this reform and instead decided to adopt a system of two municipal presidents: one would be a monolingual elder who had served civil and religious cargo positions to administer local affairs; the other would be a younger, bilingual man whose role as an *escribano* (scribe) would deal with relations between the municipal and state governments.

Salvador López Castellanos, nicknamed "Tuxum," served as the escribano president of Chamula in the 1940s. Following his service, he announced his candidacy for the civil and religious presidency. Although since 1937 the sale of alcohol had been illegal in Chamula, during the same week in 1942 that Tuxum announced his candidacy, the state government enforced a law giving religious authorities exclusive rights to sell alcohol in their municipalities. This concession guaranteed economic resources to local leaders, as they would earn money from the sale of alcohol. State authorities acknowledged this in pointing out that the concession was made "both out of respect for its ritual meaning and to help defray the costs of office" (quoted in Rus 1994). In 1943, Tuxum took power as Chamula's only municipal president. State concession of the sale of alcohol to local leaders consolidated civil and religious power in Chamula. At the same time, bilingual scribes were accepted as the sole leaders of the community (Rus 1994; Wasserstrom 1983).

By the second half of the 1950s, the Chamulan scribes had been successfully co-opted by the state and worked from within the community to serve the state against the indigenous peoples (Rus 1994). The scribes appealed to tradition and unity to defend their power. At the same time, they ensured that votes were provided to the PRI, and in exchange, the state government did not intervene in internal affairs. Cárdenas's strategy had succeeded in working from inside the indigenous communities to change leaders, to create new offices, and most important, to co-opt native leaders. Hence, in the 1950s, "the very community structures previously identified with resistance to outside intervention and exploitation . . . had become institutionalized revolutionary communities" that were part of the Mexican state (Rus 1994:267).

By the 1970s, Chamulan caciques had obtained a monopoly not only over the sale of alcohol, but also over trucking, lending money, and the sale of soft drinks (Wasserstrom 1983). These leaders had access to the most fertile land and earned large sums of money from the established monopolies, leading to stratification in wealth.[7]

When the Chamula mission was established in 1966, Father Hernández and other religious workers recognized the destructive power of the caciques. Father Hernández worked to remove caciques from power and to replace them with younger Catholic leaders. However, Father Hernández committed the critical mistake of failing to place the caciques in historical context, that is, not taking into account that identification with the PRI and support for tradition were two of the few means Chamulas had at their disposal to protect their own interests against outsiders. In addition, Father Hernández failed to address the impact of broader political and economic inequalities within Chiapas. He viewed the poverty within Chamula as an internal problem that could be solved through civilizing and Christianizing its residents and removing the caciques.

Sin of Westernization: The Chamula Mission, 1966–1969

The relationship between Chamulan authorities and the Diocese of San Cristóbal has been marked by conflict, controversy, and at times, violence. When a group of Clarist missionaries began to work in several Chamulan hamlets in the 1960s, they were accused of being Protestant evangelicals and asked to leave after two years because of conflicts with municipal authorities. On May 13, 1966, Bishop Ruiz García established Misión Chamula, a Catholic mission directed by Father Leopoldo Hernández, a diocesan priest. Father Hernández quickly established a "development plan" that included the construction of a health center, a campaign for hygiene, a school of home economics, a night school for boys and girls with classes in Spanish, and training so that the students could become educational promoters of the community. As the following description of the mission's work will illustrate, Father Hernández was a complex character who at times made ethnocentric judgments but who also seems to have had a genuine desire to better the lives of the Chamulas.[8] It is important to emphasize that there are many success stories in the diocese's work with indigenous communities, and in some ways, the case of Chamula is an anomaly. I examine this case in detail because it is critical to understanding expulsion as well as the complexities of Catholic evangelization within indigenous communities.

From the onset, Chamulan authorities resisted the mission and placed restrictions on its work in order to maintain internal control against the intrusion of outsiders and unwanted interventions. The authorities demanded that Father Hernández remain in the town center, spread Catholic doctrine only if it was freely accepted, and construct no buildings for Catholic worship (Iribarren 1980:2).

The initial work of the mission was ethnocentric and contained elements of *indigenismo,* a plan that followed the general scheme of development policies for its time, emphasizing technological, economic, and cultural change as the way to solve the poverty of the indigenous people. Rather than respecting the religious customs of Chamula, Father Hernández insisted that Chamulas had to reject many elements of their traditional culture in order to be simultaneously evangelized and modernized. *Circular a los Amigos de la Misión Chamula* (Friends of the Chamula Mission Newsletter), written by Father Hernández to inform the mission's financial backers of its activities, presents a view of Chamulas that is paternalistic at best and outrageously racist at worst. In the first bulletin, dated May 13, 1966, Father Hernández introduces the Chamulas as "obstinate and stubborn, indifferent to pain and very criminal, very susceptible to alcohol." He laments that they make *chicha*, an alcoholic drink of fermented sugarcane juice, for their "bacchanal" and refers to Chamulas as *inditos*, a pejorative term which translates literally as "little Indians." The majority of the mission's evangelical work was carried out in Spanish, a practical problem since most of the people in Chamula spoke Tzotzil and not Spanish, but it also reflects the colonial mentality of the mission. Although they had arrived in Chamula from elsewhere to teach the Word of God, the Catholic missionaries did not learn Tzotzil but required the Chamulas to learn Spanish.

The news bulletins continually contrast Catholic belief with Chamulan tradition, a comparison that carries with it a series of dichotomies: modern/primitive, good/evil, and enlightened/ignorant, to name a few. In a short article titled "Two Different Pictures of a Tribal Mission" in the news bulletin of February 1967, Father Hernández contrasted the indigenous festival of Carnival to a Catholic religious ceremony. The description of Carnival is reminiscent of a Colonial missionary view—"seven days of unending sacred orgy," with some 15,000 Chamulas flooding the central esplanade of the village and "rivers of bronzed aborigines" walking through the streets. The Temple of San Juan is characterized as a "Babylon" with people "drinking alcohol, shouting, and singing in an environment thick with the smoke of incense and dust." In contrast, the Catholic celebration is portrayed as orderly and Christian, with people recognizing the presence of the Holy Spirit, uniting in their faith, and gathering around the altar to sing spiritual songs. In another bulletin, Father Hernández describes a catechism course and laments that "we see their [the Chamulas'] misery and ignorance without a remedy close at hand" and "I put my hope for establishing the reign of Christ in Chamula in the education of these ill-mannered men" (September 6, 1969).

One of the first direct conflicts between the Chamulan authorities and the mission was over the construction of a pig shed near the Temple of San Juan.[9] Although many Chamulas do not eat pork and consider pigs to be unclean, Father Hernández commissioned their help to build a shed to raise pigs for consumption. Perhaps he was unaware of Chamulan views about pork. Nonetheless, it is clear that he did not think to ask their opinion on the project, nor did he ask what might be the best productive project for the community. Instead, the priest made the decision himself and looked for people to do the work. In his bulletin of October 12, 1968, there is a picture of eight Chamulan men holding pigs. The caption below it reads: "Eight catechists will go home with pigs. They are happy. Chamulas, according to tradition, don't eat sheep because they are sacred and don't eat pork because it is dirty. But Christians have learned that it is not what enters the mouth that stains the soul, but what enters the heart." In spite of these "happy" catechists, many Chamulas criticized the construction of the shed. The people rejected not only the pork but found the presence of the animals near the Temple of San Juan insulting. In written complaints, Chamulan authorities repeatedly criticized the pig shed and forced Father Hernández to remove it.

Father Hernández's blatant racism often obscured the mission's threat to the power of local authorities. He publicly and officially denounced the caciques, sometimes by name, and little by little began to train a younger generation of leaders who would resist the caciques. The roots of this project can be seen in the formation of catechists. Young Chamulas received religious training, along with training in literacy, Spanish, and other skills, at the catechist school in San Cristóbal de Las Casas.

Juan, a Catholic catechist who resides in Guadalupe, recalled that Father Hernández arrived at his home in Chamula the late 1960s to invite him to a catechist course in San Cristóbal. Along with his two brothers, Juan decided to attend the class and remained in the course in the city four full months, reading and studying day and night. Why did Juan decide to leave his home in Chamula to participate in the class? He was an orphan—his mother had died when he was ten months old, and his father later died from alcohol abuse. He did not have any land and had few prospects for earning a living in Chamula. Perhaps in his alliance with Father Hernández and the Catholic diocese he saw the possibility, however small, of an alternative to a life that seemed to offer only poverty.

His conversion brought a number of changes: literacy, connections with other indigenous peoples in Chiapas, and validation for his newfound work as a catechist, complete with a credential identifying him as such. In 1994, Juan recalled his first catechist course some twenty-five years earlier:

> We read in Spanish and Tzotzil. I didn't know how to read when I arrived at the course, but I studied hard. With the help of God, I learned to read and write. They had a book in the two languages, one page in Spanish and the facing page in Tzotzil.
>
> There were more than sixty people at the course. They were all in-digenous—Tzeltals, Tzotzils, Cho'ls, Tojolabals, Mams, and Zoques. I studied there for four months. During the course I made my first com-munion and my confirmation. I have my credential from 1969 that states that I am a catechist.

Faith played a strong role in his decision to remain in the course and to work as a catechist. As he told me in 1995, after working as a catechist for more than twenty-five years:

> I will be a catechist for my entire life. Some people say that they need a rest and will stop preaching the Word of God when they are older. But a catechist is a job for life; there is no rest because there is a lot of work to be done.

In Chamula, the majority of the first catechists, like Juan, were very young. Elders viewed these young male catechists as a threat to their religious and social authority, an authority gained through service in the traditional cargo system. Hence, the Chamulan Council of Elders became one of the strongest oppo-nents of the mission, and in June 1967, the council prohibited Father Hernández from celebrating mass outside the main temple under threat of death. Father Hernández failed to recognize the traditional authority and respect granted to the elders. For him they only represented an obstacle to his work. In the Febru-ary 1, 1968, newsletter, he described the elders as "impenetrable and unyield-ing to true Christianity, remaining obstinate in their traditions with profound roots in the past." [10]

In 1969, the caciques' complaints about and threats against Father Her-nández grew in intensity. On September 4, 1969, the religious authorities of Chamula wrote a letter to the Office of National Patrimony[11] and accused Fa-ther Hernández of the following:

1. Committing acts against the cultural unity of Chamula; of having been imposed by the Diocese; of exciting an immediate danger of a rupture of the religious sentiment of the community. He has tried to make us deny our Gods and is against our customs; he has introduced outsiders into the municipality.

2. Crimes against the Patrimony of the Nation; works against the aesthetics [of the community]: pig sheds, hen houses, rabbit warrens, washing-places, dining rooms, dormitories, and all of this next to the temple.

3. Other crimes in prejudice of the economic interests which are established in the zone.

Signatures and fingerprints of some five hundred people followed the letter (Iribarren 1980:6). The accusations are based on religion and culture rather than politics. The priest had entered the Chamulas' ritual and geographic space in living and working in their community, but he had done so on his own terms rather than on their terms. Father Hernández had broken even the initial agreement not to construct any religious buildings. In 1966, he attempted to build a chapel in the hamlet of Candelaria. Perhaps the Chamulan authorities found Father Hernández's ethnocentric evangelization to be the most destructive and damaging aspect of his work. Perhaps they believed that the federal government would be most sympathetic to complaints about "patrimony" rather than to complaints about the formation of new leaders. In any case, it was clear that Chamulan authorities wanted control over their space, and they demanded that Father Hernández abandon his residence in Chamula. Nonetheless, the authorities hoped that the priest would continue to visit on feast days and to perform sacraments such as baptism.

Traditional authorities threatened Father Hernández as well as numerous Catholics of Chamula. The priest's news bulletin of September 1969 reported that the only Catholic family in the hamlet of Las Ollas was violently attacked. A woman named Dominga and her eight-year-old son were assassinated. A second son was hospitalized due to wounds caused when his ear was cut off with a machete. In October 1969, Father Hernández wrote a petition asking for protection of some eight hundred Catholics in Chamula. He reported that in Candelaria, the hamlet with the largest number of converts, Chamulan authorities had violently threatened about two hundred Catholics. Threats of violence against Father Hernández continued.

Bishop Ruiz responded to the accusations and threats against the mission in a letter to the public ministry (district attorney's office) in San Cristóbal de Las Casas. Bishop Ruiz rejected all the charges against Father Hernández; noted that Chamulan authorities, rather than the overall population, were frightened by the work of the mission; and announced Father Hernández's retreat to prevent "the disgrace of a crime of uncontrollable resonance of which the community would not be responsible" (Iribarren 1980:7). Bishop Ruiz did not publicly denounce the ethnocentric errors of the Chamula mission. Rather than being removed from the region, Father Hernández continued the work of the mission from San Cristóbal. In his letter, Bishop Ruiz implies that the caciques rejected Father Hernández because he challenged their authority. Although Bishop Ruiz and Father Hernández focused exclusively on oppression caused by local leaders, this local oppression was linked to state and national government structures. Years later, other pastoral workers would criticize this lack of perspective in the work of the Chamula mission.

On October 26, 1969, Father Hernández wrote the last news bulletin from the mission. He laments having to leave their "tribe" because "the temple will remain without a priest and will return to be occupied by the curanderos and witches." Father Hernández's ethnocentric and paternalistic attitude had not changed.

Local Elections and the First Expulsion in Chamula, 1970–1974

Although Father Hernández no longer resided in Chamula after October 1969, he maintained pastoral responsibility for the municipality. He focused on training Chamulan catechists. From 1970 to 1973, Mariano Gómez López served as the municipal president of Chamula, and with Father Hernández living outside Chamula, there seems to have been a change of attitude on the part of the municipal authorities. Rather than being treated with hostility, Father Hernández was asked to visit to celebrate baptisms and other sacraments. Catechists intensified their work and held religious meetings in their homes. Meanwhile, the number of Word of God Catholics in Chamula increased (Iribarren 1980:9).

Father Hernández initiated several social development projects, including a local credit union that charged minimal interest rates and classes in health, carpentry, and home economics.[12] These projects were attempts to serve some of the specific needs of the population. Most important to the history of expulsion was a political project established in 1972 to form community and political leaders. The project, funded by the U.S.-based Catholic Relief Services, involved courses aimed at creating integral community development, laying the groundwork for an interregional indigenous alliance between Tzotzils and Tzeltals, and teaching about the Mexican constitution, individual guarantees, agrarian law, government offices, and planning of community projects (Iribarren 1980:14). The team responsible for the courses included Father Hernández, eight nuns, and specialists in certain areas. In 1972, they gave several ten-day courses, with an average of thirty-three Indians attending each one. One of the aims of the courses was to train people who would resist the political and economic power of the caciques. Father Hernández's own evaluation of the courses states, "We believe that with the assimilated knowledge (about laws) they will be able to defend themselves a little from the oppression and injustice in which they live" (Iribarren 1980:14).

The courses attracted those opposed to the caciques, and course participants began to organize for political change in Chamula. In 1973, four courses were given, each lasting ten days. According to Father Hernández, the newly trained leaders were well-received in their respective communities, and many were given important positions such as municipal *agentes* or heads of local education committees. Most important, the students in the courses formed the Unión del Pueblo (Union of the People), which organized to protest the injustices of the caciques.[13]

Father Hernández along with a small group of pastoral workers became involved in the preparation for the 1973 elections of Chamula's municipal president. For the first time in years, there was an opposition candidate, Domingo Díaz Gómez, who was an independent, not affiliated with any political party. He had received training in catechism and leadership through the Catholic mission and had a large number of supporters including Catholics and Protestants. Father Hernández and the nuns working in the area supported his campaign.

The other candidate in the election, Agustín Hernández López, was affiliated with the PRI and promised "that if I win the election, I will expel all the believers of the township." By "believers," Hernández López was surely referring to Catholics and Protestants who supported the independent candidate. He also declared his support for those who had served in the traditional cargo system and those who sold alcohol (Iribarren 1980:24). As the election neared, it seemed that Domingo Díaz Gómez would win. Witnesses stated that during the election, two lines were formed, one for the supporters of each candidate, and that the line for the independent candidate was the longer of the two. Observing this, a group of Chamulan authorities invented pretexts as to why a number of Díaz Gómez's supporters could not vote and began to pull men and women out of this line (Iribarren 1980:25).

In response to complaints about this fraud, a second election was held in November of the same year. Angel Robles, director of the government Office of Indigenous Affairs, observed the election and sent the ballots to the state capital of Tuxtla Gutiérrez, where they were to be counted. It remains unclear whether the votes were fairly counted. However, on December 30 the PRI candidate Hernández López took possession of the presidency in the presence of Angel Robles and congressman Jorge Ochoa. The next day local authorities jailed seven Chamulan men who protested the election. Two additional men were jailed in San Cristóbal for attempting to speak to the governor about the elections.[14]

Supporters of Díaz Gómez did not abandon their attempt to run a popular candidate for the local presidency. In 1974, they met with members of the right-of-center National Action Party (PAN) who agreed to open an office in Chamula. But the Mexican government continually thwarted their attempts to reach a peaceful solution to the post-election dispute. When President Echeverría visited the city of San Cristóbal in September 1974, a group of Chamulas including Domingo Gómez López tried to speak to him, only to have the dialogue interrupted by the governor of Chiapas, Velásco Suarez, who called the Chamulas "agitators of the pueblo" (Iribarren 1980:27).

Frustrated in their efforts to receive assistance from the state government, opponents of Hernández López resorted to more drastic measures. On October 13, 1974, during the Indigenous Congress, a group of three hundred Chamulas and forty students from a professional school for teachers in Tuxtla Gutiérrez occupied the municipal presidency of Chamula, arguing that Agustín Hernández López had won the local presidency by fraud. At noon, the students returned to Tuxtla Gutiérrez, leaving the Chamulas alone to defend the building. Angel Robles and Jorge Ochoa arrived in Chamula that afternoon. After making an agreement with the municipal president and the judge of Chamula, transit police violently evicted the protesters, injuring and arresting several (*El Caminante* October/November 1984; Iribarren 1980:29). The opposition group failed in its attempt to take the presidency. Perhaps most important, it was now clear to all that the state government backed Hernández López and would assure that he remained in power. His supporters began to organize to get rid of the opposition group, and plans for the first expulsion from Chamula began.

On November 1, 1974, Chamulan authorities held an assembly and began to identify members of the opposition—mostly Catholics but also Protestants—in their respective communities. In subsequent months, many dissidents were detained, robbed, wounded, threatened with death, or had their homes burned (Iribarren 1980; Morquecho Escamilla 1994:62). Municipal authorities claimed that these people were evangelicals who were going to destroy the Temple of Chamula, when in actuality they were dissidents who opposed the municipal president. At the same time, three Catholic chapels were burned. Municipal authorities arrested 161 people, who were transported to jail in the municipality of Teopisca in vehicles provided by the Office of Indigenous Affairs (Iribarren 1980; Morquecho Escamilla 1994). Authorities of the Office of Indigenous Affairs demonstrated a blatant disregard for Mexican law by participating in the arbitrary arrests of the 161 people.[15] Chamulan authorities threatened the exiled with death if they ever returned to their hamlets in Chamula. These threats finalized the first act of mass expulsion from Chamula. The event demonstrated the power of the caciques as well as their alliance with the state government. Not only did the state government fail to prevent the expulsion, it actively assisted in expulsion by transporting people to jail. The pattern would be repeated hundreds of times in the following two decades when local authorities, with the complicity of the state government, exiled political dissenters from Chamula.

Given this sequence of events, expulsion cannot be viewed exclusively as a religious conflict because political and economic interests are embedded in religious symbols (Morquecho Escamilla 1992, 1994; Pérez Enríquez 1994; Rus 1994). This point cannot be overemphasized. Jan Rus (2002b) writes of the "religious conflicts" of 1964–1976 from an economic perspective. He describes the clash between the traditional scribes and a growing group of young men who challenged their authority. This second group included a large number of entrepreneurs and elementary school graduates who refused to accept the scribes' authority (Rus 2002b). In response, the Chamulan leaders expelled all dissidents in an attempt to preserve the unity that had provided some protection to the community against outside intervention. Not wanting to jeopardize the thousands of votes that Chamulas provided to the PRI, government authorities failed to intervene to stop the expulsions.

After 1974, the expulsions continued, with Municipal President Hernández expelling six hundred people in August 1976. Most were Protestant, but Catholics also were forced to leave (Iribarren 1980:38). In response, the Catholic clergy wrote a letter to the Chamulan authorities announcing that the priest would not go to celebrate mass for the important Feast of Rosario if the exiled were not allowed to return. The authorities refused to allow the exiled to return, and the Catholic Church distanced itself from Chamula.

Protestants as Political Dissidents

In the early 1970s, at the same time that the first expulsions took place, growing numbers of Chamulas converted to Protestantism. This religious change is linked both to the growing number of Catholics within Chamula and the growing resistance to the caciques. Protestant missionaries had been in Chiapas since the 1800s and in highland communities since at least since the 1940s, when the Summer Institute of Linguistics (SIL, the international section of the Wycliffe Bible Translators) began work in highland Chiapas.[16] Protestant missionaries had minimal success in highland communities until the 1970s. Indeed, anthropologist George Collier (1994) notes that a Protestant missionary lived in Nauvenchauk, Zinacantán (a municipality adjacent to Chamula), for more than a decade before anyone joined the church.

In the late 1960s small numbers of Chamulas began to join Protestant churches. Two of the first Chamulan converts, brothers Domingo Gómez Hernández and Miguel Gómez Hernández, joined the Presbyterian church in 1964 (Gossen 1999). Poverty, politics, and religion are linked in their conversion narratives. Domingo's conversion came as the result of his job as a gardener in San Cristóbal for Kenneth and Elaine Jacobs, North American Presbyterian missionaries. Miguel, nicknamed "Miguel Kaxlan" because of his mestizo-style clothing, converted soon after his brother did, and he began to live and work at the missionary compound, where he assisted in translating the New Testament to Tzotzil. Like Juan, the Catholic catechist of Guadalupe, Domingo and Miguel had few economic prospects in Chamula. All came from very poor families with little access to land for farming.

By 1969, about 120 people—a tiny percentage of Chamula's total population—had converted to Protestantism (Gossen 2002:1097). Like the Catholic converts described in this chapter, Protestants were political dissidents. They represented a threat to traditional authorities in their rejection of alcohol, which cut into the revenues for the civil religious hierarchy, and their refusal "to recognize the moral authority of the central town government in their lives" (Gossen 1999:217). The Protestants paid a high price for their conversion. A number had their homes burned and fled to San Cristóbal (Gossen 1999; 2002).

In the 1970s, Protestantism gained increasing popularity in Chamula and other highland municipalities. Early explanations of Protestant conversion focused on the role of U.S. imperialism. Indeed, advisors close to the Reagan administration suggested that Protestant proselytism be encouraged in Latin America to counteract the supposed communist ideologies of progressive Catholicism (Pérez Enríquez 1994). However, attributing the rise in numbers of indigenous Protestants to U.S. imperialism denies converts any agency (Bastian 1983; Rivera Farfán 1998; Rus 2002b). Just as some Chamulas and other indigenous people of Chiapas allied themselves with the Catholic Church as part of the process of resisting political and economic oppression, others allied themselves with one of a number of Protestant churches. In writing of Protestant conversion in rural communities, Jean-Pierre Bastian notes that "the rise of Protestant sects, and of Pentecostalism in particular, seems to be the privileged means for large sectors of rural subalterns to express social and political protest" (Bastian 1983:152). Chamulas' ability to join Protestant churches reflects broader political and economic changes in the highlands. Rus and Wasserstrom (1981) note that in the 1970s, increasing numbers of Chamulas resisted dependence on the favoritism of the caciques. As plantation owners began to directly recruit laborers rather than work through the caciques, economic dependence on caciques lessened.

The number of Protestant converts in Chamula seems to have increased after the Catholic Church pulled out of Chamula in 1974. At this time, Miguel Kaxlan allied with the PAN to resist the political authority of Chamulan caciques. Gossen observes that Miguel Kaxlan "was able to mobilize large numbers of his compatriots for the cause of antiestablishment sentiments, for Miguel's antipathy for the ruling families was shared by many of his compatriots. With this political ploy, it was not difficult to turn religious conversion into a political statement. Indeed, many who could not have cared less about the tenets of the faith became Protestants precisely because of its antiestablishment political posture" (1999:218–219). While I would argue that tenets of the faith did matter, Gossen's observation that conversion to Protestantism was a political statement is an important one.

As it became evident to the caciques that the newly converted Protestants and Catholics opposed their authority, these converts were seen as a threat to established power relations. The caciques often failed to distinguish Catholics from Protestants, as both groups are accused of reading the Bible and threatening local tradition. In addition, both meet in homes in Chamula or churches in San Cristóbal de Las Casas, challenging the centralism maintained by the unitary Temple of Chamula in the municipal center.

The Aftermath of the Chamula Mission

Year after year, caciques continued to expel Chamulas from their lands, although the annual numbers vary depending on the decisions of each municipal president of Chamula. Diverse local and national human rights groups have denounced the complicity of the state and federal governments in indirectly supporting the expulsions through their failure to follow the Mexican constitution and punish Chamulan authorities or to take steps to stem the abuses. In other highland municipalities, local leaders have similarly expelled political and religious dissidents.[17] Current estimates cite from 20,000 to 30,000 indigenous people who have been expelled.[18] With expulsion continuing into the 1980s, Bishop Ruiz García declared that the diocese would no longer work in Chamula. At the request of local authorities, Agustín García, a priest from the Temple of San Pascual Babilón, began to visit Chamula to perform weddings and baptisms.[19]

The colonial actions of the mission were harshly criticized from within the Catholic Church, an indication that the mission's work went against the broader diocesan project described in the previous chapter. In a letter written to Bishop Ruiz García in 1975, Father Mardonio Morales—a Jesuit priest of the diocese—noted that Father Hernández's evangelizing in Chamula attacked the traditions, indigenous identity, and life of the community itself. Father Morales asserts that the mission mistakenly focused on economic oppression narrowly conceived rather than on structural injustice. The Chamula mission worked to get rid of the caciques without recognizing that "being of one soul" allowed Chamulas to receive political and economic benefits from the state.

Andrés Aubry, a historian and long-term collaborator with the diocese, wrote an extensive letter in 1980 assessing the Chamula project.[20] Aubry calls the mission "a pastoral Golochán," referring to a 1980 massacre mentioned in the previous chapter in which police and soldiers killed at least twelve people during a violent land eviction. Prior to the massacre and after a few years of advising the regional peasant movement, pastoral agents felt that they could no longer offer the necessary political advice. The Socialist Workers Party stepped in and, following a national campaign for land invasion, pushed for an invasion in Golochán. According to a description of events by Pablo Iribarren (1985), this political party "capitalized" on the situated and "directed" people to take over the finca of Golochán. In any case, the twelve killed were peasants, not advisors of the Socialist Party.

In comparing Golochán to the Chamula mission, Andrés Aubry is not in any way suggesting that the pastoral agents working in Chamula (or the political organizations in Golochán) are responsible for the repression; the blame clearly falls to the state. Instead Aubry is insisting that outsiders must take responsibility for the way they involve themselves in the defense of indigenous or peasant rights. In this regard, Aubry posits several questions: How much of the involvement—of pastoral agents or political parties—is for their own interests? How much is for indigenous people inhabiting the municipalities? Aubry adds that pastoral agents in both the Chamula mission and Golochán "embarked on a project, without knowledge of the indigenous problem and without the tools to achieve their goals, and with urban or ladino plans." His questions and comments suggest that the diocese needed to reconsider its accompaniment of the poor to avoid further mistakes. Aubry suggests that pastoral agents must work not to serve their own interests but to serve the poor as they walk beside them in their struggles. Diocesan-based projects, from the training of catechists to health clinics and schools, must be grassroots, local projects, not mestizo projects.

In response to the failure of the mission, diocesan pastoral workers changed their approach to expulsion beginning in September 1982, when they supported the foundation of the Comité de Defensa de los Amenazados, Perseguidos, y Expulsados de Chamula (Committee for the Defense of the Threatened, Persecuted, and Expelled of Chamula, or simply El Comité).[21] Initially, the group was composed of expelled Chamulan Catholics who worked to publicly denounce expulsion and other aggressions committed by caciques. Pastoral agents would not serve as representatives of the indigenous peoples. Instead, the expelled would be the agents of their own struggle. The group grew rapidly, and with the assistance of pastoral workers, members of El Comité met with then-governor Juan Sabines. Through meetings with government officials, public marches, fasts, and sit-ins, the group brought a great deal of attention to the problem of expulsion. In 1984, CRIACH, the Council of Indigenous Representatives of Highland Chiapas, was formally constituted from El Comité. Protestants who had been expelled from Chamula played an active role in the group, with some taking on leadership roles. In time, more and more Protestants joined, and expelled Chamulan Domingo López Angel, then a pastor of the Seventh Day Adventist Church, became its president. Ironically, this very group that had been established by Catholic priests and nuns became an important mobilizing point for Protestants (although Catholics remained active in the organization). This turn is the result of pastoral agents walking *with*, not in front of, the indigenous peoples.

The diocese's relationship with Chamula has changed significantly since the 1960s. Following the 1994 Zapatista uprising, Chamulan leaders asked that the Diocese of Tuxtla Gutiérrez send a priest every few weeks to perform baptisms in the Temple of San Juan. Ecclesiastically, Chamula forms part of the Diocese of San Cristóbal, so the authorities' decision to initiate relations with the Diocese of Tuxtla Gutiérrez may reflect their memory of the work of the mission in the 1960s or a rejection of the criticisms of expulsion issued by the Diocese of San Cristóbal. In this decision, it is also important that the Diocese of Tuxtla Gutiérrez is affiliated with the conservative line of the Mexican Catholic Church and is often politically aligned with the government, while the Diocese of San Cristóbal has taken an active stance opposing the political and economic repression in the state of Chiapas.

Under the leadership of Felipe Arizmendi, bishop of Chiapas since Ruiz's retirement in 2000, the Diocese of San Cristóbal has reestablished relations with Chamulan authorities. Diocesan priests and the new bishop have traveled to the town center to celebrate mass and perform baptisms in spite of the fact that expulsions continue.

Outside the town center, in dozens of hamlets, the religious panorama is significantly different. Catholic catechists within Chamula travel to San Cristóbal de Las Casas, where they participate in meetings with other Tzotzil catechists, including those from Guadalupe. These catechists preach the Word of God within Chamula and even attempted to construct two chapels in the 1990s.[22] Yet they must work with caution as their message continues to challenge the authority of caciques.

Photo and caption by Xunka' López Díaz, 2000, originally printed in color in López Díaz (2000)

My aunt is weaving a woman's black skirt.

Mi tía está tejiendo una enagua negra para mujer adulta.

Li junme'e ta sjal ik'al tsekil, sventa muk'ta ants.

5

Defining Human Rights in Context
Anthropological, Legal, and Catholic Perspectives

Only from within the poor classes of Latin American society will it be possible to grasp the true meanings of the biblical cry for the defense of human rights . . . The church may not, then, content itself with alleviating the most blatant forms of repression, as long as the cause of this brutality—institutionalized violence—remains in place.
—GUSTAVO GUTIÉRREZ (1983:87–88)

God wants all humans to live in happiness and to have that which they need for a dignified life. God made us all his sons and daughters.
—REFLECTION OF PARTICIPANTS AT A HUMAN RIGHTS
WORKSHOP, VILLA DE LAS ROSAS, CHIAPAS,
NOVEMBER 1991

In April 1992, the state government of Chiapas convened a public hearing on expulsion from indigenous communities. The event was the first of its kind and took place almost twenty years after the initial expulsions from Chamula described in the previous chapter. The motive for the hearing was a conflict in La Hormiga, one of the colonias surrounding San Cristóbal.[1] At the hearing, Governor Patrocinio González Garrido presented a legal proposal to classify expulsion as a crime with specific punishments and invited the hearing's participants to comment on the legal reform. In dozens of presentations, indigenous authorities, religious officials, academics, and human rights activists discussed a variety of issues related to expulsion. Many who opposed expulsion—religious leaders and human rights activists—argued that the new legislation was unnecessary because the Mexican Constitution protects the right to personal security, physical and moral integrity, property, and freedom of worship, rights that are clearly violated in expulsion. Indigenous authorities opposed the new legislation on grounds that it would threaten their culture and traditions. In the end, the hearing resulted in little more than a three-hundred-page publication of the presentations on expulsion (Chiapas State Congress 1992). No agreements were reached, no laws were passed, and the expulsions continued after the event.

What was missing in Governor González's act was acknowledgement of the political, economic, and historical context in which expulsion takes place. In writing about human rights in southern Mexico, anthropologist Lynn Stephen observes that rights can only be understood in context. "Thus the most important criterion for analyzing human rights from an anthropological perspective is that the analysis be grounded in a particular situation linked to the actions and intentions of specific actors within the context of institutionalized power" (Stephen 2002:29). In the case of expulsion, the institutionalized power of the PRI and the corporatist state led Chamulan caciques to ally themselves with the PRI to gain benefits at the same time that caciques expel dissidents. State and federal government officials justify their lack of involvement in expulsion through a supposed concern about preservation of indigenous custom and tradition. At the same time, officials use human rights language to justify involvement in indigenous affairs when it serves state interests, for example in the arrest of indigenous opposition leaders. Without placing specific cases in their context, human rights can become a pawn used to the benefit of those in power.

This chapter describes differing understandings of human rights that are relevant to the case of expulsion in Chiapas. The first half of the chapter examines anthropological debates surrounding universal human rights and cultural relativism, Mexican legislation regarding indigenous rights, and the concept of the "rights of the poor" in liberation theology. The second half of the chapter turns to the Fray Bartolomé de Las Casas Center for Human Rights, of the San Cristóbal diocese, and its approach to human rights in legal and educational work. The center's strategy in legal work is examined through one recent case of expulsion. The center's educational work involves presenting human rights workshops in communities throughout the diocese. The workshops illustrate indigenous Catholics' understandings of rights, which emphasize social and economic rights, or the right to a dignified life.

Human Rights and Anthropology

The legal conception of human rights has a long history going back to the Enlightenment and the revolutionary constitutions of France and the United States in the eighteenth century. Human rights gained international recognition in the contemporary period with the creation of the United Nations (UN) in 1945. In response to World War II and the massive human rights violations committed under fascism and Nazism, member states of the UN drafted the Universal Declaration of Human Rights (UDHR), which was passed in December 1948. The document contains thirty articles and in its preamble recognizes the "inherent dignity" and the "equal and inalienable rights of all members of the human family." Although the declaration is based primarily on individual political and civil rights, it also includes economic, social, and cultural rights. It is based upon the unity of human beings, which its authors saw as extending beyond races, groups, and individuals, and the universality of fundamental human values seen as transcending the particular values of diverse cultures (Beller Taboada 1994). Human rights were thereby recognized for all human beings precisely because they are human, independent of their social circumstances and the differences among individuals. Given this focus, it seems fitting that the UN declaration of 1948 does not mention indigenous peoples nor grant them specific rights.

Scholars, including anthropologists and political philosophers, concur that human rights as set out in the UN declaration are Western in origin and focus.[2] What remains in debate is whether the UN declaration can be applied universally without infringing upon the rights of societies with distinctive cultural, religious, and political traditions. A gap exists between the theoretical work of political philosophers and political scientists and the ethnographic research of anthropologists. Although scholars in the first group have advanced extensive theories regarding rights and the respective role of individuals and communities, they seldom examine ethnographic works on non-Western societies to explore how theories are played out in concrete situations. The anthropological literature provides detailed descriptions of law and rights in non-Western societies, but reference to theories of political philosophy and political science is minimal.

Theoretical questions relating to the conflict between local and universal definitions of human rights are particularly relevant to the case of expulsions in Chiapas, where some argue that Western conceptualization of human rights conflicts with the value of community cohesion. Since the proclamation of the UDHR in 1948, there has been a debate in anthropology with respect to international human rights and cultural difference (see for example Cohen 1987, Geertz 1984, and Nagengast 1994). Anthropologists criticized the international legal human rights framework for being ethnocentrically Western and for failing to recognize that different peoples have different conceptions of rights, negating the application of a cross-cultural code of rights.

Support for local, culturally based definitions of rights stems from cultural relativism, defined by Melville Herskovits as "a philosophy which, in recognizing the values set up by every society to guide its own life, lays stress on the dignity inherent in every body of custom, and on the need for tolerance of conventions though they may differ from one's own" (1950:76). On June 24, 1947, as the United Nations was drafting the UDHR in response to World War II, the Executive Board of the American Anthropological Association (AAA) rejected the idea of a universal human rights framework, arguing that different peoples have different notions of rights. The AAA statement, drafted by Herskovits, uses the concept of cultural relativism to criticize universal human rights. "Standards and values are relative to the culture from which they derive so that any attempt to formulate postulates that grow out of the beliefs or moral codes of one culture must to that extent detract from the applicability of any Declaration of Human Rights to mankind as a whole" (American Anthropological Association 1947:542). The association's opposition to the statement of the United Nations was that rights were "conceived only in terms of the values prevalent in the countries of Western Europe and America" (American Anthropological Association 1947:539).

At present, more than fifty years later, many anthropologists have criticized Herskovits's statement, and in 1999 the AAA adopted a declaration of human rights that supports the UDHR as a useful starting point for the defense of rights. Commonly critiqued is Herskovits's assumption that custom and tradition are inherently valuable and worthy of protection. As Richard Wilson points out, "Herskovits was saying that even if the political system is abusive, cultural values (as opposed to say, political values?) could be invoked to restore a balanced social order" (1997:2). Wilson emphasizes that culture itself is embedded in power relations and can be oppressive.

The universal/cultural relativism debate regarding human rights must be reframed, given that contemporary indigenous communities appropriate international human rights language as they struggle to defend their rights. For example, Sally Engle Merry (1997) describes indigenous Hawaiians' appeal to the UDHR as well as the U.S. Constitution along with local understandings of rights in their struggles for land. Throughout Latin America indigenous people have appealed to universal human rights accords to gain broad support for their demands (Kearney 1995). Similarly in Chiapas, indigenous groups appeal to the Mexican Constitution and UDHR for the protection of their rights.

More fruitful than the universal/cultural relativism debate is examination of the historical, political, and economic context of specific human rights cases. In writing of human rights abuses in Guatemala, Jennifer Schirmer (1997:162) notes that "an over-emphasis on abstract universal standards without the contextualisation and follow-up of rights-in-practice in the end, may hinder what shall be termed a climate for sustainable rights." In 1984, the Ríos Montt regime in Guatemala disbanded special tribunals established to try prisoners following intense criticism from international human rights organizations that the tribunals did not follow the Guatemalan penal code. The end of the tribunals made it appear that the Guatemalan government had made positive advances in human rights. Yet in the end, not only were the political prisoners denied a fair trial, but more than one hundred were covertly assassinated by the military. In her concluding comments on the case, Schirmer notes: "If human rights are to play a sustaining role in protecting individuals from particularly dangerous kinds of harm and injustices, the human rights and legal communities must learn not only to contextualise the perceptions and practices of rights but also to understand that momentary actions may not be lasting victories" (1997:181).

In Chiapas, the state and federal governments have used human rights discourse for their own benefit. Anthropologists Shannon Speed and Jane Fishburne Collier note:

The state government of Chiapas appears "colonialist," not just in imposing a literal interpretation of human rights documents on indigenous peoples, but, more importantly, in using the discourse of human rights to justify intervening in the affairs of indigenous communities whose leaders happen to displease government officials. Just as colonial authorities in the past justified intervening in the affairs of colonized peoples by claiming to eradicate practices that were "repugnant" to "civilized" sensibilities, so government officials in Chiapas are justifying their right to arrest indigenous leaders who (the government claims) have violated the human and constitutional rights of community members. (2000:878)

The contradictory claims made in the name of human rights necessitate consideration of rights within their political and economic context. When the "defense of human rights" is pulled from its context and accepted as an absolute, it is at risk of becoming an empty concept, or one that can be manipulated to serve the interests of the state (Malkki 1995).

Finally, emphasis on the universal/cultural relativism debate focuses on political rights and sidesteps economic and social rights. It is in this latter group of rights that many violations occur. In Chiapas, as some indigenous peoples such as Chamulan caciques ally themselves with the state to gain benefits, others join independent political groups, peasant organizations, and religiously based movements, among others, to demand access to basic economic rights. That is, all are involved in a struggle for economic resources but have chosen different political paths to achieve their aims.

Mexican Legislation and Indigenous Rights

Mexico's 1917 Constitution, written following the Mexican Revolution of 1910 to 1917, is one of the most progressive of its time. It provides for fair elections, land redistribution, the right to education, and fair wages and work conditions, among other rights. The first twenty-nine articles, known as individual guarantees, provide for the protection of basic human rights, including the right to life, equality, liberty, education, social security, and juridical security. The PRI, which held power from 1929 to 2000, worked to apply the "institutionalized revolution" of a social state. Yet the integration of the party and the state led to widespread corruption and limited the PRI's ability to realize its revolutionary program.

The 1917 Constitution contained no specific provisions for Mexico's indigenous population. At the time, prevailing ideology held that granting all citizens, indigenous and mestizos, the same rights would lead to equality.[3] In the 1940s, the Mexican government adopted a policy of *indigenismo*, an attempt to integrate indigenous peoples into a unified nation-state through assimilation. Indigenismo worked toward creating cultural homogenization in Mexico rather than a pluricultural nation, and hence the policy did not grant any specific rights to indigenous people or formally recognize their customs and laws. Programs promoting indigenismo neither integrated indigenous populations into the dominant society nor resolved poverty and political marginalization faced by indigenous communities.

President Salinas de Gortari's administration (1988–1994) introduced two important constitutional changes: one that ended agrarian reform and another that recognized Mexico as a pluricultural nation. On February 26, 1992, Salinas's administration passed reforms to Article 27 of the Mexican Constitution, which had promised agrarian reform. The changes to Article 27 declared the end of agrarian reform and denied peasants the right to solicit the endowment or extension of ejido lands, a form of community property. The second important change in the reform of Article 27 is that it allowed for the sale of ejido lands. For the first time, these lands could be bought, sold, conceded, transferred, rented, or mortgaged if the respective ejido commissions agree.

This legal reform was one of many policies carried out as part of the structural adjustment package promoted by the World Bank and International Monetary Fund. The reform to Article 27 paved the way for the passage of the North American Free Trade Agreement (NAFTA) and foreign investment in the countryside. Structural adjustment policies—begun under the administration of President Miguel de la Madrid (1982–1988) and continued under Presidents Salinas, Ernesto Zedillo (1994–2000), and Vicente Fox (2000–present)—dramatically reduced public spending on social services, privatized state industries, and reduced credit and subsidies, among other reforms. These policies break with the state's revolutionary social pact. Many indigenous and peasant organizations protested structural adjustment policies, noting that the adjustments favored large agribusiness operations at the expense of small rural producers. The EZLN (the Zapatista Army) declared that NAFTA would be a "death sentence" for Mexico's indigenous people.

A second constitutional change implemented by Salinas's administration was adding a paragraph to Article 4 to respect the rights of indigenous populations and recognize Mexico as a pluricultural nation. The new paragraph reads:

> The Mexican nation has a pluricultural composition originally sustained by the indigenous pueblos. The Law will protect and promote the development of their languages, cultures, practices, customs, resources and specific forms of social organization, and will guarantee their members effective access to the jurisdiction of the state. In the trials and agrarian procedures in which they participate, their practices and juridical customs will be taken into account in the terms that are established by the law.

Although the article begins by recognizing indigenous customs in judicial procedure, it ends noting that these will be recognized only in the "terms which are established by the law," referring to positive law, not indigenous conceptions of law (Cruz Rueda 1994).

The 1994 EZLN uprising brought the issue of indigenous rights to national and international attention. Zapatistas demanded that they, as indigenous peoples, "be allowed to organize and govern ourselves with our own autonomy, because we do not want to be subordinated to the will of the national and foreign powers any longer" and that "justice be administered by the indigenous peoples themselves, according to their own customs and traditions, without the intervention of the illegitimate and corrupt government."[4] Pressure exerted by the Zapatistas and other indigenous organizations forced the Mexican government to consider constitutional changes and new laws to protect indigenous autonomy. In February 1996, government representatives negotiating with the EZLN signed the San Andrés Accords, which redefine and expand specific cultural, territorial, and political rights for indigenous peoples. For five years, the Mexican government refused to pass the San Andrés Accords, citing concerns about sovereignty. In April 2001, the Federal Congress passed a watered-down version of the accords, contradicting commitments to support the dialogue process. For example, the Mexican Congress's version refers to "the places where communities dwell and which they occupy," while the original version recognizes indigenous peoples' right to lands, territories, and natural resources. Indigenous groups throughout Mexico protested the new law and demanded that the original San Andrés Accords be honored. Nonetheless, the Mexican Supreme Court rejected the hundreds of legal challenges it received regarding this diluted version of the law.

Progressive Catholicism and the "Rights of the Poor"
Catholic social teaching has a long history in calling for the respect of human rights. For example, Pope Leo XIII's encyclical *Rerum Novarum* issued in 1891 protests the exploitation of industrial workers. Of particular importance are the encyclicals of Pope John XXIII (1958–1963). These encyclicals define human dignity in social and structural terms as exemplified by *Pacem in Terris* (1963):

> Any human society, if it is to be well ordered and productive, must lay down as a foundation this principle, namely, that every human being is a person, that is, his nature is endowed with intelligence and free will. Indeed, precisely because he is a person he has rights and obligations flowing directly and simultaneously from his very nature. And as these rights are universal and inviolable so they cannot in any way be surrendered. (Quoted in Traer 1991:37)

The encyclical presents a list of rights including rights related to life and an adequate standard of living and rights in the area of moral and cultural values—religious activity, family life, economics (including work, humane working conditions, and a just wage), assembly and association, freedom of movement, and political participation.

As noted in Chapter 3, the historic meetings of the Second Vatican Council (1962–1965) and the Latin American Bishops Conference in Medellin, Colombia (1968) emphasized the structural roots of poverty and called on the Church to take concrete actions to end injustice. In liberation theology, one stream of progressive Catholicism, the issue of human rights became central to the work of the Catholic Church. In Latin America, Catholics worked to defend human rights, particularly against the repressive military regimes of Chile, Brazil, Guatemala, El Salvador, and Nicaragua. The military responded to Catholic-based activism by violently suppressing representatives of these movements. In many regions of Latin America, priests, nuns, and lay workers were assassinated, jailed, or exiled (Lernoux 1982).

The view of human rights in liberation theology differs significantly from that of western European legal codes. The protection of human rights follows the liberating mission of Jesus Christ and extends beyond individual conceptions of rights. Liberation theologians cite John 10:10, in which Jesus states, "I came so that they may have life, and have it abundantly," in describing God as a God of life. Following from the idea of a preferential option for the poor comes the idea of "rights of the poor," specifically concerned with basic human needs or economic and social rights. In the Latin American context, these were the most urgent concerns. As explained by theologians Boff and Boff:

> The struggle for promotion of human dignity and defense of threatened rights must begin with the rights of the poor ... first must come *basic* rights, the rights to life and to the means of sustaining life (food, work, basic health care, housing, literacy); then come the other human rights: freedom of expression, of conscience, of movement, and of religion. (1986:61)

Liberation theologians use the term "rights of the poor" rather than human rights to emphasize the relevance of social and economic rights. Gustavo Gutiérrez criticizes the "laissez-faire, liberal doctrine" of human rights that assumes that Latin American society "enjoys an equality that in fact does not exist" (1983:87). The Catholic Church, he contends, must address institutionalized violence, the cause of the most "blatant forms of repression" in working for the rights of the poor. "The church's denunciation of violations of human rights will quickly become a hollow cry if church officials rest content with the beginnings of a 'democracy' that is only for the middle class and actually only enhances the flexibility with which the prevailing system exercises its domination over the popular masses" (Gutiérrez 1983:87).

In his analysis of the use of human rights in liberation theology, Mark Engler (2000) summarizes the critiques of the western European idea of individual rights: they do not encompass economic rights or basic human needs, they support reform rather than systematic change, and they uphold the basis of capitalism through private property and other bourgeoisie concerns. Most relevant for the rights of indigenous peoples is Engler's recognition that individual conceptions of rights can deny the poor of agency, as the definition and defense of rights are managed by those with access to the legal system (2000:349). Engler suggests that the concept of the rights of the poor brings a historicization to human rights. It "draws attention to other uses of 'rights' that better allow the poor to become agents in the making of history. Human rights can function as utopian norms at the root of a vision of just relations and as a set of demands that mandate immediate historical action by many persons and groups working with the poor for a better society" (Engler 2000:358).

Liberation theology calls for a new type of society—not merely reformism—that involves both structural change and the transformation of individual human beings. Although it rejects capitalist development for creating divisions of wealth and the concentration of social power, liberation theology does not spell out exactly how the new society should look. O'Gorman notes, "There is no blueprint for the building of a new society; no map for the journey toward justness. Inspiration from faith and from the reality of daily living are the signposts but the way has to be forged as people move along together" (O'Gorman 1983:41, cited in Smith 1991:46). Liberation theology is clear, however, in its condemnation of such human rights abuses as torture, arbitrary detentions, and assassinations and in its advocacy of creating a new life based on solidarity and love among all. The concept of the rights of the poor coincides with the vision of the pastoral workers of the Diocese of San Cristóbal who saw the need for structural change in Chiapas in order that impoverished peoples could live a dignified life.

Human Rights and the Diocese of San Cristóbal de Las Casas

For the pastoral workers of the Diocese of San Cristóbal, the experience of living and working among the people of Chiapas led to the recognition of the need to promote and defend the human rights of the poor and indigenous peoples. Specific historical events such as the Indigenous Congress of 1974, the assassinations of peasants in Golochán in 1980, and the arrest of Father Joel

enty-two hours for verbally opposing the expulsion of the other families. The man paid a steep fine to be released and was threatened with expulsion himself. This jailing shows the level to which fear is propagated in Chamula and the risk involved in going against the power of caciques.

Second, the case also clearly demonstrates the complete political and economic domination maintained by the Chamulan authorities. The testimony states that because of the fear of authorities, the people of the hamlet accepted the accusations against the group without argument, although they knew the accusations were false. The fragile power held by the caciques is also evident in that they are threatened by the fact that a small group of families has received a loan from FONAES to buy instruments to play traditional music. This small cooperative in and of itself represents the possibility for further political and economic mobilization at a local level. This type of organization represents a threat to the monopoly of power held at the municipal level. Other cases have been documented in which Chamulan authorities threaten community members for participating in any type of local-level organization.[7] Chamula received significant amounts of state and federal aid in the 1990s, and caciques responsible for distributing aid within the municipality denied money to those involved in independent organizing. In order for the caciques to maintain political control, they could not allow independent groups to solicit funds.

The Las Ollas families who had taken part in the music cooperative were each required to pay a fine of three hundred pesos to the Chamulan authorities. This fine represents a punishment for their action but is also a way of returning all government funds to the hands of the municipal president.

How did the Center for Human Rights intervene in the case? When the families threatened with expulsion first arrived at the center, workers recorded their testimony and copied relevant documents. The center's lawyers proposed preparing an *amparo* (a document granting legal protection to someone under threat, similar to a restraining order) to protect the families of Las Ollas. If corresponding government authorities accepted the terms of the amparo, the families would be able to return to their homes in Las Ollas.

The lawyers explained the conditions, terms, and possible repercussions of the amparo to the families of Las Ollas, who after lengthy discussion agreed to this legal strategy. The lawyers then wrote up the legal documents. The amparo demanded that federal authorities protect the families from municipal authorities of Chamula. The documents referred to the Mexican Constitution in listing specific rights that were violated in the threat of expulsion. The lawyers then read the amparo to the group from Las Ollas, and members of each family signed each page. Because many did not know how to read or write, finger-prints served to formally identify individuals.

The papers were sent to the attorney of justice in the state capital, Tuxtla Gutiérrez, where a judge requested that the families present themselves in his office. The judge's official reason for this request was to verify the fingerprints as identification. It is likely that the request was simply a way to slow down the entire procedure, since fingerprints are commonly accepted in lieu of signa-tures. However, the center organized and paid for a trip to take the families to Tuxtla Gutiérrez. None of the women had ever been to the capital, and I ac-companied a lawyer from the center and the women on this daylong trip.

The next stumbling block was that some of the Las Ollas group had to pres-ent themselves in the same office in Tuxtla Gutiérrez to serve as witnesses to the events described in the amparo. The lawyers at the human rights center drafted the questions in advance. As several of the witnesses did not speak Spanish, the center prepared for a Spanish-Tzotzil translator to accompany them. Al-though the state is legally required to offer a competent translator, authorities commonly fail to comply. The testimony of the witnesses was successfully pre-sented, and the next step was to wait. Finally, in late June—three months after the victims had arrived in the center—the amparo was formally granted. This was the first time that any amparo had been successfully implemented against Chamulan authorities. The families returned to Las Ollas a few months later but were fearful that repression against them might continue. However, in this case, the amparo served its purpose; the families were allowed to live in peace in the community.

The case demonstrates the difficulties of working within the legal system of Chiapas to protect human rights. Without the legal assistance and financial backing of the Center for Human Rights, it would have been very difficult for the group from Las Ollas to seek legal protection. They did not have money to hire a lawyer nor the resources to make several trips to Tuxtla Gutiérrez to present the documents. The Las Ollas case demonstrates that expulsion is a phenomenon with political and economic roots. The Las Ollas families were threatened with expulsion for challenging the economic authority of caciques. Even with the threats, the families were willing to file the necessary legal docu-ments so that they could be allowed to return to their homes.[8] Although the amparo officially offers protection to the group from Las Ollas, its enforcement depends upon the political will of government authorities to carry out the or-der to protect the families.

The political context in which the events took place certainly had an impact on the response of state authorities. The conflict in Las Ollas began in April 1994, just three months after the EZLN publicly launched its uprising. The Zapatista uprising pressured state and federal authorities to directly address the issue of expulsion, at least with words if not actions. For example, the National Commission of Human Rights (CNDH) did not issue a recommendation on expulsions from Chamula until April 1994, even though it had received legal complaints about expulsion for years. In 1994, the CNDH recommended that penal action be taken against those responsible for expulsion, that the expelled be permitted to peacefully return to their communities of origin, and that exile be stopped. However, this recommendation has not been effectively implemented, as the CNDH does not have the power to enforce its recommendations.

The organizing path: Workshops and local human rights promoters
The priests, nuns, and laypeople (most of them mestizo) who work at the Center for Human Rights regularly organize workshops in different regions of the diocese. Workshops are carried out following the request of a community member, catechist, or pastoral worker. Some workshops provide a general overview of rights, while others are focused on a specific topic such as the electoral process, indigenous rights, or the rights of children or women. For the most part, workshop participants are peasants and indigenous people of rural communities. Members of the human rights center present information on the legal aspect of rights, including Mexican and international law. At the same time, workshops are a space for participants to share their own views of rights, which may differ significantly from the legal perspective. In the following, I analyze the *memorias* (literally, memories, or reports of the discussion) from thirteen courses given by the human rights center from 1989 to 1991 in various communities of the diocese. In addition, I draw from five additional courses I observed from 1993 to 1995. Analysis of these courses provides insight into both the ways the diocese attempts to promote human rights and indigenous understandings of rights.

The quote at the beginning of this chapter from a workshop held in Villa de Las Rosas, Chiapas, emphasizes that God desires equality and a dignified life for all. In the context of extreme racism and stratification in Chiapas, this is a radical view. The notion that everyone has the right to a dignified life demands structural change. The workshops described in this section promote utopian norms for building a just society, to use Mark Engler's words (2000). For example, in one workshop given in San Cristóbal, participants made lists of the rights of people (or individuals) and of communities. In a brainstorming session, participants noted that individuals have the right to

> live, be equal, be free, work, be paid a just salary, enjoy the fruits of our work, be doctors or professionals, eat, talk, think, sleep, and rest; have dignity, education, a home; marry freely and have the children that we want; have religion; have a car and go up in a plane; go to other countries; advise others; live in the country or city; enjoy protection of the law, justice; organize in our homes; travel in the street, and work for the betterment of our family.

In reflecting on their rights in communities, participants at the same workshop noted:

> We have the right to have land, request land; grow fruit trees; have cattle; form collectives; have sports facilities, roads, electricity, potable water, health clinics, schools; buy goods cheaply; receive a just price for our harvest; cooperate in the community; speak our own language; receive respect for our culture; have fiestas in the community; organize ourselves; participate in solving problems in the municipality; elect our authorities; hold demonstrations; get rid of our municipal president if he doesn't work; have a political opinion, and occupy political positions.

These two lists of "rights" begin with what are commonly defined as rights: the right to life, equality, freedom, work, a just salary, freedom of religion, political participation, and education. However, the lists go well beyond traditional definitions of rights; they include cultural rights specific to indigenous communities such as the right to "speak our own language." Inclusion of the "rights" to "be doctors or professionals" and to "have a car and go up in a plane" show a keen awareness of the existing inequality between mestizos and indigenous people as well inequality in the global system. According to course participants, indigenous people have the right to do these things, just as mestizos do. Some rights, such as the right to "cooperate in the community," are obligations (or reciprocal responsibilities) rather than entitlements.

The demand for equality is expressed in religious terms in the workshops.

For example, workshops often begin with the question Why do we have rights? The answers given in distinct communities are similar:

- Because we are human beings.
- Because we are created in the image of God.
- Because we are free people capable of loving and thinking.
- Because we are sons and daughters of God.

The statement that rights are given by God, not by the government, is a powerful one in a nation that has continually violated the rights of indigenous and poor peasants. The idea that humans are created in the image of God is empowering. It reinforces the demand for social justice as it challenges the status quo in Chiapas, where a small group of mestizos has held political and economic power for decades.

Several responses to the same question—Why do we have rights?—emphasize that people must work to defend their rights. For example, participants state that they have rights

- Because God Our Father sent his son to teach us to struggle.
- Because Jesus taught us to say the truth and taught us to defend our human rights. God formed us and made us so that all could eat.
- Because God formed the world and made all free so that the great (or powerful) don't take advantage of the small.

The link between human rights and action to defend one's rights is repeated throughout the workshops. Participants discuss problems that exist—in the terms used in workshops, "what causes suffering"—at three levels: family, community, and municipality. Problems mentioned at the family level include illness, poverty, alcohol abuse, lack of work, lack of respect for children, and inequality between men and women. At the community level, participants commonly note the lack of teachers, medical attention, roads, potable water, and organization among community members. At the municipal level corrupt authorities, divisions between communities, and lack of markets for products are discussed.

After naming these problems, workshop participants are asked to reflect on the causes of the suffering. Their responses emphasize structural factors: corrupt authorities, electoral fraud, unjust laws, capitalism, and unequal distribution of land, among others. Some of the causes have to do with local problems and conflicts; for example, alcohol is mentioned as a cause of poverty and violence. In addition, participants mention that suffering exists, in part, due to the lack of organizing among the poor.

During workshops, participants examined readings from the Bible in the context of human rights. The most common readings chosen for biblical reflection are Exodus 22:22–27; Isaiah 10:1–4; Amos 5:10–15; James 5:1–6, and I John:3, 1–2.[9] After the presentation of a reading, participants work in groups to discuss its meaning in their own lives, a method that has been used in Christian base communities in Latin America as part of the praxis of liberation theology.

An important theme in discussion of biblical readings is that of solidarity. In discussing Matthew 25:34–45, in which Jesus describes the importance of helping the needy in order to serve God, participants of a workshop in Amatán in February 1991 noted:

> It speaks to us of how God will bless our spirit of service with the most needy because in sharing with them, God makes us, and He will recompense us in the heavenly realm. On the other hand, those who don't will be condemned.

Another common theme is that injustice is wrong and goes against the will of God. In reflecting on a reading from Isaiah, course participants from a workshop in Ocosingo in April 1991 noted that the reading "tells us that there shouldn't be unjust laws that oppress the poor, the people. God made an announcement to the powerful who organize the oppression and injustice." Participants note that in contrast to inequality they experience, God's will is that all share in the riches of the world. At the course in Amatán in February 1991, a group presented this summary after discussing several readings:

> The Word of God speaks of justice, equality, and human rights. Also, God gives his word to the poor because we are those that live in a world full of corruption. He says that the rich must not be selfish and only see for their own good, but that they must become conscious of the needs of those who don't have things. Currently, we see that there are many who worship the "god of money" and for this God makes war, killing innocents, and increasing poverty.

The Word of God hinders the selfish and the powerful because it goes against their plan of making wealth. Nonetheless, the Word of God teaches us to open our eyes, because it shows us the reality and asks us to unite forces to change the world by making it better.

Another theme in the courses is the history of the struggle for the protection of human rights. The revolutions of France, the United States, Russia, and Mexico, as well as the laws that resulted, are discussed. The notion of equality among all human beings in Mexican law is emphasized; on paper, rich and poor, men and women, Indians and mestizos are equal. With regard to Mexican law, course participants focus on the fact that laws are not respected in practice. This is described both at a national level, where the indigenous are not granted the same rights as mestizos, and within indigenous communities, where the rights of women are not respected. In other words it is not enough to know one's rights. Course participants emphasize that they must work to defend their rights. For example, in concluding the discussion of laws, participants in Villa de Las Rosas in August 1991 stated:

For us in front of our oppressors, we didn't value our dignity and accepted what was done to us and we walked not for our own good, not to free ourselves of that which our ancestors worked for. The people don't realize what rights they have and continue to accept things as they are. In knowing our rights we have the obligation to demand that others respect them so that we can change society.

Few workshops in the period examined make explicit mention of the relation between human rights and culture. Perhaps due to the overwhelming number of human rights violations and extreme poverty present in indigenous communities, the defense of cultural rights did not seem to be so urgent. One course did deal directly with the issue of culture. A group of participants from Huistán in November 1990 noted that unquestionable acceptance of custom is problematic and that traditional festivals have been modified.

We have gotten rid of the customs that we used to be obligated to carry out. Before the fiestas were obligatory, it was custom to drink alcohol, and those who had to pay for the cargo [burden] of the fiesta were poor. Thank God that now we continue with fiestas, but not as before, because that caused many people to be drunk and even die. When people drink they begin to fight in front of church with yelling. For the fiesta we name those in charge who look for money and give cooperation for sweets and cookies.

More recent courses, those after 1995, have taken up the issue of indigenous rights and some courses focus exclusively on this topic.

In sum, the courses stress that rights come from God and from laws. The idea that rights are given to all as "children of God" is powerful. It illustrates that the current political and economic system of Chiapas goes against God's will. Following this reflection is another powerful idea—that people must organize to defend their rights. At the end of each course, agreements are reached and commitments are made. The most common is that the participants of the course will share their knowledge with other members of their communities. They also agree to put in practice what was learned by "following the Word of God" and working in their families and communities to see that rights are respected. The participants in one course agreed

to continue organizing ourselves and to have more communication; to unite so that we are not divided; to have hope for the future; to return to organize and to correct our errors and to be more conscientious; to put in practice [what we have learned] and to share with other communities.

The courses have a strong impact on the participants. As a result of classes, local human rights committees are created, demands are sent to government officials, and in some cases, acts of political protest are planned. Given the action-oriented focus of the courses, it is not surprising that government officials and the economic elite have accused Bishop Ruiz and diocesan workers of being "subversives" and have attempted to remove Ruiz from San Cristóbal.

The Center for Human Rights combines definitions of human rights based on legal codes, Catholic tradition, and indigenous understandings. The use of these different conceptions of human rights comes out of concrete experience. For practical reasons, legal codes are followed in the presentation of juridical denouncements of human rights violations. Workshop participants discuss the Mexican Constitution and international rights codes (both focused on the protection of individual rights) and learn about their legal rights before the state. However, a communal notion of human rights along with a Catholic view of rights is also evident in the courses. Participants state that people have rights because they are "created in the image of God" and that injustice and poverty go against God's will. Communal rights and the importance of sharing goods and knowledge are stressed. Participants leave the courses with the desire to unite in their communities and to demand that their rights be respected. Distinct notions of human rights—including those from indigenous communities, from Catholic doctrine, and from legal codes—are not treated as competing notions but rather as coexisting definitions of rights, each with its own utility.

Similarly, the Mayas of Chiapas who have been exiled from their native communities combine distinct views of human rights. They have appealed to the Mexican Constitution and international human rights groups in presenting juridical complaints in an attempt to return to their native lands. At the same time, they have decried the violation of community norms of respect and the lack of Christian brotherly love as they explore solutions to poverty and landlessness.

Photo and caption by Xunka' López Díaz, 2000, originally printed in color in López Díaz (2000)

My sister is embroidering my blouse.

Mi hermana Rosa está bordando mi blusa.

Li juix Loxae tsluchbun jchil.

6

Respect and Equality
Practicing Rights in Guadalupe

Human rights are not taught, you practice them all day long from the
moment you get up in the morning.
 —HEBE BONAFINI, MOTHERS OF THE PLAZA
 DEL MAYO (QUOTED IN BOUVARD 1994:109)

All people, Ladinos, Chamulas, Oxchuqueros, those from Chenalhó,
Mitontic, and Tenejapa, all people are from the same blood of Christ.
All humans are equal. Young and old, everyone.
 —FERNANDO, CATHOLIC OF GUADALUPE

The many human rights abuses in Chiapas are not limited to acts such as expulsion, arbitrary detention, and the abuse of authority; they include the poverty, discrimination, and marginalization that most indigenous peoples and peasants experience in daily life. It was not until the Zapatista uprising that human rights violations in Chiapas attracted national and international attention, and since then, the number of local human rights organizations has proliferated. The Zapatistas have a broad vision of human rights. They demand political rights (free and transparent elections and democracy), economic rights (agrarian reform, health clinics, access to social services), and cultural rights (official recognition of indigenous languages, respect for custom and tradition, and the right to administer justice in their own communities). For the Zapatistas, as for other marginalized peoples of Chiapas, the demands and struggles for human rights emerge from their daily experience. At the center of their demands is the "right to have rights" (Harvey 1998), that is, the end of the exclusion and oppression in which indigenous peoples of Mexico and Latin America have lived for centuries.

This chapter narrates the visions of human rights shared with me by the Catholics of Guadalupe. I first visited their homes to learn about expulsion, their understandings of human rights, and their struggles to defend their rights. In particular, I hoped to learn how their views articulated with western European notions of individual rights. As I listened to life stories of childhood, work in plantations, conversion to Roman Catholicism, expulsion, and life in Guadalupe, I learned about the violence of everyday life, the ways poverty and marginalization mark daily life.[1] In myriad conversations, the Catholics described the need for basic economic rights: health care, housing, water, education, work, and, perhaps most important, land. They described the racism of mestizos and the Mexican government. Their stories forced me to consider human rights abuses as an integral and ongoing part of daily life rather than isolated events that can be described and quantified in legal terms.

Human rights are commonly presented in dichotomies—individual versus community rights, economic versus political, culturally relative versus universal, Western versus non-Western. In rethinking theories of rights, a number of scholars emphasize that dichotomies may obscure more than they illuminate because different understandings of rights are not exclusive but interactive (see especially Pollis 2000). And as anthropologists Shannon Speed and Jane Fishburne Collier (2000) point out, mapping the ways rights are understood and used in specific contexts is more useful than exploring whether human rights are universal. My research in Guadalupe revealed a plural notion of human rights. The Catholics have a complex understanding of rights, which is internationally informed (by both the Catholic Church and universal human rights accords) but locally grounded. This understanding encompasses community solidarity, Catholic beliefs, individual rights, and national and international law.

Fernando: Struggling at the Side of God

I begin with the life story of Fernando, a Catholic of Guadalupe who earns a living by making and selling sandals from discarded automobile tires. He lives on the margins of society, a peasant without land who makes sandals from industrial society's waste. Although Fernando rarely mentioned the formal concept of human rights in our long conversations, the daily experience of poverty, racism, and political exclusion formed a central part of what Fernando told me and attempted to show me. It is this context in which he understands human rights and struggles to defend them. As anthropologist Richard Wilson (1997) points out, the political, economic, and historical contexts in which human rights are violated and defended are essential to understanding local interpretations of rights. Social history and biography intersect in Fernando's life story. Like the majority of Mexico's peasants and indigenous peoples, Fernando is excluded from political and economic power but at the same time is engaged in a constant struggle to defend his rights.

Tires and pieces of rubber mark the back gate of Fernando's house. When I found him home, he was commonly seated under a tree, measuring and cutting the rubber soles of the sandals. It takes him about two hours to make one pair of sandals, which he sells for five to seven pesos a pair (around a dollar in 1995). Most of the men in the community use these rubber sandals—they are sturdy and comfortable. Fernando would invite me to sit with him in the shade of a small tree, calling on one of his daughters to bring a chair. As he worked, we spoke about his life and his faith. He and his wife have eight children, and the youngest girls ran around and played near us as we talked. Every now and then one would sit in my lap and then run off and giggle. Fernando's house, one of the simplest in the community, had a dirt floor, walls of wooden planks, and a tar paper roof.

The stories he shared with me—of his childhood, work, religion, and expulsion—focused on the importance of the Word of God in his life. Now in his mid-thirties, Fernando had converted to Roman Catholicism when he was twenty-three and living in San Juan Chamula. He told me that it is important to "keep one's thoughts with God," and he prayed and fasted when making important decisions. When we first met, Fernando was preparing for the Catholic sacrament of confirmation and for his children's first communion. He was saving money for the event, attending classes, learning new prayers, and teaching Catholic doctrine to his children.

Fernando's life story begins with his parents. Like others, he mentioned his father's problems with alcohol—"he didn't hit my mother, he would just drink and drink until he fell asleep"—and the death of his parents when he was only eight years old. In these conditions, going to school was not an option. Instead he and his oldest brother, Santos, went to work on a plantation. Fernando told me that the work was hard and the pay minimal, but they had no other option. Reflecting on this time before he heard the Word of God, he said, "Sometimes I spent my money poorly. I bought a gun and things I sold later for a higher prices."

While living in his hamlet in Chamula, Fernando met a group of Catholic catechists and heard the Word of God. "At first, I wasn't so sure about following the Word of God," he told me. "I didn't understand it well." But little by little his faith grew. Practically landless (he owned a quarter of a hectare) and an orphan, Fernando found hope in this new religion and began to attend the Church of Caridad in San Cristóbal de Las Casas.

The Chamulan municipal authorities threw him in jail when they learned that he was attending Catholic services. "I was in jail for a day and a night, shut up with twelve or thirteen people, all of them Catholic. We played guitar and sang. We prayed to God." After his release, the authorities came to his hamlet and told him that he must stop worshipping as a Catholic or leave Chamula. "They threatened to kill me. The authorities don't know the law. But I had decided that I would obey God's commandments even if the authorities killed me." In the contention that expulsion is illegal, that the authorities do not know the law, Fernando is claiming his own rights. But his knowledge of the law could not prevent him from being expelled. He knew of the corruption of the state government that permitted the expulsions to take place year after year, and he had seen many families before him leave Chamula with no legal recourse. Eventually, he also had to sell his land and leave.

As part of his life story, Fernando described his search for land and a way to make a living, a search that began well before his exile. From Chamula to the plantation to San Cristóbal de Las Casas, the Lancandon jungle, and even Mexico City, Fernando and his family looked for a place where they could earn a living.

Like Fernando, the majority of the men in Guadalupe and many women traveled to fincas early in life. Plantation work is grueling; men and women harvest coffee, pull weeds, and trim the trees that provide shade to the coffee plants. The hours are long—work begins at four in the morning and continues through three in the afternoon—the pay minimal, illness and hunger common, and the housing barely adequate. Sebastián, another man in Guadalupe, remembered the daily abuse he experienced while working in the plantation: "The owner would throw fertilizer, water, and pesticides on the people while they were working. If you sat down to rest, they would scold you." Don Lucas complained of similar abuses, but most difficult was the strict discipline and control of having to work for someone else. He told me, "In the plantation you are not free. They don't respect people there . . . Before, I was a slave on the plantation."

Currently the residents of Guadalupe have a number of jobs. Most work as manual laborers or carpenters when they can find employment; others sell in the streets or market, wash dishes in restaurants, or carry out paid domestic work in private homes. Some travel to the state capital, Tuxtla Gutiérrez, or to cities outside Chiapas: Villahermosa, Cancún, Mexico City, and even to the United States in search of a way to earn money. Although the residents of

Guadalupe are urban Indians, they continue to identify themselves as peasants. Fernando told me that he has very little land but "thinks" like a peasant. Land carries symbolic importance, and like other peasants, he is a skilled farmer with vast knowledge of agriculture. In contrast to the exploitation of work in the cities, cultivating the land is dignified work in which one controls what is produced and consumed. While working for wages—on the plantation or in the city—the hours, pay, and labor itself are determined by one's boss. Wage labor reinforces the marginality of urban Indians as they provide a source of surplus labor for mestizo-owned businesses or households.

Immediately after being expelled, Fernando and his family were given shelter in the chapel of Domingo López Angel, a former Seventh Day Adventist pastor and important political leader of the exiled, in the city of San Cristóbal de Las Casas. Fernando remembers that forty-seven people, all of them recent exiles from Chamula, were staying in the chapel. He and his wife traveled to Betania, a community of exiles in the municipality of Teopisca, but they could not afford to buy any land there, and so they returned to San Cristóbal.

Then, one day, we met Mateo at the Church of Caridad. We decided that it would be better if we came to live here [in Guadalupe]. We saw that here there is water to drink. But we didn't have enough land to cultivate corn and beans, only this small lot.

Next, they traveled to the Lacandon jungle, where they found sufficient water and land and could plant pineapples, oranges, coffee, and corn. Unaccustomed to the heat (in contrast to the cool climate of the highlands) and the insects, they became ill. But what Fernando recalled as the most difficult was the lack of community: "There weren't any people to talk to there since we lived in the mountain." He told me that he and his family decided to move to another region of Chiapas.

So we left the jungle and went to live in the lowlands. We lived near Cintalapa and stayed there for a year and a half. We grew corn and beans. But in Cintalapa, people do not worship the Word of God the way we do. There are Evangelicals, Pentecostals, and Seventh Day Adventists, but no Catholics. We had to leave our home at five in the morning on Sunday in order to go to the celebration of the Word of God, and we did not return until almost nine at night. We had to walk a long way. We walked every week. Sometimes, my poor wife couldn't make the long trip. It was very difficult. I thought that it would be better to leave—that it would be better if we didn't stay there any longer. We returned to our home here in Guadalupe.

Community and Respect

Since his conversion to Catholicism, Fernando's faith in God remains constant and his home a place where he can share his faith with others. Although Fernando and his family regularly travel to the Grijalva Valley, where they cultivate corn, squash, and beans on rented land, Guadalupe is their home. It is the community where they have a house, where Fernando's brothers live, and where they go to church. When I visited Fernando during the summer of 1999, he explained that he had been selected to serve as one of the municipal "police" with the duty of resolving local conflicts, from drunken misbehavior to marital conflicts to theft. He explained that he spent hours listening to people's problems, searching for negotiated solutions, and assessing fines only when no other resolution could be found. Fernando lamented that this work took a great deal of time each week and that he had very little money. Considered service to the community, his work was unpaid (the honor of being recognized as a leader and mediator serving as the reward), and he was unable to leave the community to search for work elsewhere. So his only source of income was the small amount he earned selling sandals. But his service to Guadalupe is central to his belonging in the community; his service embodies the practice of respect for others, of building a local community where all have rights.

I first learned of the importance of community and rights in 1993, when I was part of a small research team that conducted a series of interviews on agrarian conflict and human rights violations.[2] My colleague and I spoke to peasants who had been detained arbitrarily, had received death threats from large landowners, had been evicted violently from lands by police or soldiers, and had been denied fair treatment by agrarian authorities. We asked peasants how they understood their right to land. One respected elder from the Tzotzil community of Tzajal-ch'en (municipality of Chenalhó) told us, "The peasant has the right to care for the land," and then he proceeded to talk of the importance of neither burning the land nor using fertilizer nor cutting down trees. In his answer, "caring for the land" was described as being important because people cannot live without the food the land provides. He described the land as a holy mother, *la Santa Madre*, who provides milk to her children, and the children in turn must care for their mother. Although the man's answer seems somewhat idealized (perhaps a longing for the past before chemical fertilizers were used, perhaps as a lesson to two young caxlan women), the reciprocal notion of rights surfaced time and time again in the interviews. The elder from Tzajalchen affirmed the peasants' struggle against the state as he criticized government authorities for perpetuating human rights abuses. But he also reaffirmed the value of community where rights are practiced as reciprocal responsibilities.

The interviews I later conducted in Guadalupe similarly revealed a deep commitment to solidarity. I was told that each member of the community has reciprocal responsibilities toward others, just as one has responsibilities toward the earth that gives life. At the center of belonging to and participating in a community is the idea of respect, which has two points of reference. One is historical: Tzotzils, like other indigenous peoples of Latin America, have not been respected by the dominant culture for more than five hundred years. They have been excluded from political and economic power. The second is that all humans are worthy of respect because they have dignity as human beings and as children of God.[3] Terms for respect in Tzotzil include *p'iso' taj muc,* which translates as regarding or measuring someone as a mature person, and *p'iso' taj vinik,* regarding someone as an adult, not as a child. Hence, treating people with respect means granting them dignity. The importance of respect has been well documented in ethnographies of highland communities. In writing of household relations in San Pedro Chenalhó, Christine Eber notes that before a daughter marries, her parents instruct her on the importance of "respecting" her new spouse. "If you and your husband both respect each other, you will be happy when you do your work. You will be very happy when you work your fields. In this way you will be true men and women" (1995:68).

Respect in Guadalupe, I was told, has meaning within the context of a community where each member carries out mutual responsibilities toward others. Most importantly, acting with respect means that one listens carefully, does not fight, and attempts to understand others. In Tzotzil, the verb *a'iel* means to listen, feel, and understand. Men and women of Guadalupe explained to me that respect begins at the level of the family.[4] A man who respects his family works in cooperation with his wife, provides food and other necessities for his family, does not fight with or beat his wife, and will not leave his wife for another woman. Likewise, a wife who respects her family works in cooperation with her husband to support her children and does not fight. Parents with respect know how to counsel their children and do not hit them. Agustín, a catechist, explained that respecting people in the community directly follows the model of respect in the family. "It is custom to respect elders and children. One must respect each elder as if they are your father or mother, and each child as if they are your son or daughter." Community members with respect are said to cooperate with others and "speak well," that is to talk things out rather than fighting. Obviously, this concept of respect is the ideal. Many conflicts exist within and among the families of Guadalupe.

Respect only has meaning in practice; it is fundamentally about how one treats others. In fact, men and women who are described as having a "good heart" are those whose words and actions are congruent, that is, they have only one heart.[5] Hence, each member of the community is responsible for respecting the rights of others. Rafael, a male resident of Guadalupe, explained how respect is put into practice:

A man with a good heart knows how to speak well. He knows how to respect his companions and will set a good example. He will take his cargo [work on behalf of the community]. He knows how to unite with others. He will work well. Those who are content are those who know how to work together.

The image of "working together" is commonly used to describe serving God. In some cases, it is symbolic, representing the need to form a community where people treat one another with respect. In other cases, working together is literal; those who respect others will carry out their duties, helping out in communal projects such as the construction of roads, schools, or chapels. This notion of respect is put into practice in the many acts of sharing food, money, or labor with those who have less. Widows and single mothers depend on other community members for their survival.

The community expected each member to work toward maintaining the survival of the community itself, and this may override individual interests. One problem discussed with me was the scarcity of water in Guadalupe. I was told that all community members should equally share the right to water to ensure that there would be enough for the basic needs of all. In 1995 none of the homes had piped water; rather there were several tanks where women and children filled plastic containers for their households' water supply. Two families who live directly below the tank used a hose to pipe out some water to their land for the cultivation of strawberries, which are sold as a cash crop. Other families saw this as problematic and complained that the household was not respecting the community, since the water used for strawberries was not essential to the families' survival. Cristóbal, who runs a small store in Guadalupe, explained, "The water is scarce, and it is for everyone. We don't think that anyone should waste the water here." He emphasized that community resources belong equally to all, and each family should have access to what is needed. However, there are no legal sanctions for using the water for cash crops, and in spite of the numerous complaints I heard about this family "wasting the water," the strawberries continued to be cultivated and watered for years.

The conflict over the use of water illustrates the link between basic economic rights (the need for water) and solidarity rights (the need for all community members to cooperate in conserving water). In Guadalupe, the practice of sharing water is not just a community or moral decision, it is a material necessity. The water conflict is the result of structural constraints imposed by poverty and marginality. There is little need to ration or "share" water in the older neighborhoods of San Cristóbal de Las Casas where scarcity of water is rarely a problem. Perhaps this small example is simply a reminder of the resourcefulness of those who live in communities with scarce resources. This is not to stereotype indigenous peoples as being innately generous, but given the circumstances of poverty and exclusion in which they live, sharing becomes a necessity.

Equality and Justice

Given the extreme economic and social stratification in the city of San Cristóbal de Las Casas, it is no surprise that I heard numerous stories in Guadalupe about the "lack of respect" that mestizos show indigenous peoples. One common complaint was that mestizos do not even look at indigenous people or exchange greetings when passing by in the streets. This seemingly simple action takes on great significance in a city where a few decades ago indigenous peoples were forced to walk in the streets instead of the sidewalk. In government offices, I was told, the mestizos pass to the front of the line, while the indigenous people wait for hours and hours. At times, I was asked to accompany people to the local clinic under the assumption (which proved to be correct) that my presence would lead to better treatment. Of course, I had seen countless examples of this discrimination myself. In the market or on the street, indigenous vendors were treated with disdain, and mestiza women sometimes refused to pay the prices requested for produce or other merchandise. In January 2001, the municipal president of San Cristóbal de Las Casas sent police to violently evict all indigenous vendors from the city's plazas in his attempt to "clean up" the city.

At the center of the indigenous Catholics' criticism of the mestizos' "lack of respect" is that it displays inequality. The Catholics denounce that they are not treated as equals of mestizos nor are they granted the same rights by the government. This inequality, I was told, goes against the will of God, who created everyone with the same flesh and blood. The religion-based notion of equality was repeated in a number of ways. In sermons and conversations, the catechist Juan reiterated, "We are all equal, men and women, rich and poor, indigenous and mestizo," and sometimes added, "In the beginning, there were only two people, Adam and Eve. All people are descended from them, and so we all have the same blood. Therefore, we are all united." As I was introduced to people in Guadalupe (and in other communities), indigenous Catholics would commonly remark that even though I am from another country and have different customs, "We are all united because we are children of God."

This seemingly simple concept of equality has great importance. It reaffirms a sense of self-esteem and self-worth, as it gives a strong justification (God's will and the Bible) for the dignity of all. Guadalupe Catholics condemn abuses suffered at the hands of mestizos and demand structural change so that indigenous peoples can have rights within the wider society. This same concept of equality underscores the necessity of uniting forces, for the most part with other Indians, to defend their rights. In Fernando's words:

In Chiapas, there are Tzeltals, Tzotzils, Zoques, and Ch'ols. We don't even speak the same language as they do, . . . but they are our brothers and sisters because we all have the same blood.

Fernando powerfully linked his struggle for liberation to his religious beliefs:

I've been living in Guadalupe for five years now. Before I heard the Word of God, I wasted my time drinking. Now, my thoughts are with God. One has to be with God to be struggling at his side . . . We have to fight. This means listening to and understanding the Word of God. God will free us from our enemies.

The statement that "God will free us from our enemies" does not take away personal responsibility to work toward change. To the contrary, Fernando told me, "Because we all are equal, we must work together following the Word of God to struggle to defend our rights." To protest injustice in his community and in Chiapas, Fernando and other Guadalupe residents participate in marches for fair rates for electricity, pilgrimages to pray for peace and justice, and sit-ins denouncing expulsions. (These activities are discussed in Chapter 8.) In these acts—some of them small, others massive—participants work toward the eradication of oppression and domination at the same time that they work to redeem their own dignity. Moreover, Fernando asserted his own dignity through his identity as a peasant and a Tzotzil Maya. In explaining his struggle for survival, he stated:

We are peasants and we know how to work the land, how to plant and harvest. The mestizos do not know how to plant. We are maintaining the mestizos. If we didn't work, the mestizos would starve to death. They have money, but they don't know how to work the land to harvest their food. It is from the work of the peasants that the mestizo lives. But they do not respect us.

In some ways, the above statement is a Marxist critique of the relationship between peasants and mestizos. The mestizos have capital, that is, they own the means of production and do not work, while the impoverished peasants work to maintain the mestizos by providing their food. Fernando's analysis mixes class with ethnicity in identifying all indigenous peoples as peasants, even those, like himself, who are forced to eke out a livelihood in the city. For him, being indigenous and working as a peasant are intrinsically linked. As an urban Indian and a landless peasant, he is fundamentally displaced, forced to take on whatever work he can find.[6] His own identification as a poor peasant links his experience to that of thousands of others in Chiapas and lays the groundwork for building networks to mobilize against oppression.

Fernando's statement in the proceeding quote that mestizos "do not respect us" is perhaps the most powerful. Not only are the peasants poor, they are not treated with respect. The work of peasants—the very work the mestizos depend upon for their daily food—is viewed with disdain. Yet Fernando reaffirms the value of his own work even in a time when his work is recognized neither by the market nor by Mexican society. His demand for equality does not mean that he wishes to work as a proletarian. Rather Fernando asserts the dignity of working the land. His identification as a peasant persists, even in an era of neoliberal reforms that leave the peasants out of the national project.

In a number of conversations, Fernando and other men of Guadalupe criticized the inequality evident in the contrast between the Indians' and mestizos' work. I was told that mestizos who work in offices and at desks do not sweat, carry heavy loads, or suffer injuries. In contrast, residents of Guadalupe who work as day laborers carry stones, pour cement, or dig ditches and receive about twenty pesos (about three U.S. dollars) for a nine-hour day. I should add that my own work in Chiapas as an academic and chronicler of human rights abuses clearly falls in the mestizo category. The very work that brought me to Guadalupe in the first place was the activity that most distanced me from indigenous Catholics. As they often reminded me, I was not at risk of injuring my back in the fields or poking my eye out on a tree branch while harvesting coffee.

The criticism of mestizos is a criticism of an unjust politico-economic system that forces indigenous peoples to work long hours without the necessary resources to live a dignified life. As Juan stated, "All of the prices are going up except the price of corn and wages. The poor peasant is going to die of hunger. And the government doesn't care. They don't respect us." Sebastian echoed this in noting that if the government really wanted to help people, it would provide land for the peasants to cultivate corn. The lack of land, of social services, of well-paid work are all injustices that contradict equality and dignity and go against the will of God.

Expulsion and Rights: The View from Guadalupe

The act of expulsion clearly violates both national and international human rights accords. In speaking with the Catholics of Guadalupe, I hoped to learn about their own understandings of expulsion and human rights. Did they view expulsion as a violation of human rights? If so, why? Given that Chamulan authorities accuse the Catholic converts of threatening community values, I was particularly interested in the Catholics' perspective on community and rights. In addressing these issues, as in all my fieldwork, I found that patiently listening to the Catholics' stories was much more revealing than asking direct questions.

Late one afternoon I sat with Agustín on his porch; he said he wanted to tell me a story about how the expulsions began. "In 1965 the problem began in Chamula in the hamlet of Sak Tzu. They burned live people." He spoke slowly, pausing for effect, and watching my face to see if I was taking in the horror of the story. Agustín had not observed these events; they were told to him by others, and he, in turn, felt the need to retell the story in order to explain his life.

> The throats of two children were cut. One woman who was eighteen years old tried to escape, and she was thrown into the *temescal* [a small room used for steam baths] with two children. They threw daggers inside. One ten-year-old child didn't die, and he reported that Don Salvador had attempted to burn him.

This burning was done because the people were religious. The authorities arrived and took the child to the town center of Chamula for interrogation. The child was very badly wounded. They asked him, "What did they do?" And the child responded that Don Salvador had burned them all. But they said that the child was telling lies. They asked him three times, but they didn't want to believe him. The child died because of his wounds.

So, what happened is that the people didn't want Catholics in their community. All the community said that they did not want people with other religions, they said "We are of the religion of before, we respect the cross, we speak to the caves. The Catholics are not going to respect us, they do not pray in caves or burn incense or candles. They don't use traditional healers, drink alcohol, or look for two wives." Then, the people with religion had to leave their land and their homes.

Agustín paused, the sun was setting, and there were chores to finish in the last moments of daylight. But he insisted that I return to visit the next day so he could tell me another story, that of the history of Guadalupe. As a Catholic who had been expelled from Chamula, his own story was inextricably linked to the one he had told me. Like thousands of others, he had to leave his land and his home.[7]

Several themes of the story underscore Agustín's strong criticism of the authorities of Chamula. First and most obvious is the brutality of the incident. The violence was ruthless: live people were burned and others were cut with knives. To make it worse, young children were killed along with their parents. Second, when the incident was reported to the authorities in Chamula's town center, nothing was done although the child identified the guilty party. The assassins were not punished, and the child was disbelieved, later dying from his wounds. The local authorities enjoyed impunity, perhaps setting the stage for further violence. Third, the only reason given for the violence was that "people didn't want Catholics in their community." Perhaps in reality, there were other motives for the violence. However, in Agustín's recounting of the event, religion was the only motive; innocent people were killed simply because they "don't use traditional healers, drink alcohol, or look for two wives."

What is left out of the story is as important as what is included. The story is framed in religious, rather than political or economic, terms. Agustín attributes his suffering—being jailed, being threatened, having their homes or crops burned, and losing their homes and land—to his religious beliefs. At the same time, religious belief is a source of strength. In Guadalupe, many recounted that throughout expulsion their "hearts were strong" and they did not give up their religious beliefs but instead suffered persecution and left Chamula.

Like Agustín, every Catholic family in Guadalupe expressed harsh criticism for the Chamulan authorities perpetuating expulsion. The families accuse the authorities of failing to comply with the local norms of respect that are essential to maintaining community. Anita told me:

> The municipal president of Chamula told us that we had to give up our religion, but we said that we would never do that. The municipal president was very angry. He doesn't respect the law. One must respect others. In Chamula there is no respect.

Anita, like other Guadalupe Catholics, denounces Chamulan authorities for failing to respect the law. People regularly cited Article 24 of the Mexican Constitution that protects freedom of religion. Yet Anita and others also criticized authorities' lack of respect for community. The complaint that the authorities lack respect for those with religion was repeated to me time and again. Emiliano explained that he was jailed for "having religion," but he questions the authorities' decision: "We weren't going to rob anyone or do anything wrong." The expelled Catholics contend that they were respecting others, but the authorities did not respect them in return, violating the norm of reciprocal obligation in community.[8] Manuela explained:

> The authorities [of Chamula] speak badly. They don't respect people. They speak with bad words. They rob and harass people. They don't listen to others ... They don't try to fix things. They don't talk things out. If they were good, they would ask questions, talk about problems, and then fix them.

In short, Manuela argues that a good authority would seek to resolve problems by building community cohesion, by working things out instead of sending people to jail and expelling them.

The stories from the Guadalupe Catholics forced me to question the utility of presenting human rights in dichotomies—universal versus local, civil and political versus social and economic, individual versus communitarian. The Catholics have a plural notion of rights that combines local norms of community solidarity, Catholic beliefs, and references to individual rights and national laws. Guadalupe residents understand their rights in the context of a community where each person has reciprocal responsibilities toward others and where solidarity is a necessity for survival. At the same time, they speak of the necessity of respecting the rights of each individual as a "child of God." Human rights as they are codified in the 1948 U.N. declaration may be western European in their origin, but indigenous peoples appeal to this declaration to gain support from national and international movements (Kearney 1995; Merry 1997). The pastoral agents of the Diocese of San Cristóbal may have brought the formal language of human rights to indigenous communities, yet the understanding of rights has been appropriated and reinterpreted within the context of each community.

In his writing on suffering, anthropologist and physician Paul Farmer (2003) emphasizes the necessity of documenting the pain of structural violence—inequality, exclusion, racism, and poverty—violence that otherwise can be hidden or disguised by the discourse of those in power. The life histories from Guadalupe force recognition of the violence of everyday life. For although these indigenous Catholics have experienced human rights violations—arbitrary detentions, physical and psychological abuse, corruption, and negligence, among others—that can be denounced nationally and internationally through the language of human rights, their understanding and defense of rights is inextricably linked to community, dignity, and ethnicity.

For decades Chamulan authorities have defended their "right" to expel using the argument that the dissidents fail to respect local custom and thereby threaten community cohesion. This defense has been accepted and replicated by Chiapas state authorities who have taken little action to prevent expulsion or punish those responsible. The case of Guadalupe suggests that it is an oversimplification to argue that expulsion involves a conflict between community rights (as defended in Chamula) and individual rights (of freedom of religion). The expelled do not reject the concept of community cohesion—they embrace it. In fact, the Guadalupe Catholics self-consciously work to build a community where each individual has rights and responsibilities. The irony is that while the caciques accuse the expelled of jeopardizing community, the expelled Catholics hold the authorities accountable for failing to practice the respect on which community is based.

Photo and caption by Xunka' López Díaz, 2000
The Presbyterian church is near my house.
La Iglesia Presbiteriana está cerca de mi casa.
Li ch'ul na Presviterianoe tey nopol ta sts'el jna.

7

"Our Culture Keeps Us Strong"
Conversion and Self-Determination

In the summer of 1993, I met Mariano and his family, Tzotzils who had been exiled from Chamula, while on a combi in the city of San Cristóbal. Recognizing that I was a foreigner, the family approached me and explained that they had traveled intermittently to the United States—to Florida and as far north as New York state—to earn money harvesting fruits and vegetables. In time, I attended several Pentecostal services with the family at a Tzotzil church and learned of their experiences in Chamula, San Cristóbal, and the United States. Mariano's stories of expulsion echoed what I heard from Guadalupe Catholics. He spoke of his religious conversion—in his case to Pentecostalism rather than Catholicism—the anger of Chamulan authorities when he stopped drinking alcohol, and his subsequent expulsion. When I asked about customs and traditions, Mariano explained the positive values of many customs but criticized their negative aspects.

> We continue with our culture, it keeps us strong. We dress as Chamulas, speak our own language, and continue to work on the land as we always have . . . We men wear our black wool ponchos, and we also have white ones . . . We don't do anything to harm anyone.
>
> The problem is alcohol—that is what has been seen as bad. It destroys our lives. Alcohol is sold in Chamula. People pass out on the ground. They drink liter after liter of alcohol and fight. It is very destructive to family life and leads to a poorly lived life. It is better that we leave that behind and search for better things.

I begin with the story of a Protestant to emphasize the commonalities between indigenous Protestants and Word of God Catholics in the social aspects of conversion. Like Mariano, the Catholics of Guadalupe emphasize the value of many customs but criticize others. Members of both groups criticize alcohol abuse and work to eradicate alcohol from their communities. Soft drinks have replaced alcohol in many social rituals. This chapter examines three domains of tradition that are re-created by indigenous Catholics of Guadalupe: alcohol use, elaborate festivals of the cargo system, and gender relations. These practices are recreated by new religious groups in Chiapas as well as by members of secular movements, most notably the EZLN. Changes in alcohol use, cargo, and gender relations do not represent narrow moralistic concerns but are a way of resisting social and economic oppression and form part of a larger project of self-determination. Hence, in this chapter I argue that the reconfiguration of tradition in Guadalupe is an attempt to create new social relations within and beyond the community rather than a rejection of indigenous identity.

The Rejection of Alcohol: Drinking versus Thinking

In writing about prohibition in several communities of the highland municipality of Chenalhó, Christine Eber notes that the Tzotzils' critical perspective on alcohol is shaped by the "search for greater autonomy" and the Zapatista movement, which provided "a broader context within which to create alternatives to the Mexican government's neoliberal economic policies which have disregarded indigenous people's beliefs and practices" (2001a:252). In addition, given the conditions of poverty in highland Chiapas, Tzotzils of Chenalhó criticize spending scarce cash on alcohol. Women have organized against problem drinking "based on their roles as household managers of meager resources and as newly empowered political actors in their communities" (Eber 2001a:252).

Guadalupe Catholics similarly resist social and economic oppression through their rejection of alcohol. Men and women told me of numerous benefits of prohibition: families no longer spend money on rum, domestic violence declines, and within Chamula, the power of municipal authorities is challenged as their profits from alcohol decline.

History of alcohol in highland communities

To understand the Catholics' rejection of drinking, the use of alcohol in indigenous communities must be placed in its historical and political context. In the pre-Columbian period, Mayan communities made fermented drinks from maize, honey, flowers, wild fruits, and other items, and alcohol was used in specific situations to cure illness and to arrive at communion with the gods (Eber 1995). However, the use of alcohol changed with the Spanish invasion. Alcohol was one of many means used to control indigenous communities. For example, beginning in the 1680s, in order to create a "market" for sugar, Spanish colonists forced indigenous people to accept rum among other commodities in exchange for cash crops such as cacao, cochineal, and indigo (Eber 1995; MacLeod 1989).[1] During the colonial and independence periods, as Europeans attempted to take control of indigenous lands, alcohol was linked to debt, taxes, and the loss of land. In the early 1840s, as mestizos migrated to highland Chiapas, some sold alcohol to the indigenous people. As traffic in alcohol increased, indigenous people fell into debt and were forced to give up their land or mortgage future harvests at great discounts (Wasserstrom 1983). Men and women who worked on the fincas in Ocosingo in the late 1800s and early 1900s recalled being paid two liters of alcohol each week in lieu of wages (Gómez Cruz and Kovic 1994:40). These examples demonstrate some of the ways in which alcohol was taken out of its ritual context and was used by Spaniards and mestizos as a means of economic and social control.

In the first half of the twentieth century, the sale of alcohol played an important role in establishing the PRI's hegemony among the local leaders in Chamula. As discussed in Chapter 4, the state granted permission for Chamulan religious officials to sell alcohol in order to support a political alliance between Chamulan authorities and the PRI.

Nonetheless, alcohol plays an important role in ritual life and social interaction in Chamula as in other highland municipalities. People drink "to create, maintain, and patch up relationships both among themselves and between them and their deities" (Rosenbaum 1993:52; see also Eber 1995, Gossen 1974, Pozas 1952, and Siverts 1973). In public and private ritual settings—particularly in important business, personal, or supernatural transactions—a drinking ceremony is held to bond participants (Gossen 1974).[2] Even though drinking is accepted and encouraged in specific ritual contexts, both women and men consider excessive drinking problematic because it consumes money that should go toward the survival of the family (Eber 1995; Rosenbaum 1993).

Alcohol in Guadalupe
In contrast to the acceptance of the ritual use of alcohol in Chamula, Guadalupe Catholics reject all use of alcohol. Although Catholic doctrine does not prohibit drinking, the indigenous Catholics associate abstinence with following the Word of God. From their personal experience, alcohol only stood in the way of living a dignified life. In conversion stories, men and women recalled the problems alcohol created in their families when they were young. Some saw their fathers beat their mothers while intoxicated, and some saw the health problems that resulted from excess consumption of alcohol.[3] For example, Juan the catechist told me about his father's drinking and early death.

My father drank a lot ... My mother died when I was ten months old. They fed me *matz* [pozol] mixed with sugar. I was often sick as a child, but thanks to God, I didn't die. My father remarried and had six children with his second wife. He continued to drink, especially on Sundays. He beat his wife and me and the other children. We often went hungry because there wasn't money for food. My father drank so much that his body swelled up from the alcohol. My father died when I was very young. His body was swollen when he died.

The story of his father's death was repeated to me several times as a sort of parable warning of the problems associated with alcohol: illness, violence, and poverty. Juan said, "Una vez que empieza la hinchazón, ya no puedes hacer más que esperar ir al panteón" (Once the swelling starts, you can't do anything but wait to go to the cemetery). Drinking is contrasted with the ability to think clearly and is seen as a key cause of oppression. Juan complained that in Chamula, "You are not free because you have to drink alcohol." Such memories of alcohol abuse override any recognition of its ritual significance.

Although expelled Catholics of Guadalupe described many cases of alcohol abuse, it is important to point out that controls are placed on drinking within Chamula. For example, a Chamulan male who is drinking too much may be given a religious cargo to moderate his drinking. The cargo both places drinking in a religious context and forces him to begin to save money for the expense of the cargo (Rosenbaum 1993). Perhaps Word of God Catholicism has particular appeal to those who suffered from their own or a family member's abuse of alcohol.

Guadalupe Catholics describe drinking as antithetical to thinking. Emiliano explained that someone who drinks heavily cannot think, work, or learn the Word of God.

When you drink a lot, you lose your ability to think clearly. The president [municipal president of Chamula] drinks daily, so he does not think clearly. We want to work. We want to learn the Word of God. The drunkards are not going to work. They are going to lose their ability to think.

Drinking, I was told, prevents one from having respect, that is, from carrying out one's responsibilities toward family and community members and from listening carefully to and trying to understand others. As Emiliano notes, a man who drinks cannot work, and his family will suffer as a result. In addition, the purchase of alcohol consumes precious money that could go toward household necessities.

Domestic violence is another problem associated with alcohol. Josefina, like many other women in Guadalupe, recounted how her husband stopped beating her when he gave up drinking:

> Without the Word of God, people continue to drink. When my husband and I arrived here [in Guadalupe], we gave up drinking. In our hamlet in Chamula, my husband hit me. He drank. Now, he doesn't drink, he has changed his heart. He used to hit me and his friends when he was drunk. Sometimes he would grab a machete and threaten people with it. Here we are at peace; my husband gave up drinking.

Indigenous Protestants in Chiapas, like their Catholic counterparts, link abstinence to their religion and denounce the problems associated with drinking. Xunka' López Díaz, a Protestant Tzotzil woman whose family was expelled from Chamula when she was a child and a photographer whose photographs illustrate this book, recalls stories from her parents about problem drinking. She writes of her childhood in Joltzemen, Chamula: "My dad told me that for a long time he drank a lot and got angry with my mom. They say that one day my dad had a machete and a gun and nearly killed my mom! One time my grandparents and my aunt defended my mom" (López Díaz 2000:35). Her parents began to attend a Presbyterian church in San Cristóbal where they presumably were pressured to stop drinking.

The important role that the rejection of alcohol plays in conversion has been documented for Protestant converts in Chiapas as well as in other areas of Latin America.[4] Along with Word of God Catholics, Protestant converts and Zapatista supporters have mobilized to limit drinking. Groups of indigenous peoples reject alcohol as they link drinking to economic oppression, violence, and other negative effects within their communities. Although many reject alcohol primarily on religious grounds, their refusal to purchase rum challenges the economic power of local leaders within communities including Chamula. Scholars, indigenous leaders, and human rights organizations have observed that the rejection alcohol erodes the economic power of local leaders.[5]

For the most part, women are at the front of movements against alcohol, and they cite its detrimental impact on their own lives and their family members' lives. For example, in the summer of 1994, I attended a meeting of a Catholic women's group in the northeastern municipality of Yajalón where participants worked in small groups to discuss problems they faced. Both mestiza and Tzeltal Mayan women were present. Each group of women reported alcohol as a central problem. They linked alcohol to domestic violence, needless expenditure of money, and other issues, and they discussed ways to combat it.

In workshops coordinated by the Fray Bartolomé de Las Casas Center for Human Rights, alcohol is commonly listed as a cause of community suffering. Reasons for prohibiting alcohol are not narrowly moralistic. During a 1990 course in the highland municipality of Huixtán, indigenous participants poignantly linked alcohol use to oppression: "We see that the poor stay poor because of alcohol and look for problems with others and sell their land to buy alcohol. In this, the authorities don't help us, they divide the community."

In many Zapatista base communities of highland Chiapas and the Lacandon jungle, alcohol use is strictly prohibited. Members of Zapatista base communities have set up checkpoints where cars are searched for alcohol and drugs.[6] With the dramatic militarization of highland communities and the Lacandon jungle, an ongoing complaint from rural communities is that the presence of soldiers has increased the sale of alcohol in the region. According to Christine Eber (2001a:257), Zapatistas as well as members of civil society in Chenalhó "maintain that alcohol is disruptive to community relations and thwarts the path to peace and justice." In response, community members have implemented harsh punishments for excessive drinking. Tzotzil residents of Chenalhó "see alcohol and other drugs as handmaidens of political and economic domination" (Eber 2001a). Like Chamula, authorities of Chenalhó have gained a monopoly over alcohol sales through their alliance with PRI officials. Members of Zapatista base communities and civil society who oppose the PRI recognize alcohol's link to political and economic power in their municipality.

Redefining Cargo: Serving God and Community
In highland Chiapas a cargo is a burden or responsibility carried out to serve one's community. In the traditional cargo system, indigenous men, together with their wives, occupy various civil and religious posts to publicly serve their community and their saints. The cargo system of San Juan Chamula, one of the most elaborate in highland Chiapas, is the cornerstone of religious and political life. In working for the Chamulan Town Council (a civil post) or sponsoring a festival in honor of important saints (a religious post), the cargo holder and his family sacrifice time and money but gain respect and prestige.

In contrast to Chamula, no elaborate festivals to honor the saints are held in Guadalupe. Yet Guadalupe Catholics continue to emphasize the importance of cargo as service to the community. The work of catechists, health promoters, prayer leaders, and local officials is described as a cargo. Like traditional cargo holders of Chamula, those who serve their community in Guadalupe gain respect and prestige.

The cargo system in Chamula

Numerous anthropologists argue that the cargo system is a critical expression of Chamula's commitment to community and tradition (see for example Earle 1990, Gossen 1974, and Rosenbaum 1993). In religious festivals honoring important saints, thousands of Chamulas, along with tourists and indigenous peoples from neighboring municipalities, crowd into the town square to celebrate. The festival is a community event and an expression of ethnic identity.

> In reacting to the negative experience [Chamulas] face daily because of their disadvantaged position in the *Ladino* world, they have carved out a space where they can make a bid for power in local arenas. Men and women feel they can affect, to some extent, the way in which they live their lives by establishing a network of people who respect them and who they, in turn, can influence (Rosenbaum 1993:151).

The religious hierarchy is composed of dozens of officials responsible for sponsoring festivals to honor saints. The expenditures for festival sponsorship can be exorbitant. Religious cargo holders must purchase corn, beans, alcohol, candles, incense, firecrackers, flowers, and other items. Religious and civil cargo holders may recuperate some of these costs through the sale of alcohol. Nonetheless, many have to borrow money to have the necessary capital. Supposedly all Chamulas will participate in the cargo system. However, only the wealthiest will sponsor important festivals, as poor families cannot afford to do so.[7]

Religious cargos are tied to political and economic power within Chamula, as local leaders have effective monopolies on the sale of alcohol, soft drinks, candles, and other items used in festivals. As Chamulas purchase these items, the leaders benefit. Further, the cost of bearing a cargo and the purchase of alcohol can quickly place community members in debt, and interest charged by local lenders accumulates very rapidly, sometimes at the rate of 10 percent monthly, forcing some to sell their land. In some cases those accused of being religious converts are given cargos either to reincorporate converts into traditional religious life or as punishment for their transgression.[8]

Cargo in Guadalupe

Guadalupe Catholics criticize the large festivals of Chamula because of the consumption of alcohol and huge expenditures of cargo holders, but they do not reject the festivals outright. In fact, a number of families continue to attend religious festivals in Chamula, particularly for important events such as the feast day of Saint John, even after they have been expelled. Guadalupe residents insisted that they always supported the festivals while living in Chamula through the obligatory *cooperación,* or monetary donation, provided by each family to help cover expenses.[9] In some cases, Chamulan authorities refused to accept contributions from Catholic families, only to later accuse these families of threatening community and tradition. One woman, Mónica, echoes a common complaint:

> The authorities [in Chamula] don't like religion because they say people are going to lose their customs. The municipal president gets angry when you don't drink; he thinks you have another religion. It's not true that we are going to lose our customs. We are still going to cooperate with the festival, we respect others, and help out with the festival. Sometimes the authorities don't want to receive our contributions [for the festival]. If they say we are not keeping the custom, it is their fault, not ours.[10]

At the same time, Guadalupe Catholics point to what they see as problems with the festivals. Josefina, for example, criticized the cooperación. She contrasted life in Guadalupe to Chamula by saying, "Here, there is money to buy food. We aren't forced to buy soft drinks for the fiesta."

Nonetheless, cargo defined as service toward the community continues to hold great importance in Guadalupe. Don Lucas's role as sacristan, Juan's work as a catechist, and Fernando's position as a local official are each described as a cargo.[11] All of these duties require a significant investment of time and energy. Like the traditional cargo holders of Chamula, catechists must be respected community members to be selected for this religious cargo. As catechists visit Catholics in their community and other villages to offer counsel and moral support and to share the Word of God, they are recognized as important community leaders and are listened to for advice and sought out to mediate conflicts. These cargos do not require the same financial sacrifice as the religious posts in Chamula, yet Guadalupe cargo holders give up many days of work to fulfill their community responsibilities.

While there are no festivals in Guadalupe honoring the saints, festivals for life-cycle events such as baptisms, weddings, and first communion are common, as are community-wide festivals on Christmas, Easter, and New Year's Eve.[12] After a baptism or wedding, godparents invite Catholics to their homes to share bread and coffee or a meal of chicken soup, tortillas, and soft drinks, which have replaced alcohol. These small local festivals are important in maintaining community relationships and facilitate building the base for networks. In addition, weekly participation in the celebration of the Word of God—like the cargo system of Chamula—serves to ritualize the individual's dependence on the community for survival.

Gender Relations and the Word of God

One morning in Guadalupe I found families talking about a recent fight between two Protestant women.[13] After inquiring about the event, I learned that the women had been yelling at one another and pulling each other's hair. Such fighting was rare in Guadalupe, and to make matters worse, the fight had taken place in front of one woman's home and many had witnessed the event. Community members felt a need to assist in resolving the conflict, and the local agente called a public meeting. Later that day, Protestants and Catholics gathered in the town hall, where the two women were asked to explain what had happened. It turned out that one woman's husband had left her to live with the other woman. After attempting to sort out the story, the agente asked the people in attendance to make a decision as to what to do. Much discussion ensued, but eventually all agreed that the man who had left his wife to live with the other woman had made a mistake and should return to live with his wife. He agreed to this and in addition agreed to pay a fine of three truckloads of sand that would be placed on the road in the community to help prevent erosion. His "punishment" prevented the erosion of the road during the coming rainy season at the same time that it prevented a symbolic erosion within the community by reincorporating the man into community life. Of course, the man could have refused to abide by the community decision. Divorce is legal in Mexico, and he could have gone to live with the second woman. Yet it probably would have been necessary for him to live in another colonia to escape the strong disapproval from the community.

A major factor behind the decision in this case is that, to a certain extent, the community itself takes on the responsibility to care for single women. Hence, the man's fine served the entire community, reflecting the implications that his action had for all. Because the case was decided in a public audience, it served as a warning to all men about the consequences of failing to provide for their families. This story illustrates the complexity of gender relations in Guadalupe. For although Catholic and Protestant women are at once dependent on and protected by men, women also are described as equal partners, and community controls on drinking, domestic violence, and abandonment represent a dramatic change from life in Chamula in women's experience of marriage.

It could be said that the Catholics of Guadalupe live in a patriarchal society. Women's domestic work allows men to work for wages outside the home, and money is kept in the hands of men. Widows and women who have left or been left by their husbands in Chamula are dependent on the assistance of their older sons or other men in the community. However, both men and women have power in the community and are interdependent in daily life. For women in Chenalhó, Christine Eber notes, "Although no patriarchy allows women to act freely, the kind of patriarchy I saw in Chenalhó makes men and women partners in most aspects of life, not just those necessary for survival" (1995:239). Women in Guadalupe are protected and have rights. Men are expected to provide money for food and other necessities.

The distinct yet complementary roles carried out by men and women are evident in the division of labor at the household level. The gendered division of labor in Guadalupe is similar to that in Chamula (see Rosenbaum 1983, Chapter 6). Women's work includes preparing food, primarily tortillas. This process starts with cleaning maize, soaking it with calcium, grinding the corn or taking it to a house with an electric grinder, making the dough, and forming and cooking the tortillas over a fire in the small smoke-filled kitchen. As already noted, women must obtain water for cooking, cleaning, and drinking from one of two tanks on the road of the community, carrying it home in plastic jugs. Firewood for cooking is cut from the forest above the hill. Women, with the help of their older children, wash clothing, care for sheep and take them out to graze in a pasture below the hill for several hours every day, and weave and sew clothing for themselves and their families, all while watching their young children. In addition, women participate in income-producing activities such as making friendship bracelets, belts, woven cloths, wool jackets, vests, and other items that are sold for small amounts of cash. The income from these ventures is used for household expenses such as the purchase of food and materials for clothing.

Men work in the city in paid occupations as described in Chapter 2. Through wage labor, men have access to money. However, the money they earn is expected to go toward the maintenance of the family. Spending money on alcohol, described as "wasting" money, is strongly criticized. The jobs performed by the vast majority of men provide irregular employment at best, while the artisan work sold by women provides regular, if very small, sums of money.

For the most part, men are better able to negotiate relations in the mestizo-dominated city of San Cristóbal than women are. Most men of Guadalupe speak at least some Spanish, while few of the women do. Men's knowledge of Spanish permits and reflects male negotiation with mestizos. However, the process of exile and making a life in a new setting permits or forces women to leave the community. They go to town to buy thread and yarn for embroidery, to sell their finished products, and to buy goods in the market. In the community, meanwhile, men have specific domestic tasks. They are responsible for building their homes and repairing them as the roofs and walls are in need of replacement. Sometimes men help in gathering firewood. Both girls and boys are sent to school. However, girls may stay at home to help their mothers with child care and other domestic tasks.[14]

The gendered division of labor is well established in Guadalupe. It is rare that a man will perform a woman's task and vice versa. The exception is boys, who sometimes make bracelets to sell. Scholars have pointed out that a gendered division of labor in and of itself does not indicate inequality between men and women. What is important is the status of the work assigned to each sex (Bourque and Warren 1981). In Guadalupe, the work of both men and women is considered indispensable for survival. Just as a woman cannot survive on her own, a man cannot survive without the work of a woman. However, as single men can pay women to perform domestic tasks or can buy tortillas in the city, they can—at least to a certain extent—circumvent their dependence on women. This significantly reduces women's power in the society. Nonetheless, a number of men in Guadalupe told me that women's work is very valuable and that women have more work than men. Juan emphasized the difficulty of women's work without questioning the gendered division of labor:

Men have less work, women have more. Women have to care for sheep, prepare maize, and carry water and firewood. There is a lot of work for women. They have to wash clothes, grind maize, weave clothes, make food for their husbands, and make tortillas. Sometimes men will threaten and grab their wives to make them work . . . Men have less work. They plant, burn the land to prepare for planting.

Gender relations changed dramatically within households after couples heard the Word of God. The key change, I was told, is that men now "respect" their wives, meaning that husbands must work together with their wives in supporting their families and that verbal and physical abuse is rejected. The conversion narratives clearly separate the before and the after: before is a time of violence, fighting, and drinking, and after is a time of peace, although poverty and problems continue.

In her research on gender relations within Chamula, Brenda Rosenbaum found that domestic violence was common in Tzajal Vitz, the Chamulan hamlet where she conducted fieldwork. She notes, "In some marriages, wife beating occurs only a few times in the woman's life; in other marriages, it happens frequently. Women often excuse mistreatment by a drunken spouse when it occurs on the husband's return from wage labor on the plantations. They interpret it as a backlash from the abuse men suffer when working away from home" (1993:51).[15] A woman in Chamula who suffers domestic violence has several options: she can return to her parents' home, especially if she does not have any children; she can leave her husband; or she can take her husband to court. A man may be thrown in jail overnight and publicly shamed for beating his wife. A woman who decides to leave her husband may receive a one-time payment for each child. However, this does not leave a mother with enough money to support a child for even a year. Rosenbaum notes that while Chamulan women are expected to attempt to help their husbands change, they are not expected to be martyrs. "Indeed, people think that a woman who puts up indefinitely with a husband who drinks constantly, mistreats her harshly, and fails to support her economically must be under a spell of witchcraft" (Rosenbaum 1993:55).

Jan Rus and Diane Rus (personal communication) note that drinking and domestic violence in Chamula cannot be seen only as an internal problem. Important economic factors affect alcohol use and domestic violence. The harsh conditions of life on the finca and the economic insecurity faced by males struggling to support their families lead to an increase in drinking and domestic violence. A woman named Juana recounts a story much like those of several other women in Guadalupe who reported that their fathers or husbands drank more after they returned from the finca:

When I was young, my father left to work on the finca. When he returned, he hit my mother and spent money on alcohol. My mother said that it would be better if he stayed on the finca because then he wouldn't hit us.

My father also hit us children, he would throw a whip. I was hit with a stick on the head, in the eye. My face was swollen. It is the custom of old. Now, things have changed. You have to teach your children well with the Word of God. Parents beat their children when they are drunk.

I was told that domestic violence is not accepted in Guadalupe. The local agente can jail a man for twenty-four hours for beating his wife. This happened to several men during the time I conducted fieldwork in Guadalupe. The sanctions against hitting women are communal as well as juridical. A man who beats his wife is strongly criticized. Women are not expected to put up with abuse forever; a number of single mothers living in Guadalupe have left abusive husbands because of excessive drinking and domestic violence and receive support from the community. One single mother, Martha, lives with her three children in a simple home on the same plot of land as her sister and brother-in-law. Her brother-in-law built her home and assists her financially and in other ways while Martha earns what she can selling her artisan work.

Verónica left Chamula with her four children to escape an abusive husband. She explained to me how things should be between husband and wife: "According to the Word of God, a husband must respect his wife. Husband and wife must live together united. A man should not hit his wife." She went on to describe the difficulties she had encountered in Guadalupe and in Chamula:

Here, there is much suffering because I have to support my children alone. We need food; there are not enough clothes. I left my husband in Chamula four years ago. My husband beat me a lot. He beat me even when he wasn't drinking. When he returned [from the fields] in the afternoon, I said to him, "Here is your food, your pozol, your tortilla and beans." But he didn't want to eat. He hit me and kicked me. My face swelled up from being beaten.

He didn't give me money to buy maize, beans, and clothes. He would go to work on the finca and return to scold me. However, I forgave my husband. But he continued to beat me. So I left him. I left because I didn't want to be beaten any longer. I was without food and went to live in another hamlet in Chamula.

My husband now lives in Tlaxcala [a settlement in the north of San Cristóbal de Las Casas]. When we were married, he looked for another wife. My husband now has five wives.

Verónica stopped to laugh as she noted that her husband "only lacks one more wife to make a half-dozen." She continued to tell me how she was expelled from Chamula:

When I had to leave, it was because my husband spoke to the authorities in Chamula. He told them that I was following another religion [Catholicism]. I was thrown into jail; it was my husband's fault. I was in jail one night. Then I returned to the hamlet for two more months. I waited for my children to finish school, and then we left and came to Guadalupe.

I am praying to God, asking for forgiveness. I have made my first communion as well. My son helps me out when he can.

Neither Martha nor Verónica is criticized in Guadalupe for leaving her husband. Their decisions to work to "follow the Word of God" are praised. Although Verónica prays for forgiveness for leaving her husband, Catholics of Guadalupe criticize a man who does not provide for his wife, "looks for another wife," or beats his wife. She is considered an upstanding member of the local chapel and regularly sits on the front bench, a place reserved for the wives of catechists and other honored members. Verónica earns money from a small store where she sells such items as rice, oil, and soft drinks to members of the community, and her oldest son, married with two children of his own, also offers financial support. The fact that the catechists and others take the side of a woman who is being mistreated is perhaps the strongest sanction against abusive husbands. In other words, women's rights are enforced by the community's disapproval of mistreating women.

Respecting one's wife in Guadalupe means that a married man must support his family. Hence, he should not abandon her to take another wife. Both men and women recalled the difficulties they faced as children when their fathers left their mothers. Central to their memories is the poverty they experienced without the support of a male. For example, when Lorenza's father left her mother, she was left without an inheritance and endured the pain of rejection:

My father has five wives. He left my mother to look for another wife when I was young. We suffered a lot. My father is rich; he has his own truck. I don't know him well because he left my mother when I was a little girl. When I see him in San Cristóbal, he doesn't talk to me. Now he has another wife. He didn't leave me any land in our hamlet. When I was little I lived with my mother. She had to work to buy tortillas. She sold firewood in San Cristóbal and made wool jackets to sell in the market. My father didn't leave us anything—not a single soft drink or even a sweet. There was no money. My father married a third time to a mestizo woman, and then twice more.

My mother looked for another husband and married again when I was nine years old. The second husband drank a lot; he hit us and kicked us the same as my father did. He died.

In Guadalupe, the agente may jail men who leave their wives, a sanction that applies to both Catholics and Protestants. When Mateo, former catechist and founder of Guadalupe, took a second wife, he lost his moral authority in the community and was forced to leave to avoid further conflict (see Chapter 2). More recently, Antonio left his wife and took up with a Catholic widow of the community. When his wife, Manuela, complained to the agente, Antonio was put in the local jail for twenty-four hours as punishment. Since being in jail, he has returned to Manuela, has asked forgiveness for what he did, and told me that he feels ashamed of his actions.

The changing gender relations resulting from conversion to Catholicism are similar to that described for Protestant converts. Scholars studying Protestant conversion in Chiapas and other parts of Latin America note the way the religion responds in some ways to women's needs. For the case of Tzeltals in Tenejapa, Chiapas, Susanna Rostas argues that Protestantism empowers women by giving them a new arena to express themselves, although it does not "give them a place in the male world" (1999:327). Elizabeth Brusco's work on evangelical Protestants in Colombia demonstrates that this religion can be an "antidote to machismo," that is, it encourages men to orient themselves toward church and home rather than toward the public sphere (1993:148). In their work on Pentecostals in Brazil, John Burdick (1993) and Andrew Chesnut (1997) argue that this religion appeals to women because of its rejection of alcohol, gambling, and other "vices." What is interesting about the case of Guadalupe is that these very same changes are taking place as people convert to Catholicism. Rejection of alcohol, domestic violence, and abandonment are common changes implemented by religious converts. These changes are not limited to one religious denomination.

Furthermore, the push for reconfiguring gender relations in indigenous communities has come from diverse groups of women, not only from Catholics and Protestants. To give one example, in May 1994, several nongovernmental organizations convened a workshop on women's rights and customs in San

Cristóbal de Las Casas.[16] More than fifty indigenous women attended the event, and the 1994 document *El grito de la luna* (Cry of the Moon) was prepared for presentation at a public forum for discussion on constitutional reform regarding indigenous rights. The women affirmed the value of some aspects of customs, such as language, weaving, traditional healing practices, and working the land. However, the women criticized several aspects of custom:

> The customs that we have should not do harm to anyone. We do not like the custom when the authorities make crooked deals and they are the ones who decide how to distribute the land. The authorities do what they want and we cannot always defend them. (*El grito de la luna* 1994:31)

Women denounced the use of "custom" to permit gender discrimination. They noted that at times land inheritance is given only to males, and donations taken from the community for the ill are only taken for males. Their criticisms of being forced to marry against one's will, domestic violence, and alcohol abuse are echoed by the Guadalupe Catholics.

Women of the EZLN are also demanding that they be granted respect and equality. Women have participated as Zapatista soldiers and commanders, one of the most visible examples being Ramona, a Tzotzil woman who participated in the February 1994 peace talks in San Cristóbal de Las Casas. The much-publicized Revolutionary Laws of Zapatista Women drafted in 1993 demand comprehensive rights for women, including the right to choose their work and to earn fair wages; to decide the number of children they will have; to take part in community affairs; to choose their partners in marriage; to be free of domestic violence; and to occupy positions of leadership in the EZLN.

Gender roles are changing in Zapatista support bases. Women have organized to limit domestic violence and alcohol sales (Eber 1995; Forbis 2003). They are active as health promoters and community leaders and have carried out collective projects such as farming, raising chickens, and making bread. Collective projects provide extra food or cash for women as well as a space for women to share their experiences. Lucinda, a Tojolabal woman in a Zapatista base community in the Lacandon jungle, describes changes that have taken place since the Zapatista uprising:

> Before most women didn't go to meetings, the men wouldn't let their spouses leave, but now it's changing, we are all meeting together. Now we all have rights to participate and say what we want, men and women.

But before the men didn't pay attention to us. The government said that women didn't have the right to participate and say things. And the men thought that way too, and didn't open spaces for us. (Quoted in Forbis 2003:246)

For the Guadalupe Catholics, changes in gender relations and the use of alcohol are part of conversion. Giving up drinking and treating women with respect are religious practices, just as attending mass, reading the Bible, or visiting the ill are. Indeed, it was their experience of conversion, expulsion, and finding a new life in Guadalupe that brought about and solidified these changes, changes that are linked to their search for a dignified life. Yet this community of Catholics is not unique in its search for a dignified life. Many indigenous Catholics throughout the Diocese of San Cristóbal de Las Casas as well as indigenous Protestants are fighting for self-determination. They reject alcohol, and women's roles are changing. At the same time, the Zapatistas, who rally behind the defense of indigenous culture and insist on the importance of their way of life, are also demanding that these two domains be reconfigured. They reject alcohol, insist that women should not be forced to marry against their will, and denounce domestic violence. In this indigenous peoples are actors in building their own traditions, rejecting a static view of culture, and searching for ways that traditions can be a source of liberation.

Photo and caption by Xunka' López Díaz, 2000
Women from Chamula near the cathedral during the celebration of the 40th anniversary of Bishop Samuel Ruiz's pastoral service.
Mujeres de Chamula cerca de la catedral para la celebración de 40 años de aniversario de servicio pastoral de Don Samuel Ruiz. Chamula antsetik ta nopol Ch'ul na kateral sventa sk'inal yu'un ts'aki cha'vinik a'vil ochem ta mol ovixpo li Samuel Ruise.

8

Working and Walking to Serve God
Building a Community of Faith

For you have delivered my soul from death,
my eyes from tears,
my feet from stumbling.
I walk before the Lord
in the land of the living.

—PSALM 116:8–9

As peasants we have to walk a lot. Sometimes there are no roads,
sometimes we don't have money to pay for transportation . . . Cate-
chists have to walk to visit families and communities to share the
Word of God. The work of the catechist never ends.

—JUAN, CATECHIST OF GUADALUPE

One Saturday in July 1995, a group of thirty people from Guadalupe traveled to Buena Vista to celebrate the inauguration of a new Catholic chapel. Buena Vista, the pseudonym of a hamlet in the highland municipality of Chenalhó, is at the top of a steep hill and can be reached by a difficult walk from the town center or by taking a truck up a rocky dirt road. Nonetheless, Guadalupe Catholics regularly visit Buena Vista to share their prayers and to offer material and moral support. On this cold and rainy day the group from Guadalupe boarded a rented a truck so they could ride together and transport the musical instruments that would be played during the ceremony. On the way, the truck stopped in the center of Chenalhó to pick up the parish priest, Father Miguel Chanteau, who would bless the new chapel. To cover the cost of truck rental, each family contributed thirty pesos, more than a day's wages. Moreover, a number of families had given a *cooperación* of money for a festival with food and soft drinks for all attending the inauguration.

On the following Sunday during the religious celebration in Guadalupe, the men and women who had visited Buena Vista gave a lively report of the chapel's inauguration, including a detailed account of the events, from the colors of the chapel—bright pink, yellow, and blue—to the meal of chicken soup, homemade tortillas, and soft drinks provided for all. The strength of the Buena Vista congregation that had worked so long to found a new chapel greatly impressed the Catholics of Guadalupe. But what most impressed me was the way the Guadalupe Catholics committed themselves to Buena Vista and to many other communities, offering their time, moral support, spiritual guidance, and material donations. In addition to the many trips to Buena Vista, Guadalupe residents traveled to a number of hamlets in the municipalities of San Juan Chamula and Teopisca and constantly visited chapels in San Cristóbal de Las Casas where Tzotzil Catholics congregate for worship. At the same time, indigenous Catholics from other communities regularly visit Guadalupe to preach, join in worship, and exchange information on local events. The discourse on equality and unity among human beings, a fundamental part of the Tzotzil definition of human rights, is put into practice through these visits.

In this chapter I detail two sets of networks: first, the local networks (micro-level) of indigenous Catholics emanating from Guadalupe, and second, the diocesan-wide networks (macro-level) built through Pueblo Creyente, a group of diocesan Catholics who work to build unity and to address poverty and political repression.[1] I explore the ways faith, ethnicity, and poverty serve to create ties and the ways networks can lay the groundwork for the defense of human rights. The chapter also presents the ways religion can promote divisions within and among communities. An in-depth exploration of these local networks reveals their fragility; that is, local networks within and among communities can break down due to religious and/or political conflicts. Yet these local networks can become integrated into broader (macro-level) networks such as those of the diocese, especially in the group Pueblo Creyente.

Faith, Networks, and Social Capital

The Indigenous Congress of 1974 was a historic event that contributed to a collective indigenous consciousness and facilitated ties between indigenous peoples of different ethnic groups. One of the most important outcomes of the congress was that Tzotzils, Tzeltals, Tojolabals, and Ch'ols saw that they all experienced similar oppression and could work together to change their situation. The congress allowed for the creation of social networks within and between these ethnic groups as it empowered the participants. For the first time the four ethnic groups united in public spaces that had been dominated by mestizos and some participants went on to form political organizations. For others, empowerment was less dramatic, but no less important. They saw that others experienced similar problems, making poverty a social rather than an individual issue. They saw a shared desire for equality and justice.

For those excluded from national political and economic projects, connections with others who share visions for a better future are highly valued and paramount to survival. On the material level, Guadalupe Catholics rely on networks for mutual aid, and their links with others in their community are an economic necessity, a sort of safety net, in the fragility of their everyday lives. On a social level, these networks connect them to others with a shared vision for justice and dignity. In the long run, these ties may lay the groundwork for political mobilization. These networks are primarily religious; that is, indigenous Catholics are connected to one another because of their faith, and the Catholics unite to celebrate their faith. At the same time, the formation of the networks is constitutive of their faith. In the words of the catechists and prayer leaders of Guadalupe, sharing one's faith and supporting those in need is part of "working and walking" to serve God. It is through these networks that the Catholics build a community of faith and create social bonds that lay the basis for a shared path of resistance.

Anthropologists have long noted the social, political, and economic relevance of informal networks, particularly for the poor living in urban areas.[2] My research adds to this literature in demonstrating the central role religion plays in creating and maintaining networks. Larissa Lomnitz (1977) describes the extensive networks formed among the poor in a Mexico City neighborhood. Through networks people exchange information (including opportunities for residence and employment and general orientation to urban life); lend money, food, work instruments, and other items; share services such as lodging and care for family members; and give moral support to one another. These networks, which include kin and non-kin, are critical to the survival of the families.

The political importance of informal networks is also well documented. Networks can provide a space for political participation in areas where access to formal political organizations is closed to the poor. Furthermore, networks can provide a space for people to discuss common problems and aspirations, and this space may, in turn, facilitate a base for political mobilization.[3] In their examination of contemporary Latin American social movements, Sonia Alvarez, Evelina Dagnino, and Arturo Escobar note that study of social movement networks or webs can be useful in exploring "how social movements' political interventions extend into and beyond political society and the state"

(1998:14).[4] Social movements at once draw strength from the networks of daily life—such as family, community, and ethnicities—as they create new networks or reconfigure old ones. It is important to point out, however, that involvement in networks does not necessarily lead to political mobilization. In fact, networks may exert a "stabilizing" rather than mobilizing influence when they cut across income differences, preempting class consciousness among the poor (Denoeux 1993). In the case of Guadalupe, some networks serve economic and religious purposes but have little direct relationship to politics.

A number of scholars have described the ways religion can strengthen ties of solidarity and promote the formation of networks that facilitate ties within and among communities (see for example Denoeux 1993, Levine 1992, and Peterson, Vásquez, and Williams 2001). In the Catholic context, Christian base communities (*comunidades eclesiales de base,* or CEBs), established as prayer and reflection groups in Latin America from the late 1960s onward, connected people in neighborhoods and parishes as they promoted trust among their participants. The terms "base" and "community" have double meanings that reinforce the idea of building bonds of trust. "Base" refers both to the base of the Church, the people of God who make up the Church, and to the base of society, that is, the poor. "Community" refers to a geographically defined social group and to the fundamental goal of CEBs, which is to create community. Although CEBs were not created for political motives, through participation in CEBs people often recognize that they share problems, learn leadership skills, and can mobilize to change their situation. In several Latin American countries, particularly Nicaragua, Brazil, Chile, Guatemala, and El Salvador, CEBs supported social movements challenging repressive regimes. Certainly not all who join CEBs become politically mobilized: "People participate in base communities not out of some desire to change the society at large, but rather because of their religious faith" (Mainwaring and Wilde 1989:5). Nonetheless, participation in CEBs has led to political participation in many cases. For example, Nicaraguan CEBs played an important role in mobilizing people in the Sandinista revolution.[5]

In the 1980s, members of the Diocese of San Cristóbal attempted to establish Christian base communities in rural and urban areas following the model of other Latin American countries. Although the base communities grew in urban areas, particularly among mestizos, pastoral workers realized that rural indigenous communities were in many ways de facto base communities. In indigenous communities like Guadalupe, there are no formal CEBs, but Catholics meet regularly to read the Bible and have established broad social networks based on connections through the Catholic Church.

In their article on religion in Peru and Guatemala, Daniel Levine and David Stoll describe some of the ways that religious institutions create and transmit social capital, "a constellation of orientations, social skills, and cooperative experiences that alter the basic landscape of politics by creating and encouraging the spread of trust as a social value" (1997:65). Over time, this trust sets the groundwork for the foundation of networks that "provide a practical basis for embedding any social activity in a supportive and mutually reinforcing context" (1997:65). Social capital may be created through religious institutions such as CEBs, development agencies, human rights networks, study centers, and other types of organizations. This type of social capital involves vertical networks, as it provides resources and institutional support through legal advice, training in leadership skills, contacts with government officials, and access to the media, among other resources. In a similar vein, Susan Eckstein (1989) notes that progressive sectors of the Latin American Catholic Church serve as an intermediary that provides an institutional connection for political mobilization and that urban social movements which succeed in resisting co-optation are often initiated by outside groups such as clergy, student militants, political parties, and Catholic base communities. Although protest grows out of dissatisfaction with local conditions, national movements depend on alliances with urban intelligentsia. Daniel Levine notes that pastoral workers may serve as mediators who "provide structured access to resources, valued alliances, and a sense of legitimacy. They help constitute spaces (often literally, as in buildings or arrangements for meetings) where innovations can be tried out" (1992:335).

The cases of Guadalupe and Pueblo Creyente described below demonstrate that religion plays a central role in the creation of networks, and the institutional structure of the Church supports and facilitates links among Catholics. Yet it is not only the institutional support of the Church that strengthens networks but faith itself (an issue seldom addressed in the network literature). Faith inspires and legitimizes social networks as it influences the types of actions taken by those involved. Following Anna Peterson, I focus on the role of faith (religious belief) to explore "how religion enables people to make sense of the world and act in it" (1997:11). I do so with the hope of contributing to the understanding of the relationship between religion and political mobilization.

Intercommunity Networks

Working and walking, two oft-repeated themes during my conversations in Guadalupe, are a necessity for the poor of Chiapas—they mark the rhythm of daily life as they mark identity. People walk long distances to reach communities where the only means of access is narrow dirt paths; they walk to market and to the city of San Cristóbal de Las Casas when they lack the money to pay bus fare; they remember walking for days to the coffee plantations to find work; and many walk for hours on Sundays to attend religious celebrations. Likewise, people must work to survive. They cultivate their cornfields, make tortillas and artisan products, and perform wage labor. The long hours of walking and the difficult conditions of work are two aspects of life that Tzotzils use to describe the difference between the mestizo and indigenous populations, and these two aspects also refer to the poverty that, in some ways, unites many of the indigenous and peasant communities throughout Chiapas.

Guadalupe residents, especially catechist and prayer leaders, are constantly walking as they visit indigenous Catholics in San Cristóbal de Las Casas and neighboring highland communities. They consider this work of serving others to be service to God. For example, one week Juan and Agustín spent four full days fasting, along with twenty-five men and women, to give moral support to the lone catechist of a community in Teopisca. The Teopisca catechist and father of six was newly widowed. Afraid that the catechist would lose his faith during the crisis, community members organized a fast to show him their support and to pray for strength. Juan and Agustín gave up four days pay as well. With their support, the community held a celebration of the Word of God three times each day during the fast. The presence of two men from Guadalupe served as a visible reminder of the network of Catholics who were willing to give their time to make a physical sacrifice by participating in the fast and to offer material support.

One of the strongest ties is with residents of Buena Vista, Chenalhó, who like the Guadalupe Catholics belong to the Tzotzil Maya linguistic group. Chenalhó, like other highland municipalities, contains three primary religious groups: Traditionalists, diocesan Catholics, and Protestant groups (see Eber 1995). Church leaders from Guadalupe make regular visits to assist the diocesan Catholics of Buena Vista, and sometimes people from Buena Vista arrive in Guadalupe to attend religious celebrations. The notion of a community of faith facilitates the exchange of economic support, religious ideas, and information on current events. As described in the following narrative, the link with Buena Vista demonstrates both the strength and weakness of building networks through shared faith.

I first heard of Buena Vista in the chapel of Guadalupe, where Catholics discussed their many visits to the community. One day I asked Agustín, the lead catechist, how and why the people of Guadalupe had become involved in the hamlet of Buena Vista in Chenalhó. He began to tell me the history of his work in the community:

> About a year ago, I was visiting the center of Chenalhó; I was playing music for the Sunday mass. Some people came up to me to tell me about a group of Catholics in the hamlet, and they asked if I couldn't go visit in order to help preach. There were three catechists in Buena Vista. When I got there, the people were suspicious. They said to me, "Who is this man who has come to preach from San Cristóbal? Is he here to make trouble for us?" I said, "No, I'm not here to make trouble. We are all equal, we're all children of God, and I've only come to preach." But there was a group of people who didn't want me to preach. They said that I had been expelled from Chamula for being Evangelical and that I would cause more problems in Chenalhó, just like there were problems in Chamula. They said that we don't use candles the same as they do, that we don't respect the images of the saints. So this group decided that they didn't want me there. They wanted me to leave. So, I said "OK, I'll leave, but first I am going to preach because that is why I'm here, I've come to preach and can't leave without preaching." So after I preached, and I did well, they decided to ask who wanted me to keep coming and who didn't. Well, thirty-five people wanted me to keep coming and five people didn't. So they said that I could still come but that the thirty-five people in favor of my preaching would have to leave to go to another church, and so the community split in two, and since then we have been going to the hamlet.

Agustín continued to make regular visits to Buena Vista, and later other members of Guadalupe joined him. In June 1995, about a year after Agustín's first visit to the community, the new chapel was constructed and, as described at the beginning of this chapter, a group from Guadalupe participated in its inauguration.

When I asked Agustín to explain the causes for the division in the church, he said the division was religious and political. He told me that those who stayed in the original church categorized themselves as Traditionalists and affiliated with the PRI. The thirty-five people in favor of his preaching belonged to *sociedad civil*, or civil society, a term used in Chiapas since the Zapatista uprising of 1994 to refer to those who oppose the PRI government but do not form part of the Zapatista Army of National Liberation. In Buena Vista as elsewhere, a complex relationship exists between religion and politics. Although government officials assume that a direct correlation exists between one's religious and political affiliation, political diversity exists within each religious group. Many Word of God Catholics affiliate with civil society, and some Catholics affiliate with the PRI. Although Protestants have commonly been stereotyped as politically conservative, they may affiliate with the PRI, civil society, or even the Zapatistas. Agustín's version of the divisions in Buena Vista suggests that he contributed to the split in the community. Clearly, political division in Buena Vista existed prior to Agustín's arrival, but the addition of another church likely exacerbated the rift.

One day in July 1995 as Juan recounted his work in Buena Vista, I asked if it would be possible to accompany him on a future visit. I was not sure how Juan would respond and worried that perhaps the presence of an outsider would aggravate existing conflicts. However, Juan did not see this as a problem at all and decided that we should go that Sunday. His one concern was that I be prepared to walk up the steep hill to Buena Vista once we arrived in Chenalhó. As he had repeated to me time and time again, he like other peasants was accustomed to walking long distances, but he knew that I wasn't. I assured him that I thought I would be able to walk up the hill, although perhaps not as quickly as he.

On Sunday, Juan, his two oldest daughters (ages ten and twelve), and I walked through the market of San Cristóbal de Las Casas, where we stopped to buy a kilogram of tortillas and boarded a Volkswagen van headed for Chenalhó. After traveling for an hour we arrived at the municipal town center, and Juan suggested that we eat something in the market to give us strength for the steep climb to Buena Vista. We searched for a place to wash our hands, and after finding a spigot in front of a house, we washed and ate the tortillas with cooked chicken and potatoes we had packed for the trip.

When we began the ascent, Juan looked at his watch to check the time. We climbed at a fast pace, and I slipped several times in the mud but did not fall. Unlike me, Juan's daughters did not have any trouble climbing, even though the youngest was barefoot. I asked Juan what I should say when we reached the community, and he told me that I should just greet the people and introduce myself. When we reached the top of the hill, Juan looked at his watch again and smiled. I had been able to reach the top in forty-five minutes, Juan informed me, the same as he usually does, and he was impressed that I had been able to walk so quickly. He commented that we had been lucky to be able to make the first part of the trip in a van. Years earlier, he remembered, before the road was built, the walk from the town center of Chenalhó to San Cristóbal de Las Casas took five hours.

I was glad to hear that we would no longer be climbing uphill, just following the path to the community. We walked another forty-five minutes, which was actually more climbing, but it was not as steep as the first part of the walk. We could see the town of Chenalhó below, and the countryside was beautiful. Juan began to tell me about the community of Buena Vista to prepare me for our arrival:

The people in Buena Vista don't grow coffee; it's too cold at the top of the hill. Only the people who live below where it is warmer can grow coffee. Life in the hamlet is very difficult because the people have to walk up the hill. There is a road that reaches the community, but you need a truck because there is no public transportation. No one in the community has a truck, and furthermore, you can't get by in a truck during the rainy season.

On the path, we passed several people and stopped to exchange greetings. All of the women were wearing their traditional dress, red-striped blouses with embroidered designs and woven blue cotton skirts. Most of the men and almost all the boys were also wearing traditional dress—short white cotton pants and shirts.

Finally, we arrived in Buena Vista. It was 9:30 A.M., and the religious celebration was to commence at 10. People had already congregated outside the chapel, some sitting on benches, some standing, and children were talking and laughing. Juan introduced me to Diego, a catechist, and to another prayer leader. As always, I noted that it was important that Juan give more than my name—he needed to identify me, to locate me as it were, in a place where I was clearly an outsider. Juan emphasized that I am a believer (Catholic) and that I had contacts with the human rights center of Bishop Samuel Ruiz. The catechist, prayer leader, and other members of the church seemed happy that I had come to visit and to share in worship. My religious affiliation connected me in a small way to members of the community. The community of faith extends well beyond the local community. People told me with pride that those from other countries like Chenalhó parish priest Father Chanteau, who is from France, and I are all their brothers and sisters in God's family.

The chapel, built of wooden boards with a roof of corrugated metal, was brightly painted in pink, yellow, and blue. A sign painted above the door read, "Second Catholic Church, John 14,6." The Bible verse that inspired the name of the church reads, "I am the way and the truth, and the life. No one comes to the

Father except through me." The original Catholic church, built of adobe, stood about a hundred yards away, and people were preparing to begin their Sunday celebration there. Reinforcing the story I had already heard, Juan explained to me that the people in the first chapel are PRI supporters and Traditionalists, and for that reason, the members of civil society had built the second chapel. Because religion is an integral part of everyday life in indigenous communities like Buena Vista, political divisions cannot be ignored in church.

Inside the chapel, women sat on the left side and men on the right, as was customary, so I prepared to sit with the women. I was told to sit at the altar and complied, even though I felt uncomfortable as the only woman seated there. Asked to introduce myself at the beginning of the ceremony, I explained that I was happy to be present to learn about their community and to celebrate the Word of God with them. Then, three men began to play guitar and another the tambourine, and the congregation sang several songs that I had heard in Guadalupe celebrations. The chapel was almost full, but even so, there were only about thirty people inside. The women wore the traditional blouses of Chenalhó. Two Chamulan women attended the celebration, their blue blouses standing out in stark contrast to the red and white blouses of the other women. Juan later explained that they had walked to Buena Vista from a neighboring hamlet in Chamula.

After the music, everyone knelt to participate in a collective prayer, at once individual and communal, in which each person prayed out loud, offering personal desires, faults, and wishes to God. The entire service was conducted in Tzotzil. After the initial prayer, Juan was asked to share a reading from the Bible. He had selected the first letter of John 4:7–12 and began: "Beloved, let us love one another because love is from God; everyone who loves is born of God and knows God. Whoever does not love does not know God, for God is love." Following this reading, Juan discussed its meaning and also explained that Agustín had not come this Sunday because he was visiting another community in Teopisca.

Next, Diego (the prayer leader of Buena Vista) began to talk, and soon he started to cry. He expressed his sorrow that the people of the chapel are no longer united, that a respected leader had left the chapel and begun to drink, that the catechists do not follow the agreements about who will lead prayer. Multiple bonds unite members of the congregation—they are neighbors, kin, and friends. Yet these bonds can break at their weakest point, so that a personal dispute, disagreement, or other action can threaten a wider division. When people left the Catholic chapel of Guadalupe, the catechists of the chapel said the faith of those who left was not that strong. Yet I observed that other divisions (particularly personal or political rifts) underscored the decision to worship elsewhere.

After the celebration in Buena Vista, we sat on the benches outside the chapel. The man beside me began to explain how poor they were, how they had nothing but a little land on which they cultivated their cornfields, and I saw corn and beans planted all the way up the hill and in every corner. The small adobe homes had the words "Civil Society, Neutral Zone" painted on their exterior walls in large white letters. These words, announcing their status as civilians rather than as Zapatistas, demonstrated the fear of possible military conflict in the region. Indeed, Zapatista support bases exist in some thirty-eight communities of Chenalhó (Eber 2001b:54). Two and a half years after my visit to Buena Vista, the tension between those supporting the PRI and those of civil society escalated tragically, but I will return to this in the following section.

As visitors, Juan, his daughters, and I were invited to eat in the house of a family, and we all walked together up the hill to their home. We sat on small stools and were each given tortillas, scrambled eggs, and a soft drink. While the women and girls made tortillas, the father of the family talked nonstop with Juan about the problems in the chapel and the importance of maintaining unity. It was clearly of great importance that Juan had attended the celebration; he led the opening and closing prayers. Older than the other catechists and with much more experience in the Church, he was respected for his age and knowledge. After we ate and thanked the man and his wife, we began to go down the hill, stopping at the chapel to say good-bye to the people who were still talking at the benches a good hour after the celebration had finished.

After walking for more than an hour, we reached the place where vans depart for San Cristóbal de Las Casas. Juan and his daughters waited with me until a bus arrived, and then they said good-bye. It was after 2 P.M. and I was exhausted, but Juan explained that he would not go home until the next day. Instead, he was going to visit his brother-in-law in another hamlet, a walk of another hour and a half. By this time in the afternoon, it had started to rain, and I wondered how far Juan and his daughters had walked out of their way to assure that I safely reached the van to get back San Cristóbal.

The reasons for Juan's visits to Buena Vista are complex. Although he has to pay for transportation (the equivalent of half a day's labor if he makes the trip alone), make the steep climb uphill, and leave his family and community for the day, he goes to Buena Vista at least once a month. The catechist Agustín as well as other Guadalupe Catholics also make regular visits. Aside from these, there are regular visits to communities in San Juan Chamula and Teopisca. The primary reason behind the visits is religious; Juan and others arrive to preach the Word of God and to offer moral support to the Catholic community in formation. For the people of Buena Vista, the time and effort given by Guadalupe residents is a public affirmation of the importance of their project. While I was in the chapel of Buena Vista and Juan preached about the necessity of loving one another in order to know God, I realized that one important motive for supporting other communities was serving God by loving and serving his brothers and sisters in Christ. In short, the visits to Buena Vista make visible the community of faith.

Ethnic identification and poverty unite the two communities. Both are comprised of Tzotzils who share a common language, tradition, and history as well as the discrimination they suffer at the hands of mestizos. Members of the church in Guadalupe and Buena Vista recognize their shared situation of poverty and marginalization as well as their common goals. Their commonalities and ties strengthened by visits create networks that can serve as a foundation for political mobilization.

The political dimension of the link between the two communities cannot be ignored. The community of Buena Vista is divided along both political and religious lines. I was told that the largest group in the community is Traditionalists—in this case, those who follow traditional Mayan religious beliefs, who explicitly forbid participation in Protestant religions and diocesan Catholicism. Traditionalists of Buena Vista are affiliated with the PRI and distance themselves from diocesan Catholics. There is also a small group of Protestants in the community, and finally, the diocesan Catholics I visited.[6] The people of Guadalupe made the decision to support the Catholics of Buena Vista who consider themselves to be part of civil society. The visits from Guadalupe serve not only for preaching but also for sharing information on political events, including the process of negotiations between the government and Zapatistas, and concrete information on marches, pilgrimages, and other events that support the process of peace in Chiapas.

Limits of Networks: Protestants and Catholics

In the summer of 1997, I returned to Chenalhó with Juan. This time we stayed in the town center where Juan planned to join a religious celebration with a group of Catholics. Instead, he found the catechists engaged in a lively discussion about the validity of the Zapatistas' decision to take up arms. The meeting lasted for several hours, and a range of opinions was voiced, but in the end, the catechists reached an agreement—as servers of the Church they could not take up arms. I asked Juan if he still visited Buena Vista. "No, they have all become Presbyterians." Without any frustration or anger he added, "The new chapel is no longer Catholic." Why did they convert? Juan told me that they now believed that this was the true way to worship God. When I asked a priest who worked in the region about the change in Buena Vista, he suggested that the conversion resulted from a concerted effort of the state government to provide economic incentives to encourage the growth of Protestant churches. The first explanation (from Juan) emphasizes religious belief, the second (from a priest), rational choice. The move to Protestantism in this community must be placed within the political context of the region. In some ways it had become dangerous to be affiliated with the Catholic Church in Chenalhó. Beginning in the 1970s, Word of God Catholics in Chenalhó, catechists in particular, represented one group that resisted the PRI's dominance. As conflicts between those supporting the PRI and those supporting civil society escalated after 1994, local leaders commonly associated diocesan Catholics with the opposition or even with the Zapatistas. The dangers of being affiliated with the Catholic Church were made painfully evident in the 1997 massacre in Acteal, Chenalhó. Paramilitaries killed forty-five members of Las Abejas, a predominantly Catholic group dedicated to nonviolent resistance, while they were praying in a local chapel.[7] Several communities in Chenalhó suffered violence in the months before the massacre, yet Buena Vista (according to the accounts I read) had remained untouched and was presumed to be a PRI stronghold. I do not want to suggest that the people of the new chapel decided to convert to Protestantism only because it was a safer choice. In fact, I think it is telling that Juan emphasized religious belief. However, their decision cannot be separated from their political context.

Even though the Guadalupe Catholics no longer visit Buena Vista, they continue to visit and support other communities in Chenalhó and San Cristóbal de Las Casas. Their visits to Chamula ended unexpectedly in 1997. In August of that year—having just moved to the United States—I received news that one of the prayer leaders of Guadalupe had died in a car accident. Talking to friends, I was able to piece together the story. Several months before the accident, a group of men from Guadalupe had begun to visit their own native municipality, San Juan Chamula, to preach the Word of God, and they were encouraged to return weekly. These visits carried great significance for the Guadalupe Catholics, most of whom had first heard the Word of God while living in Chamula. Their visits are evidence of the religious heterogeneity in Chamula, even as local authorities insist that all are Traditionalists. The Guadalupe Catholics knew they were at risk of detention by local authorities but went to Chamula anyway. On one trip, a Volkswagen van carrying a group of men and women from Guadalupe overturned as it rounded one of the sharp curves on the mountain road while they were returning to San Cristóbal de Las Casas. A prayer leader died and others were injured in the accident, which was symptomatic of the dangers of travel to highland communities. The worn and poorly maintained Volkswagen vans commonly used for travel are subject to breakdowns, and the risk of faulty breaks presents a grave danger on the mountainous roads. In addition, roads are poorly built and in need of repair, and warning signs are practically nonexistent. A few days after the accident, Guadalupe residents met with a priest to carry out a quiet religious celebration at the site of the accident. Community members took up a collection to support the prayer leader's widow and the couple's five children. Discouraged, the Guadalupe Catholics decided that they could no longer visit Chamula, but they continued to work with Chamulas through meetings in San Cristóbal de Las Casas.

While the shared community of faith is an important basis of unity for the diocesan Catholics, the obvious limit of faith-based links is that non-Catholics (Traditionalists as well as Protestants) are seldom included in this shared community. While the faith-based networks lay an important groundwork for political mobilization, an unintended consequence is that political differences sometimes lead to religious divisions.

The Catholics of Guadalupe, particularly the religious leaders, have a well-established discourse on the unity of Catholics and Protestants and the necessity of working together. During my first visit to Guadalupe, the religious leaders gathered to talk about the community and the work I hoped to do. It was of great importance to the men that I understood that the Protestants and Catholics have to work together. "We are all children of God," they told me, "and we all read the same Bible, the same version in our language [Tzotzil]. The caciques of Chamula exiled both Catholics and Evangelicals for having religion." People often repeated this idea of unity, explaining that all had been expelled, all were indigenous, and all were believers, so that divisions between Protestants and Catholics were a mistake and do not follow the Word of God. Furthermore, (as noted in the previous chapter) there are several factors uniting both religious groups—both share the beliefs that drinking is wrong, that one must "respect" women and only take one wife, and that one should not be forced to go into debt due to participation in the cargo system. These three beliefs are the most common reasons given for conversion to Catholicism and Protestant religions. Although religious differences greatly limited networking between the two groups, I did observe several examples of cooperation between Catholics and Protestants. In one instance, a child of a Protestant family died while I was conducting fieldwork, and Catholics as well as Protestants made financial contributions to assist in the costs of burial. In another instance of collaboration, Catholic and Protestant women attempted to form a weaving cooperative to sell their textiles at a fair price. Several important community projects such as the construction of a new school or a road included both Protestants and Catholics. Many conflicts were resolved by group meetings in the town hall. Catholics work alongside Protestants as local authorities in the community.

However, the divisions between Catholics and Protestants in Guadalupe are, at times, stronger than the ties uniting them. The Catholics repeat that "all are equal in God," and hence all must work together, but they see this ideology as part of Catholicism, the "true" religion. Therefore, at times Catholics unite as Catholics, excluding Protestants. In spite of reasons for unity, some Guadalupe Catholics complained about the Protestants, accusing them of drinking, of taking more than one wife, or even of not understanding the Bible. More broadly, indigenous communities of Chiapas have multireligious affiliations, making political mobilization through Catholic identity problematic. In his description of the work of the Catholic Church in organizing the 1974 Indigenous Congress, George Collier notes that "the catechists' effort met with the limitations of their association with the Catholic Church in a landscape of religious pluralism. However much the Catholic Church hoped to speak with a universal voice, it could not do so persuasively while attempting to win people away from other religions. Only a truly secular movement appealing broadly to pluralism and democracy could hope to galvanize the indigenous and peasant community across its religious diversity" (1994:64–65).

Perhaps a secular movement such as the EZLN—which includes people from a range of religious affiliations, from diocesan Catholics to Presbyterians, Pentecostals, Seventh Day Adventists, and Traditionalists, among others—was necessary to bring together people with such diverse religious options. Yet, the EZLN, a secular movement, necessarily respects the religious option of each member, a change from previous revolutionary models.

The clergy of the Diocese of San Cristóbal have engaged in efforts to make their work more ecumenical. In the 1990s, Bishop Ruiz García made an effort to include Protestants and Catholics in his work, and in fact, some Protestants praise his work in support of the expelled and refer to him as "our friend" and even "our bishop." When the diocese became directly involved in the process of mediation and reconciliation following the Zapatista uprising, pastoral workers were forced to recognize the importance of following an ecumenical approach. Recent ecumenical projects include the Ecumenical Bible School established in 1998 with support from the diocese and Protestant groups. This school brings together diverse religious groups for prayer and courses in topics of practical concern, such as health and human rights. In addition, there are many examples of grassroots efforts to promote reconciliation at the community level. Given the many cases of people of different religions working side by side, it is a mistake to attribute violence to religious divisions. I turn from the very local and grassroots networks emanating from Guadalupe to a diocesan-wide group—Pueblo Creyente.

Growing Like a Mustard Seed: The Formation of Pueblo Creyente

The kingdom of heaven is like a mustard seed that someone took and sowed in his field: it is the smallest of the seeds, but when it has grown it is the greatest of shrubs and becomes a tree, so that the birds of the air come and make nests in its branches.

—MATTHEW 13:31–32

[In May 1991] the Tzotzils, Tzeltals, Tojolabals, and Ch'ols met. And it was a very important moment in our journey. We found that our suffering was similar in different areas, and we also felt the strength to walk together. The Pueblo Creyente grew like a mustard seed that has become a tree in which the birds of the sky come to eat its seeds. In it are different brothers and sisters from many organizations so that we can see how to live in unity without being demanding on one another and to understand that unity covers up our differences when we have only one united heart. We want to dialogue and it is easy because we don't do it with our own strength, but with strength from God. Unity is a gift from God, but it is also the work of humans, and with the help of God we can achieve it

—STATEMENT FROM MEETING OF PUEBLO CREYENTE, FEBRUARY 25–27, 1993

Pueblo Creyente was born from a diocesan concern about including the voice of the poor within the institutional structure of the Church. In the diocesan assembly of 1991, pastoral workers decided to formally incorporate members of local communities in their meetings and for the first time invited indigenous peoples and peasants to attend the assembly.[8] While the initiative for the Guadalupe networks emerges directly from the communities, Catholic clergy have played a central role in the creation of Pueblo Creyente. The group formed to select local representatives and to hold meetings to bring the word from the communities to the diocesan assembly became Pueblo Creyente. To use the terms of Daniel Levine (1992) and Susan Eckstein (1989), the clergy served as a "mediator" or "intermediary" in providing resources, strategic support, and even theological validation to the group. However, in spite of this involvement, the people of Pueblo Creyente were neither controlled nor manipulated by the diocese. While pastoral workers influence indigenous Catholics, members of Pueblo Creyente and other such groups make their own decisions regarding the actions and direction of the organization.

Pueblo Creyente began to grow in strength and number as a result of the mass mobilizations following the arrest of diocesan priest Joel Padrón in September 1991. As described in Chapter 3, Father Padrón was released largely as a result of these mobilizations, and it was out of their success that members of Pueblo Creyente saw the power they had as a united group. Following the success of a pilgrimage, Pueblo Creyente grew rapidly, attracting members from twenty-five municipalities in the San Cristóbal diocese.

The institutional structure of the Diocese of San Cristóbal facilitates the mobilization of thousands of people through Pueblo Creyente. Through the Catholic Church, people at the base learn leadership skills, establish relations with members of diverse communities, and perhaps most importantly, hold regular meetings at the local and regional levels, where decisions are made. Before further discussion of Pueblo Creyente, it is necessary to explain the organization of the diocese. Guadalupe, like other communities in the diocese, belongs to a complex network that embraces the levels of the diocese and the Catholic Church, as is illustrated in the figure on page 166. This structure legitimates and institutionalizes the informal networks that members of Guadalupe establish with other communities.

Guadalupe is one of thirty-five communities that comprise the diocesan group called Diaconías. This name refers to the first indigenous deacons (*diáconos*) from this area. It includes Tzotzil-speaking communities, both urban and rural, mostly in the municipality of San Cristóbal de Las Casas. Many of the communities are comprised of Chamulas who separated from the municipality for economic or political reasons. The catechists of Diaconías hold bimonthly meetings to make decisions, share information, and discuss biblical readings.

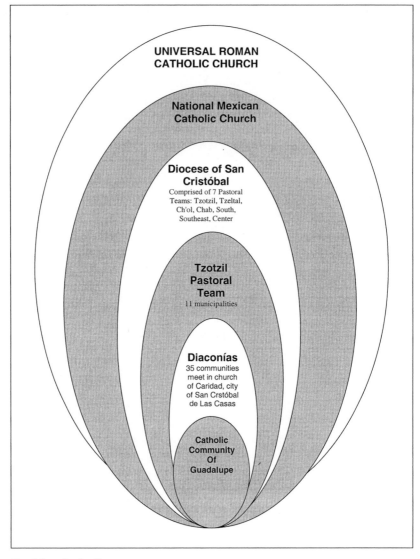

Guadalupe in the diocesan structure

Two representatives from each community, including Guadalupe, are expected to attend these meetings. In addition, two representatives attend an annual catechist course at which members share news of community achievements and attempt to work through difficulties, discuss changes or innovations in liturgy, and study specific readings from the Bible.

Several families from Guadalupe regularly attend mass or service at Caridad, a chapel in the center of San Cristóbal de Las Casas that serves as a central meeting place for Tzotzil Catholics residing in or near the city. Their connection to this chapel brings news of activities of indigenous Catholics in the region and the state. For example, one Sunday in February 1995, several catechists from Guadalupe took up a collection of maize and beans from their community to bring to Caridad, where they would be distributed to the poor communities in the Lacandon jungle suffering from a strong military presence. The catechists of Diaconías had organized the collection. At times, catechists from other communities within Diaconías attend the chapel in Guadalupe to preach and to share news from their communities.

Diaconías forms part of the Tzotzil pastoral team, one of seven such teams in the diocese, consisting of parishes from eleven municipalities in the Tzotzil-speaking region. The photo on page 148 depicts women and men from Chamula joining thousands of other indigenous people beside San Cristóbal's cathedral to celebrate Bishop Ruiz's fortieth anniversary of working in the region. Indigenous representatives from throughout the region meet annually to discuss problems in their communities to share information and to make decisions on united actions, and a lay representative from each of the teams attends the annual diocesan assembly. Committees such as Pueblo Creyente, Indigenous Theology, and the areas of women, health, and human rights are organized through these seven pastoral teams, each of which has lay representatives. Meetings are held at the community level, at the level of the team, and at the diocesan level, with elected representatives attending each assembly. It is this structure that allows Pueblo Creyente to have participating members throughout the diocese. Catholics meet within their communities, then send representatives to meetings organized at the level of pastoral teams and finally, send representatives to the diocesan-wide meetings held at least once a year. This facilitates a fluid exchange of information among the communities and Pueblo Creyente. When planning an event—a special mass, pilgrimage, meeting, fast, or other activity—all communities are quickly informed, promoting broad-based participation.

The diocesan structure also links Pueblo Creyente to the national and international Catholic Church. This link is most visible in work of the bishop, priests, and nuns. The diocese sends out news of important events to bishops and other church leaders from throughout the world. At times, pleas for prayer and others forms of solidarity are made through the international network of people who support the diocese's work. Bishops, theologians, and other religious figures are invited to attend important events such as pilgrimages, the synod (a diocesan-wide meeting process to reflect on and make decisions about the direction of pastoral work), and annual diocesan assemblies.

People at the base, such as Guadalupe Catholics, rarely see the national and international network of Catholics. Nonetheless, I found that people perceive the Catholic Church as a universal institution and feel part of a wider community of faith. The Catholics of Guadalupe feel connected to Catholics around the world because they share similar beliefs and participate in similar rituals. This was expressed to me many times when I was conducting fieldwork. For example, on Ash Wednesday, Juan told me that he would go to church that day to be marked with ashes symbolizing the beginning of Lent. Juan pointed out that Catholics in the United States, in Chenalhó, and in Guadalupe all receive ashes on the same day to commemorate a single event and that this common act unites Catholics all over the world. Although the Catholic Church as an institution is based on a hierarchical structure of authority, Guadalupe residents recognize themselves as equal to all other Catholics. When bishops and church figures from other parts of Mexico and foreign countries visit the Diocese of San Cristóbal, people from Guadalupe actually observe evidence of a universal Church. More importantly, the community of faith of Catholics— who share religious belief and sacraments—serves to legitimate the struggle of the indigenous people for justice. Their project in Chiapas, namely to work to help construct the Kingdom of God, is viewed as being shared by Catholics throughout the world. This project is intimately linked to the defense of human rights, that is, to promote a dignified life for all. The notion of the community of faith carries with it the idea that all humans are worthy of "life and life in abundance."

The Work of Pueblo Creyente

Just a year after the march in protest of the detention of Father Padrón, on the five-hundredth anniversary of Christopher Columbus's arrival in Latin America—October 12, 1992—more than ten thousand indigenous people from throughout the state of Chiapas marched into the city of San Cristóbal de Las Casas. The march began in the plaza of the San Francisco church at the monument to Fray Bartolomé de Las Casas, remembered as the Dominican priest who defended the rights of indigenous peoples against the interests of the Spanish, and moved to the plaza of Santo Domingo, where the statue of Diego de Mazariegos, the Spanish conqueror who founded the city of San Cristóbal, was dismantled in an important symbolic event. Although Pueblo Creyente did not organize this historic event, many of its members participated and were impressed with the power resulting from the unity of peasants and indigenous people of different ethnic backgrounds.

The objective of Pueblo Creyente is to "search for unity among the poor." Participants in this group have no set political affiliation and selected the name Pueblo Creyente to include all Christians, and although the vast majority are Catholic, Protestants participate in meetings and actions of the group.[9] The group is formed primarily of indigenous peoples—Tzotzils, Tzeltals, Tojolabals, and Ch'ols—but also includes mestizos. According to representatives of the group, what unites them is their faith. In the words of Bishop Ruiz García,

> Pueblo Creyente is made up of the lay people who are organized in the Diocese, in parochial structures or from a political commitment, which is non-partisan. In other words, they are expressing a political dimension of their faith, but without belonging to a determined political movement. Beginning with the incident of Father Joel [Padrón] when they just began to meet, they found spirit and illumination in their faith for their commitment to life. And so this Pueblo Creyente has grown, with its subsequent actions, and with a very wide articulation. (Quoted in Fazio 1994:184)

In a meeting of Pueblo Creyente in February 1993, participants discussed the differences and similarities between their group and political organizations. They noted that Pueblo Creyente differs fundamentally from political organizations in that it "was born from the Word of God." This links religion, human rights, and politics, since according to Pueblo Creyente, the Word of God recognizes the fundamental dignity of all human beings and the necessity of working to defend one's rights. In defining how Pueblo Creyente is similar to political organizations, they noted:

> We want to be free and we are all brothers. We all want liberty, unity, life, social change, a new system. We fight for our communities, we want equality, we fight for human rights. We are all human beings, we are all children of God. (Minutes of Pueblo Creyente meeting, February 25–27, 1993)

Bishop Ruiz García, like Pueblo Creyente, does not separate politics from faith. Instead he speaks of "a political dimension" of faith with a "commitment to life." The goals and actions of Pueblo Creyente—that is, working for life, equality, unity, and social change—are explicitly political but come from their faith.

Those who participate in Pueblo Creyente note that the divisions in rural communities cause weakness; their goals, similar to those of the Indigenous Congress of 1974, are to create unity and justice. As recorded in the minutes of the February 1993 meeting, participants spoke of the formation of the group as "a very important moment in our path where we felt that our suffering was similar in different places, but we felt the strength to walk together." They further noted, "This is a difficult moment in Mexico and Chiapas. Some want us to be divided, one against another, so that we will not be able to effect change. We have to walk together in our difference, but [also] in our unity." Pueblo Creyente has been important in uniting peasants from different ethnic groups, municipalities, and political organizations. At the 1993 assembly, people recalled the goals established by Pueblo Creyente in 1991:

1. To dialogue with other organizations in order to help us to know what our objectives are.

2. To reach agreements on how we can support ourselves and create solidarity out of our problems that arise from our poverty. Respect for others is necessary when we take into account that the Pueblo Creyente and organizations have different ways of working.

3. To maintain constant communication in order to know the problems and progress and hence, to walk united to advance our communities. (Minutes of Pueblo Creyente meeting, February 25–27, 1993)

All of these goals focus on unity and agreement. The second emphasizes creating solidarity based on poverty. Members of Pueblo Creyente may differ in their political affiliation and ethnic group, but they are united in poverty. They know that their shared poverty is a unifying force and that unity among different ethnic groups is essential in order to overcome their problems.

The growing strength of Pueblo Creyente presents a threat to the state and federal governments. Because Bishop Ruiz has supported Pueblo Creyente, the bishop was attacked. To government officials at the center of federal power, Bishop Ruiz was "a democratic leader of civil society of the state of Chiapas, a state where a semi-feudal regime still prevailed, tacitly" (Fazio 1994:185). Government officials expressed their concern to the papal nuncio of Mexico,

Monsignor Girolamo Prigione. According to journalist Carlos Fazio, this was the beginning of the offensive against Bishop Ruiz, which culminated in the appointment of a coadjutor bishop in 1995. The government's annoyance with Pueblo Creyente was also expressed in February 1995 when Jorge Santiago Santiago, a key advisor of the group, was arrested and taken to the maximum security prison in Tuxtla Gutiérrez. Santiago was accused of being one of the military commanders of the Zapatista Army for National Liberation, when in reality he is the director of DESMI, Desarrollo Económico Social de los Mexicanos Indígenas (Social Economic Development for Indigenous Mexicans), a nongovernmental organization in San Cristóbal de Las Casas. There were countless irregularities in juridical procedure, and on April 14, 1995, Santiago was released due to a lack of evidence that he was guilty of the charges against him.[10]

Pilgrimages of Pueblo Creyente

Pilgrimages are among the most public actions of Pueblo Creyente, and the Catholics of Guadalupe usually go as a group to these events. These religious events unite hundreds and at times thousands of people. Pilgrimages demonstrate how the poor walk with one heart. At a literal level, the pilgrims walk for hours from their communities to the site where the event is to begin; then they walk as a united group to their destination, usually a church. At another level, the pilgrims walk with one heart in the struggle to defend their human rights. In their journey, they pray together, asking for peace and justice at the same time that they demonstrate to the government their numbers and strength. The pilgrimages demonstrate two ways Guadalupe Catholics mobilize. First, the events mix political and religious motives, as well as class and ethnic identity. Second, the pilgrimages represent the most important public action of Pueblo Creyente and have a political impact on state and national government authorities. In fact, the Pueblo Creyente pilgrimages are often the largest in Chiapas. In numbers alone, they have more mobilizing force than any other political organization in Chiapas.[11] This group can rapidly recruit thousands of participants because of the diocesan structure and networks. Furthermore, since Pueblo Creyente is not officially affiliated with any one political party, it reaches a broad base of supporters.

The pilgrimage, a journey to a sacred shrine for religious purposes incorporating elaborate rituals and symbols, is common throughout Latin America. Pilgrimages are common among the Mayan populations of Chiapas. They are carried out to commemorate important dates in Catholicism (such as the second Friday of Lent) but also have occurred historically during critical stages of the growing season for maize (Adams 1991).

Crumrine and Morinis (1991) as well as Victor Turner (1992) note that although the pilgrimage is not a true rite of passage, the two events share important features. First, both are transformative processes that mediate between the sacred and the profane. The sacred is the goal of the pilgrimage—the shrine or sacred place—while the profane "is located in the mundane, everyday home life of the believer, with all its entanglements, confusion, and sorrows" (Crumrine and Morinis 1991:10). The sacred pole is accessible through pilgrimage. The pilgrim must separate from home and the profane in order to be transformed to the sacred. Turner describes pilgrimage as a transformative process that is a metaphorical death or separation from "the negative alienating aspects of system and structure," leading to a metaphorical rebirth of the spirit (Turner 1992:31–32). During the journey, the pilgrims no longer "occupy social positions in a hierarchical or segmentary structure of localized status roles; now they are assigned to a class of anonymous novices or plainly and uniformly garbed pilgrims, all torn or self-torn from their familiar systemic environment" (Turner 1992:30).

The pilgrims of Pueblo Creyente are united in their journey, both symbolically and in practice. Members of indigenous communities walk for hours—some walk all night—to reach the city of San Cristóbal, while others arrange to ride together in buses and vans. Commonly, participants convene at two or more places at the outskirts of the city and form groups based on their respective pastoral team. People walk together, carrying banners, singing songs, burning incense, and playing traditional music. After a journey of about two hours, all the pilgrims meet in the cathedral in the center of the city to attend mass.

Another important aspect of the pilgrimage is that it "is conceived of as an important means by which individuals can gain access to the sources of power believed to control their destiny"; this way they seek goals that "do not appear to be attainable without the direct blessing of the grace of God" (Crumrine and Morinis 1991:14). The pilgrims often ask for the intercession of a mediator, such as a saint, to reach their goal. The pilgrims in Chiapas appeal to the Virgin of Guadalupe, the dark-skinned manifestation of the Virgin Mary. Pilgrims carry banners bearing the face of the Virgin of Guadalupe, chant *Viva la Virgen de Guadalupe,* and sing a song called *La Guadalupana,* which tells the story of her appearance to Juan Diego.[12]

The pilgrimages organized by Pueblo Creyente are both religious and political events. They are differentiated from *manifestaciones* (demonstrations), which are explicitly and exclusively political. In some ways the pilgrimages are separated from political parties. This is evident in that members are not allowed to show their support of parties during their walk and no party propaganda or political chants are allowed. At the same time, religious acts are noteworthy: people carry crosses, burn incense, sing religious songs, and finish their journey in a church, usually the main cathedral of the city of San Cristóbal de Las Casas, where a mass is held. Bishop Ruiz often celebrated mass, but indigenous pilgrims participated by translating the biblical readings into their languages, speaking during the homily, giving out communion, playing traditional music, and sometimes performing traditional dance. Important church leaders including bishops and priests from other parts of Mexico, and even from other countries, attended masses.

Members of Pueblo Creyente recognize the political as well as the spiritual importance of the pilgrimage. This is evident in the motives for pilgrimage, which often include a critique of government actions. Furthermore, press bulletins are sent to the media on the day of the march, and members of Pueblo Creyente hold press conferences. Working with the media clearly goes beyond asking for the intercession of God.

While I was in Chiapas, I observed numerous pilgrimages, including the massive ones of November 24, 1993, and March 26, 1995.[13] Well over twenty thousand people—indigenous and mestizo pilgrims—from throughout the Diocese of San Cristóbal de Las Casas participated in each of these events. The pilgrimage of 1993 was organized in support of Bishop Samuel Ruiz García in response to a threat of separating him from the diocese. In 1995, the pilgrimage similarly supported the work of the bishop and called for peace in Chiapas. I also observed three smaller pilgrimages: one in August 1993 in celebration of the bishop's receipt of an international human rights award, one in March 1995 in celebration of the opening of the synod, and one in July 1995 to ask for the return of three foreign priests of the diocese who had been expelled from Mexico.[14] On these three dates, pilgrimages and religious celebrations were simultaneously held in all the parishes of the diocese.

In the pilgrimage of March 26, 1995, more than 20,000 members of Pueblo Creyente walked from diverse points in the city to the cathedral. I observed this pilgrimage as part of my fieldwork and mention it in the opening pages of this book. The pilgrimage took place at a time when political tension was high.

In February of the same year, thousands of soldiers had entered the Lacandon jungle and committed numerous human rights violations against indigenous communities, Jorge Santiago had been arrested as a political prisoner, and the pastoral work of the diocese was under increasing attack. The day of the pilgrimage, leaders of Pueblo Creyente distributed a press bulletin explaining the motive for the event:

> Our life today continues to be diminished and threatened because the pueblo continues to endure persecution, arbitrary detention, slander, aggression, torture, assassination, confrontations between brothers, defamation, threats, hunger, imprisonment, and human rights violations. The force of this pilgrimage is so that we can pray together, in order to support and show our solidarity with *Tatic* Samuel Ruiz García, and his pastoral work. We are participating in this pilgrimage also to ask for the unconditional liberty of our brother Jorge Santiago and of other brothers who are prisoners for their commitment to justice and truth.

A week before the event, the Catholics of Guadalupe met to discuss who would go to the pilgrimage and to make the necessary arrangements. A group of about fifteen men and a handful of women and children walked from Guadalupe to the Chapel of Caridad, where they met up with other Tzotzils who live on the outskirts of San Cristóbal. Trucks were provided to transport people to a gathering point north of the center of town. There, people from Guadalupe met up with others from Diaconías and the Tzotzil pastoral team. As we waited, a large truck filled with men and women from Zinacantán arrived. A huge sign on the truck reading "PRD" (Party of the Democratic Revolution, a left-of-center opposition party in Mexico) generated much discussion. It was decided that the people could participate in the pilgrimage but that they could not bring the sign. A large group of people from CRIACH also arrived, led by Domingo López Angel, to join in the pilgrimage.

Participants formed a single-file line, and pastoral workers assisted in organizing people into groups. Although the initial planning of the pilgrimage was done by Pueblo Creyente, pastoral workers played an instrumental role in assisting in the logistics of its organization, such as helping with security arrangements, media contacts, and invitations to national and international religious figures. Each community walked together as part of its pastoral team. Hence, residents of Guadalupe walked in a group that comprised part of Diaconías, which in turn comprised part of the Tzotzil pastoral team.

The different pastoral teams arrived at the plaza of the cathedral at the same time. A temporary stage had been set up in the plaza in front of the church, since all the pilgrims could not fit inside. Bishop Ruiz García welcomed the pilgrims and officiated at the mass. Bishops from other Latin American countries and from Europe were present on the stage and expressed their support of the bishop and the struggle for justice in Chiapas. Indigenous representatives from each of the pastoral teams had prepared a part of the celebration. This pilgrimage was important in demonstrating the power of the indigenous voice both to the indigenous communities themselves and to the dominant mestizo society. As the streets of San Cristóbal filled with indigenous peoples peacefully demonstrating and realizing the power in their numbers, the mestizos of the city began to fear revolt. A number of shops were closed the morning of the march for fear that events might become violent or dangerous. In Guadalupe, there was much discussion and excitement after the event, with emphasis on the large number of people from so many different communities in Chiapas and even from other countries.

The Catholics of Chiapas feel connected to Catholics around the world because they all share similar beliefs, participate in similar rituals, and are (or should be) helping to construct the Kingdom of God. This community of faith begins at the local level and extends to the regional, the state, and—at least ideologically—the international level because Catholicism is an international religion. The geographic and organizational structure of the diocese facilitates the formation of both formal and informal networks among the indigenous communities. In Guadalupe, the notion of belonging to a community of faith facilitates involvement in networks. Catholics within the community share economic and moral support with their "brothers and sisters" in Christ. At the same time, belonging to a community of faith aids the creation of networks beyond the community. Catechists and prayer leaders walk to other communities to share the Word of God with Tzotzils. People participate in political mobilizations with other indigenous groups—including Tzeltals, Tojolabals, and Zoques— of Chiapas. Through the community of faith, people are united in their common vision of working toward the establishment of the Kingdom of God, a world with justice and equality for all.

In the end, do these connections and networks alter the situation of the indigenous Catholics? Levine and Stoll (1997) argue that while churches may aid in creating social capital and hence in empowering the poor, this does not lead to power, begging the question of why people remain poor and oppressed. They cite a variety of factors including a conservative Catholic hierarchy at the local and international level, participants' reluctance to move beyond local goals, and poorly formed ideas about politics. In short, Levine and Stoll conclude that social capital is incompletely formed; before engaging in politics, groups "need to consolidate their own identity and to found their inner life on enduring bonds of solidarity, trust, and the experience of common effort" (1997:92). What is absent from Levine and Stoll's analysis are the structural reasons that explain why people remain poor and oppressed. Neoliberal economic reforms, authoritarian policies, and political violence certainly play a role in grassroots movements' ability to promote change. In Chiapas, a repressive state government, increased militarization, and an economic model that has little space for peasant livelihood limit the power of indigenous Catholics. The networks emanating from Guadalupe are not overtly political—they serve as a basis for economic and moral support. The overtly political events organized by Pueblo Creyente, in particular the massive pilgrimages, draw great attention to the plight of indigenous peoples in Chiapas, but they do not necessarily change policy. Yet the importance of empowerment itself, even if it is not immediately transformed into power, cannot be overemphasized. Those who participate in these networks or events are often changed by the experience. Taking over the streets of the mestizo-dominated city of San Cristóbal de Las Casas, even for a few hours, makes pilgrims aware of their unity and strength. Walking with others, in pilgrimages or to visit Catholics for worship, reaffirms the goal of assisting the construction the Kingdom of God where all can live a dignified life.

Photo and caption by Juana López López, 1999
These dolls dressed as Zapatistas wearing Chamula clothing are for sale.
Estas muñecas están vestidas como Zapatistas de ropa chamula y sirven para vender.
Li ixtolal ololetik li'e slapojik jech k'u cha'al j-ak' k'ok', ja' sk'u' chamula, xchi'uk ta
xtun ta sventa jchonel.

9

Conclusion

The exiled Tzotzils of Guadalupe have created an indigenous Catholic community in which they identify a broad range of human rights and work to defend these rights. Central to the creation of community consciousness are local notions of working and walking with one heart. Walking is a physical act shared by the poor in Chiapas. People walk because they are poor and cannot pay for transportation or because they must reach communities where there are no roads. On a symbolic level, impoverished Catholics state that their situation forces them to walk to make the path that will lead to respect, equality, and a dignified life. In Guadalupe people recalled walking for hours to attend religious celebrations, to visit indigenous Catholics in other communities, and to work in the fincas, the Grijalva Valley, or the city. Walking is also work. Women and men carry their children and belongings on slippery, narrow paths up and down steep hills. In addition, physical labor—be it washing clothes while bent over a stream, planting and harvesting in their cornfields, working on the fincas, or constructing roads, houses, and chapels—is also part of daily life.

For those resisting poverty and marginalization, the defense of human rights is part of the work of everyday life. This work involves not only the struggle against arbitrary detention, torture, and other abuses but also the struggle to resist structural violence and to produce spaces for dignity. This final chapter places the work of Mayan Catholics for rights within the broader context of debates on indigenous rights and religion.

Writing Rights

A central concern of this book has been to humanize rights, that is, to write about rights without essentializing, sentimentalizing, or exoticizing those who suffer abuses (Kleinman and Kleinman 1997). The discourse of human rights can dehumanize when it simplifies conflicts and divides people into innocent and guilty, powerless victims and powerful violators (Wilson 1997). In an attempt to humanize rights, I describe not only the structural constraints affecting indigenous people in Chiapas (from racism to poverty to political marginality), but the ways indigenous people, even in extraordinarily difficult situations, have worked to defend their human rights. Mayan Catholics are not only resisting abuses; they are affirming their own dignity as children of God, their own definition of rights, and their own way of life.

Jan Rus writes that the model of "resistance" is necessarily incomplete for describing indigenous actions in response to the colonial world. He notes that the attempt "to restore indigenous people's subjectivity, or 'agency,' by calling on resistance makes it seem that the initiative was always on the colonialists' side—that Spanish speakers were the active, positive side of the colonial dyad and that Indians were reactive and negative" (2002a:1025). The model of resistance, then, can assume that there was no indigenous way of life or community to defend. Rus states:

> In everyday social life, sharing a world of beliefs and knowledge— like speaking a common language—provides a source of solidarity and identification. In more extraordinary circumstances, sharing a world of meanings can raise "resistance" from an ad hoc, tactical maneuver ("protecting my fields from invasion by outsiders today") to a long-term strategic commitment ("saving the lands our ancestors received at the beginning of the Fourth Creation for our descendants through all time"). (2002a:1026)

This long-term strategic commitment is evident in the struggles of Mayan Catholics. The methods of ethnographic fieldwork—conducing in-depth interviews, listening to life histories, and observing day-to-day events—reveal indigenous agency in the definition and defense of rights. The Catholics of Guadalupe appropriate the international concept of human rights, and it takes on new meaning in their hands. Most important, the Catholics emphasize (a) rights as reciprocal responsibilities existing within a community, (b) equality and respect, which are justified in religious terms, (c) economic and social rights, and (d) the need for structural change to address national and international inequalities.

Regarding rights as responsibilities, it is within the community of Guadalupe that people work to define and defend their rights. Each person is expected to work toward maintenance of the survival of the community itself, and, in many cases, this should override individual interests. Each person belongs to and gives to the community while the community, in turn, gives something to each of its members. In criticizing those responsible for expulsion, the Guadalupe Catholics note that caciques lack respect for others, the same respect on which the Catholics base their notion of community.

Guadalupe Catholics defend their struggle for rights in religious terms. They note that all humans have dignity and the right to a dignified life because they are children of God. Part of respecting each person within the community is recognizing his or her inherent dignity. The demands of indigenous people for respect is a call for the government as well as mestizos to recognize the rightful place of indigenous peoples in the national society, just as each indigenous person is given a place in the local community.

Of great importance to the people of Guadalupe are fundamental economic and social rights, rights that are undervalued in western European doctrine, which emphasizes civil and political rights. Mayan Catholics demand the right to land, water, health care, and other resources. They criticize the government for its racism in refusing to listen to indigenous demands. In interviews, people commonly emphasized the problem of poverty over expulsion itself. Most Guadalupe families lived in poverty in Chamula, and their struggle to make a living continued in San Cristóbal. Viewing rights from the perspective of the poor necessitates an emphasis on economic and social rights, as has been pointed out by a number of anthropologists who have conducted fieldwork among marginalized people (see for example Binford 1996, Farmer 2003, Green 1999, and Scheper-Hughes 1992).

Implementation of the economic and social rights of the 1948 UDHR necessitates fundamental structural change, both within nation-states and among them (Hollenbach 1979). Without structural change, it is impossible to guarantee equal access to rights and freedoms "without distinction of any kind, such as race, colour, sex, language, religion, political or other option, national or social origin, property, birth or other status" (UDHR, Article 2); the right to social security (Article 22); the right to work and just pay (Article 23); the right to education (Article 26); and the right to "a standard of living adequate for the health and well-being of himself and of his family" (Article 25).

It is difficult to imagine that these rights can be protected within the current global economic system, particularly with neoliberal reforms being implemented in Mexico and market economies virtually unchallenged by alternatives. During negotiation of NAFTA in the early 1990s, the human rights situation in Mexico became a point of concern for U.S. and Canadian policy makers. They viewed the respect of human rights—primarily civil and political rights—as an important element in Mexico's transition to democracy. At the same time, neoliberal reforms in response to global integration are reversing

Mexico's postrevolutionary promise of social and economic rights. Since the term of President de la Madrid, subsidies and loans to rural producers have been cut, President Salinas de Gortari declared the end of agrarian reform with the changes to Article 27 of the Mexican Constitution, and President Vicente Fox has promoted a model of small businesses and maquiladoras as an alternative way of life for peasants. In this context, Guadalupe Catholics complain that although they perform hours of physical labor daily, they do not have the material means to live a dignified life. In response, they unite with poor people in Chiapas to demand economic and social rights.

"We Come to Dialogue": The Zapatista Demand for Justice

Mayan Catholics are among many groups of indigenous people in Chiapas working to defend human rights. The best-known political group is the Zapatista Army of National Liberation, but there are hundreds of others from peasant and labor organizations to cooperatives. In spite of the many differences between the EZLN and the Mayan Catholics, there are important similarities. Both groups denounce the centuries-long oppression and racism at the hands of the Spanish and mestizos. Both groups reject global capitalism and its exploitation. Both groups demand dignity and rights as Mexican citizens. Both groups insist on an alternative model of development that respects their right to a dignified life and demand that their voices be heard.

A group of twenty-three Zapatista *comandantes* (commanders) entered Mexico's National Congress on March 28, 2001.[1] In an event of symbolic importance, Comandanta Esther, an indigenous woman wearing the traditional blouse of Huistán, led the delegation and spoke to the Congress:

> Through my voice speaks the voice of the Zapatista Army of National Liberation. The word that our voice brings is outcry. But our word is one of respect for this Congress and for all those who hear us. You will receive from us neither insults nor rudeness . . . The word we bring is true. We do not come to humiliate anyone. We do not come to supplant anyone. We come to be heard and to listen. We come to dialogue. (*La Jornada* March 29, 2001)

Marcos—the mestizo "subcommander," poet, national hero, and media spokesperson—was in Mexico City but did not enter the Congress. Instead, members of Congress were forced to listen to an indigenous voice.

The Zapatistas' journey to the Congress had been a long one. Following the election of Vicente Fox, who broke the PRI's seventy-one-year monopoly on political power in Mexico, the Zapatistas announced that they would march to Mexico City to speak with the government and civil society. While in Mexico City, the Zapatista delegation hoped to enter Mexico's Congress to speak to senators about indigenous rights and the San Andrés Accords. Numerous members of Congress, led by PAN Senator Diego de Fernández de Cevallos, rejected the delegation, arguing that the "sacred" space of Congress would be violated by the presence of Zapatistas. Pressured by civil society, a group of senators called a vote to decide whether to receive the Zapatista delegation. By a narrow margin, 220 in favor and 210 opposed, Congress agreed to hear from the delegation. The results of the vote illustrate the extreme reluctance of elected government officials to listen to the voices of a group of indigenous people from Chiapas.

When the Zapatista delegation entered the Congress on March 28, it was half-empty. A group of PAN and PRI senators had boycotted the event. The senators' absence contrasts with politicians' visits to the Tzotzil community of San Juan Chamula during presidential or gubernatorial campaigns, such as Eduardo Robledo's visit to Chamula described in the opening pages of this book. In seeking votes, politicians put on the traditional clothing of Chamulas and promise to respect indigenous customs and traditions. Government officials support indigenous people when they serve political needs and only then, when the indigenous "know their place." The Zapatista visitors would presumably corrupt the "honorable" halls of Congress.

Comandanta Esther addressed the half-empty Congress, noting that the absent senators refused to listen to her voice, the voice of an indigenous woman. She denounced the racism of Mexican society and the marginalization of indigenous peoples: "We suffer from indifference because no one remembers us. They send us to live in the corner of the mountains of the country so that no one will arrive to visit or see how we live."

She denounced the structural violence experienced in everyday life: "[W]e do not have services of potable water, electricity, schools, dignified housing, roads, clinic, not even hospitals, while many of our sisters, women, children, and elders die of curable illnesses, malnutrition, and childbirth, because there are neither clinics nor hospitals where they can be taken care of."

In her closing, Esther proclaimed: "My voice doesn't lack respect for anyone, but we didn't come to ask for handouts. My voice comes to seek justice, liberty, and democracy for all the indigenous peoples." In sum, her speech was a call for the respect of indigenous rights, most important among them an end to the racism, poverty, and marginality that has characterized indigenous life for five hundred years.

Vicente Fox provoked anger and resentment during his presidential campaign of 2000 by stating that he could resolve the Chiapas conflict in "fifteen minutes." His dismissive attitude minimized the significance of Zapatista demands and denied the long-term oppression of indigenous peoples in Chiapas and throughout Mexico. Fox's response similarly denied the structural changes demanded by Zapatistas in order to live a dignified life.

The Zapatistas cry: "We come to be heard and to listen. We come to dialogue." In spite of a growing awareness of the situation of indigenous peoples and the willingness of certain sectors to attempt to address indigenous concerns, racism powerfully pervades Mexican society, and there is a refusal to dialogue with indigenous peoples, listen to their demands, and accept them on their own terms.

The Catholic Diocese of San Cristóbal de Las Casas: Voice of the Voiceless?

When Bishop Ruiz García arrived in Chiapas in 1960, he hoped to assimilate and Westernize indigenous peoples. He wished to convert them to be Catholic (and Mexican) on his own terms, rather than accepting them on their terms. The work of the Chamulan mission from 1966 to 1969 also followed this model of modernization. Indigenous custom and tradition were criticized, even ridiculed, and viewed as an impediment to evangelization.

However, the work of the Catholic Church changed in the 1970s due to the influence of the historic meetings of the Second Vatican Council (1962–1965) and the Latin American Bishops Conference of Medellin (1968) as well as the pastoral workers' encounter with the indigenous poor. So, rather than converting the poor, the poor converted Bishop Ruiz and the pastoral agents, who committed themselves to work with and for the poor. Liberation was viewed as being fundamental to this conversion, as was learning to respect indigenous culture. However, the process of conversion was not without its errors, as is indicated by the Chamulan mission, among other examples.

In working with people in Guadalupe, I saw that people introduce ideas from the Catholic Church in their conceptions of human rights and that the Church provides an institutional link through which people mobilize to defend their rights. Notions of equality and community were predicated upon and defended by religious doctrine. In mobilizing to defend their rights, the Catholics in Guadalupe believe that they are united with other Catholics through their shared beliefs and ritual practices and are (or should be) helping to construct the Kingdom of God.

The Tzotzil term *Sc'op Dios* (Word of God) is important because it unites indigenous Catholics well beyond the community of Guadalupe. In contrast, the language of Tzotzil is called *batsil c'op*, or "the true language," and is spoken by *batsil vinic*, "the true men," indicating the simultaneous glorification and isolation of this ethnic group. Sc'op Dios provides the framework for unity with other indigenous groups (including Tzeltals, Tojolabals, Ch'ols, and Zoques) and with mestizos, since all are seen as "children of God." Inter-ethnic unity was explicitly promoted by the Diocese of San Cristóbal beginning with the 1974 Indigenous Congress, at which participants began to work together to obtain liberation. The obvious limit of this type of unity is its exclusion of other religious groups, namely Protestants and Traditionalists.

Unity is the foundation of a community of faith that begins at the local level and extends to the regional, the state, and the international level.[2] Furthermore, the organizational structure of the diocese—with its pastoral teams, meetings, and economic resources—facilitates the formation of both formal and informal networks among the indigenous communities, including a community of faith in Guadalupe. A broad definition of rights also sets the goals for mobilization, as is shown in the example of Pueblo Creyente and its struggles for justice, dignity, and economic equality. The fact that the indigenous of Chiapas believe that political mobilization is not only necessary but willed by God legitimates these struggles.

What is most innovative about the diocesan project is the willingness to listen to and dialogue with the indigenous peoples rather than speaking for them. As Daniel Levine comments on the option for the poor, "Being a voice for the voiceless is less difficult and demanding for institutions like the churches than is listening to what the hitherto voiceless have to say and giving them space and tools with which to act" (1992:6). The idea of speaking for the voiceless follows the colonialist paradigm: indigenous peoples are unable to speak for themselves and need a mestizo or Western interlocutor to speak for them. Yet poor people can and always have been able to speak; it is just that those in power refuse to listen. The Diocese of San Cristóbal became a new interlocutor that sought dialogue with the indigenous people and supported them in their struggle to affirm their dignity. Instead of a voice for the voiceless, perhaps a better metaphor is "ear of the earless," with "the earless" referring to a church and society that historically have refused to listen to indigenous peoples. This dialogical process redefined both actors (the Church and indigenous peoples), and the diocese supported dozens of grassroots groups that work for human rights, women's empowerment, access to land, and participation in the political system, among other issues. By 1998, there were some 8,000 catechists in the diocese who took the Word of God into their own hands; that is, they are protagonists who announce the Word of God and denounce injustice in their communities. With changes in the diocesan project under the new bishop, Felipe Arizmendi, and what some see as the demise of liberation theology throughout Latin America, these catechists continue their work at a grassroots level.

The Diocese of San Cristóbal de Las Casas is not unique in its support of indigenous rights, nor are Mayan Catholics unique in their alliance with the Catholic Church in defending their rights. The Catholic Church as a transnational institution has played an important role in facilitating indigenous movements in many regions of Latin America (see Brysk 2000 and Cleary and Steigenga 2004). The Catholic Church has served as an ally for human rights movements in being an ear of the "earless" and is engaged in a mutual dialogue. It has provided material resources, offered training in literacy and community organizing, facilitated networks for indigenous activists, and provided social legitimacy and a language to justify struggles for justice. Yet the Catholic Church's role in indigenous rights is not without contradictions. Pastoral workers can lose sight of their own privilege based on class and ethnicity and the ways privilege distances them from Mayan Catholics. This privilege can also limit clergy's ability to listen to indigenous voices. Because many pastoral agents spent time in rural communities listening to Mayan Catholics, they were able to transcend, at least partially, the paternalistic role of being voice of the voiceless. In their role of accompaniment, pastoral agents served as an ear of the earless.

Racism, Expulsion, and Everyday Forms of State Violence

Various anthropologists (and other observers) have remarked on the hostility toward dissenting opinions to be found in a number of communities within the Chiapas region. In the extreme case of San Juan Chamula, for instance, "traditionalist" Indians have expelled practi-

cally all Protestants and orthodox Catholics. This kind of intolerance
has fed much of the present tinderbox situation in Chiapas and, in my
opinion, has intensified in the wake of the Zapatista uprising.
— ENRIQUE KRAUZE, LETTER IN
NEW YORK REVIEW OF BOOKS (2000)

The case of expulsions from Chamula has been used for diverse political purposes. Enrique Krauze uses it as an example of indigenous peoples' intolerance.
George Collier and Jane Collier responded to his characterization of indigenous people:

If indigenous leaders sometimes get carried away with their power and
violate the human rights of their opponents, they are only doing what
powerful leaders in Mexico and around the world also do. In our experience, indigenous Maya peoples are no more or less prone than other
Mexicans — or North Americans, or Europeans — to be intolerant of dissident opinions. (Letter in *New York Review of Books,* 2000)

Indigenous leaders in Chamula and elsewhere have committed human
rights violations. However, the violence of expulsion must be situated within
the broader context of the place of indigenous peoples in Mexican society. Historically, Chamulan leaders made a political pact with the state: in exchange for
a grant of some autonomy in governing their own affairs, they would serve PRI
interests. The pact can be understood as a form of resistance in the sense that
it was an attempt to preserve their land, livelihood, and way of life. In contrast,
a growing number of Chamulas affiliate with opposition parties, independent
peasant organizations, the EZLN, and Protestant or Catholic churches in their
struggle for land, social services, and human rights. These affiliations threaten
the caciques' pact with the PRI, not only because they represent an alternative
political position but also because the caciques' power depends on unity, or at
least its appearance, to defend themselves from outside interference. In addition, the government placed its full support behind the caciques, human rights
abuses and all.

One of the most tragic cases of violence in Chiapas in recent years took
place in the Chamulan hamlet of Arvenza I on the night of November 18, 1995,
"the night that Chamula cried." On this night, shooting broke out between two
rival groups. The gunfire lasted all night, and official reports indicated that at

least six people were killed, four were wounded, and four homes and trucks were burned.[3] A press release from the Fray Bartolomé de Las Casas Center for Human Rights placed the number killed at twenty-eight. To understand the confrontation at Arvenza, it is necessary to examine the violence in Chamula in the 1990s. In 1993, an unusually high number of people were expelled and, under the leadership of Domingo López Angel (then president of CRIACH), they began a sit-in at the government Office of Indigenous Affairs in the city of San Cristóbal. Rather than searching for homes in the outskirts of the city, this group of exiles chose to live in the patio of a government office to pressure government officials to take action to resolve the problem. The protestors sent out press releases denouncing the government's negligence and filed more than fifty legal denunciations before Chiapas's attorney general of justice. The sit-in lasted for eleven months, from September 1993 to August 1994 and, according to its organizers, involved more than five hundred protesters.

Even with the direct pressure of a public sit-in, the government took no action to address the problem of expulsion, and a large group of protestors decided to return to their homes in Chamula in August, just before the federal elections. Government officials insisted that they could offer no protection for those returning, and the protestors themselves took on the responsibility for "security" and carried guns hidden in the returning vehicles (Aramoni Calderón and Morquecho Escamilla 1998:251). Less than a month after this group arrived in Chamula, there were threats of violence in the hamlet of Ik'al Lumtik, and the expelled informed the secretary of government and the National Commission of Human Rights, but no action was taken. On September 19, 1994, three of the "returned" Chamulas were killed and a number injured in Icalumtic. The returned Chamulas named those responsible for the homicides, and the government released an arrest warrant, yet no one was arrested. Following the murders at Icalumtic, the violence continued, and the dissidents continued to arm themselves. The PRI supporters were also armed. Indeed, some Chamulas claimed that funds from a national government program, PROCAMPO (National Program for Direct Aid to the Countryside), had been used to purchase automatic weapons within the municipality to defend PRI supporters (Rus and Collier 2003:54). So, when the conflict began in Arvenza in November 1995, both sides were well armed.

Although the violence at Arvenza and Ik'al Lumtik took place between two groups of Chamulas, the state is clearly implicated in the violence. Time and again the government failed to take any action to stem the conflict, and furthermore, the PRI had allied itself with Chamulan caciques. As Carole Nagengast notes, political violence includes not only actions directly taken by the state, but other acts in which the state is complicit. The state "tolerates or encourages" violence "in order to create, justify, excuse, explain, or enforce hierarchies of difference and relations of inequality, [which] are acts of state violence, even though states themselves may not appear on the surface to be primary agents" (Nagengast 1994:114). Nagengast gives the examples of conflicts between the Hutus and Tutsis in Rwanda, Ladinos and indigenous people in Guatemala, and Israelis and Palestinians in Israel, among others.

Although the violence in Chiapas is much smaller in scale, government authorities similarly allow expulsions to continue through negligence and impunity. As the violence escalates, mestizos stereotype Chamulas as being dangerous and unruly, further reinforcing the inequality between mestizos and indigenous people. In this context, the failure of government officials to prevent expulsion and punish those responsible has caused the expelled to take "justice" into their own hands, with tragic consequences.

The murders at Arvenza, Chamula, are similar to the massacre of forty-five people in a chapel at Acteal, Chenalhó, on December 22, 1997. In both cases, indigenous peoples were killed at the hands of members of the same community. In both cases the murders were "foretold," that is, there was ample warning of escalating violence, and community members requested government intervention. In both cases government officials failed to take action to stem the violence. Denying any responsibility for the events, government authorities perversely blamed indigenous "custom and tradition" as the cause of the violence. In the case of Acteal, the "official" version of the events put forth in the attorney general's *Libro blanco* notes,

The specific motive [of the massacre] was vengeance, as a culmination of a sequence of mutual grievances. An unjustifiable vengeance, but one whose genesis is explained in light of the accumulated offenses and of the predominance of certain *usos y costumbres* [practices and customs] in the indigenous communities of the region. (Procuraduría General de la República 1998:96)

A combination of impunity and racism allows the state to respond in this way, to define indigenous peoples, again, as "an Other" whose odd customs include the practice of mass killing. Placing the events in their historical and political context can unravel the government misinformation and reveal state complicity in the violence.

Peace with Justice and Dignity

The problem with focusing on expulsion is that it calls attention to the actions of a small group of Chamulan caciques and ignores the thousands of Chamulas, living within and beyond the municipality, who are engaged in a struggle for justice (Rus 2002b). In addition, the focus on caciques and internal community dynamics obscures the broader picture of indigenous marginality and the struggle for access to resources that underlies expulsion. To return to the two scenes described at the opening of this book: Chamulan leaders have historically allied with the PRI to receive political and economic benefits and to be able to govern their own affairs with limited outside intervention, while those labeled "dissidents" have opposed domination by the caciques as well as by the PRI. These dissidents have engaged in a variety of strategies to defend their human rights; they have joined independent artisan cooperatives, peasant organizations, opposition parties, and faith-based movements.

The tens of thousands of indigenous people who inhabit the colonias surrounding San Cristóbal provide a powerful example of people with diverse religious and political affiliations living side by side and working to build new communities. The existence of these communities contradicts the portrayal of indigenous people as inherently intolerant and bound to tradition.

Within Chamula, there are many examples of Catholics, Presbyterians, Pentecostals, Seventh Day Adventists, Traditionalists, and other groups living and working together. Miguel Rolland (2000) describes numerous examples of Catholics and Protestants coming together for worship in Chamula as well as cases in which local Chamulan authorities have supported the construction of Catholic and Protestant churches in their hamlets. These collaborations serve as a reminder that the expulsions from Chamula have always been much more about politics than religion. In recent years, Tzotzil catechists, including those from Guadalupe, and clergy of the Diocese of San Cristóbal have made many low-profile pastoral visits to Chamula. A very public visit took place on May 28, 2003, when Felipe Arizmendi, bishop of the Diocese of San Cristóbal, went to the hamlet of Ya'al Tem, Chamula.[4] Some five hundred Tzotzils attended the mass, among them Protestants as well as Catholics, and Bishop Arizmendi welcomed the ecumenical spirit of collaboration. The actions of the pastoral workers of the diocese suggest that by walking side by side with the poor, the Catholic Church has been able to transcend some of its own intolerance. The church still has the potential to continue accompanying the work of indigenous peoples and to serve as an ally in the struggle for indigenous rights. That is, it can serve as an ear of the earless rather than a voice of the voiceless.

The voices of Mayan Catholics of Guadalupe are some of the many Mayan voices for human rights. In contemporary Mexico, Mayan Catholics demand an end to expulsion as well as equality, respect, and a broad range of economic rights. Their voices make an important contribution toward the construction of a society based on peace with justice and dignity.

Notes

CHAPTER 1

1. All translations from Spanish to English are the author's unless otherwise indicated.

2. A *municipio* (municipality or township) is a sociopolitical unit defined by Mexican law. For the most part, residents of each highland municipio have a shared ethnic identity and maintain their own dress and festivals to honor patron saints.

3. I thank Gary Gossen and Jan Rus for encouraging me to link expulsion to broader changes in Chiapas. Important sources on political and economic change in Chiapas since the 1970s include Cancian 1992, Collier 1994, and Rus and Collier 2003.

4. On the change to cattle production and the resulting impact on highland communities see Gómez Cruz and Kovic 1994, 51–53, and Collier 1994.

5. During the presidency of Miguel de la Madrid (1982–1988), subsidies to rural producers declined an average of 13 percent a year (Harvey 1998:179).

6. By the 1990s as many as 15,000 Mayas of Chiapas had migrated to the United States, primarily to Florida and California (Rus and Collier 2003; Rus and Guzmán López 1996).

7. Estimates of numbers of expelled vary greatly, depending on the definition of "expelled." Government figures are often low in an attempt to minimize the problem. Anthropologist and journalist Gaspar Morquecho Escamilla placed the total at 20,000 in a 1994 article. In a 2001 report on expulsion, the Fray Bartolomé de Las Casas Center for Human Rights placed the number at 25,000.

8. Samuel Ruiz submitted his resignation to the Vatican on his seventy-fifth birthday, November 3, 1999, in accordance with canonical law. Ruiz remained bishop until March 31, 2000, when the Vatican named Felipe Arizmendi as his successor. Enrique Díaz Díaz was consecrated auxiliary bishop in July 2003.

9. The term *caxlan* is used in several Mayan languages to refer to Westerners or people of European descent and comes from the term *castellano*, Spaniard. *Caxlan* is used in highland communities to refer to non-indigenous peoples including Mexican mestizos and foreigners like myself.

10. Heidi Moksnes observes that the concept of suffering is central to the identity of the Tzotzil Catholics of the highland community San Pedro Chenalhó. These Catholics describe themselves as belonging to a special category. "They represent the Indigenous, the Poor Peasants, for whom God holds a special love and a particular interest" (2003:207).

Like the Catholics of Guadalupe, those of Chenalhó contrast their own situation as a "suffering people" with the situation of the wealthy and mestizos.

CHAPTER 2

1. I use pseudonyms for the residents of Guadalupe.

2. In highland communities, municipal presidents frequently punish people with short jail sentences for various crimes. Legally, the municipal president can jail someone for seventy-two hours while determining whether there is sufficient evidence to charge the person with a crime. Jane Fishburne Collier (1973) notes that stiff jail sentences were given in Zinacantán for adultery, fighting, or witchcraft. These sentences were given in part to protect the offender from acts of revenge.

3. A study of wage labor in eight hamlets of Chamula revealed that a total of 77 percent of male heads of household engaged in wage labor outside the municipality, including 52 percent who worked on coffee plantations and 25 percent who worked as day laborers in the cities of San Cristóbal and Tuxtla and the oilfields of La Reforma (Wasserstrom 1983:202–203).

4. See Edelman (2000) for a discussion of diverse economic activities carried out by peasants under capitalism.

5. Another reason that women may not sell artisan products directly to tourists in the streets is to avoid domestic conflicts. Christine Eber and Brenda Rosenbaum (1993) note that marital tension increased when women in Chamula and Chenalhó began to sell artisan products. Women who sell products directly

to customers may be accused of being "women of the street." Their spouses or fathers may become angry if women keep their money from sales.

6. Caciques of Chamula commonly accuse Word of God Catholics of being "evangelicals" and claim that evangelicals must be expelled because they threaten local customs and traditions. Perhaps this is because caciques believe the state government would be more sympathetic to the expulsion of Protestants. Since traditional Chamulas mix Catholic beliefs with Mayan ritual, it would be more difficult to claim that Catholics following the line of the Diocese of San Cristóbal de Las Casas threaten the community.

7. The land Mateo purchased was uninhabited forest. When people began to settle, they cut down trees to clear space for and construct their homes.

8. In many of the masses I observed in indigenous communities in the Diocese of San Cristóbal, members of the congregation were called on to comment on the readings.

CHAPTER 3

1. In numerous diocesan documents and meetings of the 1970s, the term "the poor" (los pobres in Spanish) was used to describe an undifferentiated group of people suffering similarly from structures of inequality. This designation reifies a heterogeneous group of people. In time, the pastoral workers recognized the specific role of ethnicity in structuring the marginality and poverty of indigenous peoples of Chiapas. That is, they recognized the necessity of seeing the intersection of class and ethnicity. Nonetheless, the labeling of all oppressed peoples in

the diocese as "the poor" (or at times *los hermanos*, the brothers) would continue.

2. See Berryman (1994, Chapter 6) for a discussion of the role of accompaniment in liberation theology, especially in Central America.

3. The Spanish term *tomar consciencia*, like the Portuguese term *conscientização*, has no direct translation in English. Paulo Freire (1970) uses the term *conscientização* to describe the awakening of a critical consciousness as the oppressed question the injustices of their reality and begin to work to transform them.

4. Gayatri Spivak (1988) writes of the colonialism inherent in Western academics' claim to "speak for" or give voice to non-Western peoples with considerably less power. Because of the imbalance of power between indigenous peoples and mestizo pastoral workers, dialogue between the two groups (rather than the Church pretending to speak for and defend "its people") suggests the beginning of a new relationship of equals. Similarly, Paulo Freire (1970) emphasizes that "revolutionary leaders" should dialogue with the oppressed rather than bring (or impose) a message of "salvation."

5. In writing of the "discovery and conquest" of America, Tzevtan Todorov (1984) describes the ways the Spaniards view the Indians as an other, radically separate and alien from themselves. Hence, the Spanish failed to humanize or understand the Indians on their own terms.

6. Quoted in *El Caminante* 17 (April 1978), "Aportes de la Diócesis de San Cristóbal a la Reunión Pacífico-Sur en Tehuantepec en visitas a CELAM III, Puebla."

7. "Marco teológico de la opción diocesana," *El Caminante* 44 (1987), cited in Floyd (1997).

8. *Gaudium et Spes* no. 69.1, quoted in Dorr 1983:122.

9. It is important to point out that the meetings of Vatican II were not the first time the Catholic Church had addressed issues of human rights and social justice. Of particular importance is Pope Leo XIII's 1891 encyclical *Rerum Novarum*, which "affirms as conditions of human dignity the right to a just wage, the right to use one's earned wages to purchase and own property, and the rights to adequate food, clothing and shelter" (cited in Traer 1991:34).

10. Some of the key writings on liberation theology include Gutiérrez (1973), Sobrino (1978), Boff and Boff (1986), and Ricard (1987). For an overview of liberation theology and its critics see McGovern (1989).

11. The interview appeared in the Mexican magazine *El Proceso*, June 7, 1998.

12. Las Casas played a critical role in securing the passage of laws to protect indigenous people from exploitation at the hands of colonizers. Although Las Casas criticized the Spaniards' brutal treatment of indigenous people, he did not criticize the enslavement of Africans in the New World.

13. In the Plan de Ayala of 1911, Mexican Revolutionary leader Emiliano Zapata used this slogan in the struggle to recuperate communal lands controlled by owners of sugarcane plantations in the state of Morelos.

14. Prior to the Indigenous Congress, the dominant organization in the state

was the National Federation of Peasants (Confederación Nacional Campesina, CNC), a group affiliated with the PRI.

15. This event is also recounted in Morales Bermúdez (1992).

16. After this important meeting of all pastoral workers, a diocesan assembly was called each year to examine and revise the pastoral work. Occasional "extraordinary assemblies" are called for discussion of special events.

17. The ordination of indigenous deacons led to conflicts with the Catholic hierarchy in the 1990s to the present. The Vatican sent a letter to Bishop Arizmendi (Ruiz's successor) to express concern about Bishop Ruiz's final ordination of indigenous deacons, which took place in January 2000. The prominent presence of the deacons' wives at the ordination and the fact that Bishop Ruiz placed his hands over the heads of the deacons as well as their wives was criticized. According to the Vatican letter, this created confusion and ambiguity as to whether the women were also being ordained. The letter recommends that Bishop Arizmendi suspend ordination pending further investigation. (*La Jornada,* July 12, 2001).

18. In 1978, members of the Maoist-inspired Política Popular, the PP (People's Politics), began to work with Quiptic and other organizations in the Cañadas region of the Lacandon jungle. The PP was founded in Mexico City during the 1968 student movements; Adolfo Orive Berlinguer, then a professor of the Universidad Nacional Autónoma de México, was one of its key leaders (Harvey 1998:81). Initially, many pastoral workers of the diocese supported the political work of the PP. Indeed, Bishop Ruiz had invited

members of the PP, commonly called the Pepes, to come to Chiapas. Yet, in a short time, conflict between the Pepes and pastoral workers developed, as diocesan workers felt that the Pepes began to displace and take advantage of the Church's work. After just a year, the diocese broke off its relationship with the Pepes. The lack of endorsement from the diocese closed the door to the Pepes in many rural communities. Reflecting on this event, Jan De Vos (2002:260) notes: "Their [the Pepes'] greatest mistake was abusing the trust of Don Samuel in infiltrating the cadres of the diocese and wanting to take immediate advantage of someone else's long term work." The diocesan conflict with the PP foreshadowed future tensions. The infrastructure created by the diocesan organizing effort was attractive to many political groups. Pastoral workers feared that groups would use these structures for their own purposes without taking into account the interests of the residents of rural communities and their long-term struggles.

19. The case is summarized in the diocesan newsletter *El Caminante* of June/July 1985.

20. Donal Dorr notes that recent popes have insisted that politics should remain in the hands of laypeople. Nonetheless, the Church "as a community of people" rather than as an institution of clergy "is called to promote justice in society as an essential element in its work of evangelisation" (Dorr 1983:273).

21. Not all of the Protestant groups in Chiapas can be categorized as sects. The use of this term reflects the lack of an ecumenical project on the part of the Catholic Church.

22. The Guatemalan army made sixty-four raids on refugee camps between 1981 and 1984 to find supposed guerrillas in Mexico (Benjamin 1989:238).

23. The details of this case are documented in Gómez Cruz and Kovic (1994:154–157).

24. The arrest of Father Padrón was based on political motives, as demonstrated by the fact that the government agreed to release him only under the following conditions: (1) that the pastoral workers force peasants to evacuate lands that had recently been taken in Chiapas; (2) that the diocese emit a declaration stating that no human rights violations had occurred in Padrón's arrest; (3) that the diocese condemn the occupation of lands by peasants; and (4) that after his release Father Padrón not be allowed to preach in Mexico. None of the demands legally corresponds to the duties of the diocese, and all were rejected (Gómez Cruz and Kovic 1994; Fazio 1994).

25. The work of Pueblo Creyente is discussed in depth in Chapter 8.

26. For more information on Xi' Nich' see SERPAJ 1996; on Las Abejas see Kovic 2003b and Moksnes 2003.

27. On CODIMUJ see Kovic 2003a. For a life history of one CODIMUJ participant see Gil Tébar 2003.

28. Much has been written on the uniqueness of the Zapatistas as a guerrilla movement. They are unique among Latin American guerrilla groups in that they demand democracy but do not propose taking power themselves. They insist that their leaders obey the needs and desires of local communities in sending out orders. Subcomandante Marcos's poetic communiqués have been globally distrib-uted through the Internet. For detailed accounts of the reasons behind the uprising see Collier (1994) and Harvey (1998).

29. The bishops' statement appeared in CENCOS of January 1994 and is quoted in Floyd 1997:211.

30. For example, Enrique Krauze (1999) attributes some of the violence in contemporary Chiapas to actions of the Catholic Diocese of San Cristóbal under the leadership of Bishop Ruiz García. Others have stated that the diocese is directly responsible for the Zapatista movement (Pazos 1994).

CHAPTER 4

1. Pablo Iribarren describes this evaluation in "Experiencia: Proceso de la Diócesis de San Cristóbal de Las Casas" (1985).

2. Pastoral methods varied greatly depending on the socioeconomic context of the region and the approach taken by each religious order, i.e., Jesuit, Dominican, Marist, and others, as well as by diocesan priests. The pastoral work carried out by the Dominican mission of the Ocosingo region has been well documented (Coello Castro 1991; De Vos 2002; Iribarren 1991; Leyva Solano 1995).

3. For historical accounts of Chamula during the colonial and post-independence periods see Bricker 1981, Favre 1984, MacLeod 1973, and Wasser-strom 1983.

4. Historical accounts on the Cuscat Rebellion include those of Victoria Bricker (1981), Antonio García de León (1985), Jan Rus (1983). Chamulan writer Enrique Pérez López includes an account of the rebellion in his book *Chamula: Un pueblo indígena tzotzil* (1990).

5. A number of indigenous people joined the Ladino troops in their attacks on Chamula. Men from Mitontic, Chenalhó, and even Chamula participated in killing fellow Indians.

6. In a classic work based on research in the northern sierra of Puebla, Mexico, Luisa Paré defines *caciquismo* as "a phenomenon of political mediation characterized by the informal and personal exercise of power in order to protect the economic interests of an individual or a faction" (Paré 1979, quoted in Pineda 1993:25). Paré argues that caciques became the agents of capitalism as the traditional peasant economy of autoconsumption was transformed into a simple mercantile economy.

7. In 1977, about 25 percent of the men in Chamula had an annual income of 20,000 to 50,000 pesos from transportation, the production of rum, and the sale of agricultural products. In contrast, 50 percent of the men had an annual income below 3,800 pesos, primarily from working as wage laborers (Wasserstrom 1977).

8. Aside from Father Hernández, the personnel of the mission included three religious women of the Catholic order Sacred Hearts of Jesus and Mary, two mestizo catechists (who also taught sewing and literacy), and two female indigenous catechists who had studied at the missionary school of the city of San Cristóbal (Iribarren 1980).

9. The term "temple" is commonly used to refer to a Catholic church or chapel.

10. Similar conflicts between elders and the first indigenous catechists developed in the region of Ocosingo. As Pablo Iribarren (1991) recounts, the conflicts arose in part because pastoral agents rather than local communities selected catechists. In addition, the early catechist training opposed local symbols, rites, and customs as it challenged the authority of traditional elders. As pastoral agents recognized these problems, the catechist movement changed dramatically in the 1970s.

11. This office is dedicated to the administration of government possessions, including historic monuments. According to the Mexican Constitution, all churches were property of the state prior to legal reforms of the 1990s.

12. Clearly the new credit union significantly cut profits of the caciques, who charged monthly interest rates of 10 to 15 percent.

13. The third phase of the project was completed in 1974 with four new courses. In two years, hundreds of indigenous people had been trained through these courses.

14. These events are reported in a letter from Bishop Ruiz to Governor Velasco Suárez, December 31, 1973.

15. Government authorities of the Office of Indigenous Affairs tried to defend their involvement in transporting the expelled to Teopisca by claiming that they wanted to protect the detained and prevent their mistreatment in Chamulan jails (Iribarren 1980). Nonetheless, these authorities openly participated in an illegal act rather than attempting to stop it. One could ask why they transported the detained to a jail in Teopisca rather than releasing them.

16. In 1951, the Mexican Ministry of Education signed an agreement to support SIL's work investigating indigenous language, culture, and biology as well as SIL's work to benefit Indians (Rus and Wasserstrom 1981). Protestant churches have a long history in Mexico dating back to the nineteenth century (Martin 1990).

17. Local authorities have expelled Tzeltal and Tzotzil Mayas from Amatenango del Valle, Oxchuc, Mitontic, Tenejapa, and Zinacantán, among other locations.

18. This number does not include the thousands of people who have been displaced from their communities due to recent violence in Chiapas related to the activities of paramilitary groups beginning in 1994.

19. There is some disagreement as to the affiliation of this priest. Some claim that he belongs to the Mexican Orthodox Church, and others claim that the Church of San Pascual Babilón was formed by a dissident seminary student.

20. The letter was written to Pablo Iribarren and is dated September 30, 1980.

21. Father Hernández did not participate in El Comité or work in Chamula in the 1980s.

22. Municipal authorities have thwarted many of these efforts. On February 24, 1999, five Chamulan Catholics in the hamlet of Ucumtic were detained for attempting to build a chapel. In a similar case, on May 30, 1999, Chamulan authorities detained three Pentecostal and two Catholic males in the hamlet of Bautista Chica because they did not destroy a recently constructed chapel as they had been ordered.

CHAPTER 5

1. Following the detention of fifty Protestants in Chamula, residents of La Hormiga had detained a number of Chamulan authorities in San Cristóbal. On March 31, 1992, some 3,000 Chamulas traveled to San Cristóbal to liberate the detainees, assaulting La Hormiga residents and firing arms in the process (Aramoni Calderón and Morquecho Escamilla 1998). Politically, it was easy for Governor González to ignore the violence of expulsion when it took place within indigenous municipalities, but when violence spilled over into mestizos' spaces, such as San Cristóbal, the governor was forced to take action.

2. There is significant variation in Western notions of rights, just as there is variation in non-Western definitions of rights. I use the term "Western" to refer to rights codes coming out of the western European tradition, such as the French Declaration of the Rights of Man and the U.S. Bill of Rights, which protect individual rights to equality, liberty, and justice.

3. Article 27 of the Mexican Constitution recognizes ejidal and communal populations and protects their ownership of land. Although the article does not directly refer to indigenous peoples, this population has been identified with ejidal and communal land ownership (Cruz Rueda 1994).

4. *La Jornada*, February 21, 1994.

5. This was one of nine cases of abuse of authority in Chamula documented by the center for the first six months of 1994. In these nine cases, a total of 367 people were affected by abuse of authority, ac-

cording to documents in the archives of the Fray Bartolomé de Las Casas Center for Human Rights.

6. Domingo López Angel was the leader of CRIACH, an organization of the expelled that works to protect the rights of the indigenous people in Chiapas. CRIACH strongly opposes the power of Chamulan caciques and at times has opposed the PRI at the regional, state, and federal levels.

7. For example, women involved in an artisan cooperative founded in Chamula in the 1970s were intimidated by municipal authorities concerned that the women were linked to independent organizations (Gómez Monte and Rus 1990; Rus and Collier 2003). In another case, in March 1995, a group of women working as traditional midwives and involved with the cooperative J'Pas Joloviletic were threatened with expulsion from Bautista Chico and Tres Cruces, Chamula (Fray Bartolomé de Las Casas Center for Human Rights 1995a).

8. Several months after the case of Las Ollas, another group of Chamulan families who had been threatened with expulsion visited the human rights center. They were Catholics affiliated with the San Cristóbal diocese and explained that they did not want to return to Chamula because they were afraid that they might be killed. They described a case in which three exiled Protestants were killed when they returned to their homes.

9. Other biblical readings that were discussed include Deuteronomy 24:12–15; Proverbs 6:3; Isaiah 25:6; Matthew 25:34–45; Luke 3:1–14; and John 3:27; 15:1–6, and 19:11.

CHAPTER 6

1. The term "violence of everyday life" comes from Nancy Scheper-Hughes's *Death without Weeping* (1992), an ethnography of northeastern Brazil. Everyday violence includes fears of "disappearance," kidnapping, or arrest, institutional violence, and structural violence—hunger, illness, and poverty.

2. These interviews on agrarian conflict were conducted for the book *Con un pueblo vivo en tierra negada* (Gómez Cruz and Kovic 1994).

3. As previously noted, the concept of human dignity has deep roots in Catholic tradition: all humans have the right to a dignified life as children of God. The similarity between Tzotzil and Catholic notions of rights may reflect the impact of evangelization in indigenous communities.

4. In her ethnography of Amatenango del Valle (a Tzeltal community in Highland Chiapas), anthropologist June Nash (1970) describes the importance of respect in morality in Amatenango del Valle. In family, children are expected to respect their parents throughout their lives. A highly regarded elder in the community expresses a reciprocal notion of respect and responsibility in community: "I pay respect to my elders. I greet my brothers and my children [extension of kinship terms]. To all I give respect. Thus I fare well. I have not been killed, nor have I been sick" (Nash 1970:282).

5. June Nash (1970) describes the ways speech is linked to action in Amatenango del Valle. Those with a "good heart" were described as knowing how to "speak well," while those with "two hearts" say

one thing and do another—they are two-faced. Jane Fishburne Collier (1973) describes the importance of speech in the highland community of Zinacantán. Men who speak well, that is, those who are able to resolve conflicts between community members or recite prayers for rituals, have more prestige.

6. It is important to point out that the identities peasant and Indian are not always synonymous. Some mestizos are peasants. However, many urban Mexicans correlate peasants and rural life with Indians. Anyone from the countryside may be labeled *indio* or even *indito,* "little Indian."

7. The story is similar to the incident described in Chapter 4 in which the only Catholic family in the Chamulan hamlet Las Ollas is victim of violence—a mother and her eight-year-old son are assassinated. Similarly, Gary Gossen (2002:997–1015) presents Xalik López Castellanos's narrative about the burning of the home of one of the first Protestant converts in Chamula in 1967. While I cannot verify Agustín's story, similar events have been documented. I am interested in the fact that Agustín felt the need to tell me the story some thirty years after it took place.

8. From the Catholics' point of view, Chamulan Traditionalists do not have religion. At times Traditionalists describe themselves as being "without religion" as a way of distancing themselves from diocesan Catholics and Protestants. However, from an anthropological perspective, Traditionalists have complex religious beliefs. Religion has tremendous significance in the daily political and social life in Chamula. The view of the expelled is exclusive—only Christians (be they diocesan Catholic or Protestants)—are considered to have religion. The experience of expulsion has made the Catholics of Guadalupe hostile toward the religious beliefs of Traditionalists.

CHAPTER 7

1. See Taylor 1979 for a discussion of indigenous use of alcohol during the colonial period in central Mexico and Oaxaca.

2. Local obligations and traditions in indigenous communities are often tied to the exchange of liquor. For example, June Nash (1973) shows how the distribution and formalized drinking of liquor was important to courtship proceedings in the Tzeltal municipality of Amatenango del Valle; liquor was given as a betrothal gift. Similarly, Carter Wilson (1973) notes that in Chamula a litigant may present liquor to the town president after a satisfactory agreement in a legal dispute. Fines for misconduct are also paid in alcohol. Moreover, during funerals, the musicians, families of the deceased, and guests drink liquor as an expression of mutual obligation, status, and rank.

3. Juan Pérez Jolote, a Chamulan leader, recounts that his father died from excess consumption of alcohol. In the end of his biography, Juan Pérez Jolote recalls that many arrived at his house to drink, he cannot stop drinking, and he is afraid of dying from alcohol (Pozas 1952).

4. On alcohol and indigenous Protestants in Chiapas see Eber 1995, Robledo Hernández 2003, Rostas 2003, and

Sullivan 1998. Elizabeth Brusco (1995) describes the role of alcohol in changing gender roles among Colombian evangelicals. On the role of alcohol in Protestant conversion in Brazil see Burdick (1993) and Chesnut (1997).

5. Interview with the political leader of the expelled, Domingo López Angel, June 14, 1995. See Gossen (1999) and Tickell (1991).

6. *La Jornada*, April 24, 1996.

7. Since the 1950s, scholars have debated the religious cargo system and the distribution of wealth in peasant communities. In a classic article, Eric Wolf (1957) wrote of the civil religious hierarchy as a mechanism for leveling wealth differences, since surplus was redistributed through the sponsorship of the festivals. Several anthropologists continue to emphasize the ways the cargo system maintains community cohesion (see for example Earle 1990, Fabregas Puig 1991, and Rosenbaum 1993). Duncan Earle (1990) argues that the system is critical to ethnic solidarity and slowing class divisions. Through the festivals,

> [i]nequalities in productive potential are translated into status inequalities, ones that are blessed by the saint in exchange for proper "care and feeding." This inhibits the process of external appropriation of resources, as people are motivated to produce, distribute, and consume them locally, and also slows class divisions within the community through partial leveling and the periodic ritual reiteration of religiously based ethnic solidarity, symbolized in the public honoring of the saints. (1990:118)

However, other anthropologists argue that although the cargo system does redistribute surplus, it does not necessarily level wealth or class differences. In his study of the religious cargo system in Zinacantán, Frank Cancian (1965) notes that rather than preventing social and economic difference, the system validates accumulation of capital by the wealthy who invest in public ritual, thereby displaying a commitment toward the community and justifying their position. While promoting internal social integration, the hierarchy may also serve the political interests of the state against the local community. As indigenous people go into debt to pay for cargo service, they are increasingly dependent on wage labor, assuring a cheap labor supply for commercial agriculture (Wasserstrom 1983).

8. In one case documented by the Fray Bartolomé de Las Casas Center for Human Rights (1993:32), Chamulan authorities threatened to expel a Word of God Catholic if he failed to serve a religious cargo. Although the man completed his obligation, he was later expelled because he did not give up his religion.

9. Christine Eber (1995) writes of the conflicts that took place over monetary cooperaciones for festivals in Chenalhó. Many Protestants did not want to give any cooperación for the festivals, while Catholic catechists saw traditional festivals as an important part of community life.

10. A similar complaint was repeated by Chamulan exiles who occupied the

· Office of Indigenous Affairs in a 1993 protest in an attempt to force government action to prevent expulsion. The protest leaders informed me during an interview in September 1994 that both Protestants and Word of God Catholics were in agreement with giving cooperaciones for the fiestas but that once the Chamulan caciques learned of the contributor's religion, they refused to accept the money.

11. Melissa Forbis (2003) notes that women in Zapatista base communities of autonomous townships use the term *cargo* to describe a number of positions that serve the community. For example, health promoters and local and regional authorities describe their work as cargos.

12. Lynn Stephen (1991) describes a similar transition from community-wide festivals for saints to smaller festivals for life-cycle events in the Zapotec region of Oaxaca.

13. Although the families involved in the case are Protestant, Catholics and Protestants worked together to resolve the conflict. This particular conflict involved a man who had left his wife, but the situation is not unique to Protestants. I describe also how Antonio, a Catholic, left his wife.

14. When I taught a literacy class in the community, my students included eight to ten adolescent female students, one adult male, and one boy. The adolescent girls had never learned to read or write because they had attended school for a few years, if at all. Nonetheless, the girls' parents encouraged them to leave domestic tasks for four hours a week to attend the literacy class. The value of education for girls is even more apparent in the urban setting (see Nash and Sullivan 1992).

15. Christine Eber documents domestic violence in the municipality of Chenalhó and describes its close relationship to alcohol (1995, especially Chapter 6). June Nash notes that in the municipality of Amatenango del Valle, beating one's wife is tolerated, especially if it is done in drunkenness (1970:281). However, women beaten by men who were not their husbands were allowed to beat those men in court.

16. The Women's Group of San Cristóbal de Las Casas, the Organization of Indigenous Doctors (OMIECH), the Artisan Union J'pas Joloviletik, and the Women's Commission of the Coordinadora de Organismos No Gubernamentales por la Paz (CONPAZ) organized the event.

CHAPTER 8

1. Following Denoeux, the term "network" refers to "informally organized groups of individuals linked to one another by noncontractual and highly personal bonds and loyalties" (1993:147).

2. Of particular importance are the studies of British social anthropologists of the Manchester School that examine the ways social networks create ties among people and influence behavior. See for example Barnes 1969, Cohen 1969, and Mitchell 1969.

3. To give just one example, in *Rituals of Marginality: Politics, Process, and Culture Change in Urban Central Mexico, 1969–1974*, Carlos Vélez-Ibañez (1983) demonstrates how networks based on kinship, fictive kin, residence, and friendship were central to gathering support for

the political struggle for land and services in a poor Mexico City neighborhood.

4. These authors suggest the term "webs" rather than networks to draw attention to the complexity and precariousness of the networks, as each actor in the network has ties with institutions, political parties, nongovernmental organizations, churches, and other groups (Alvarez, Dagnino, and Escobar 1998: 15–16).

5. On Christian base communities and political mobilization in Latin America see Azevedo 1987, Cleary 1985, Hewitt 1991, and Lancaster 1989.

6. It is possible that some residents of Buena Vista are directly or indirectly involved with the EZLN. For obvious reasons, I did not ask about their involvement in the armed uprising.

7. For more information on Las Abejas and the massacre at Acteal see Eber 2001b, Kovic 2003b, and Moksnes 2003. For a woman-centered perspective see Hernández Castillo 1998.

8. Before the birth of Pueblo Creyente, concerns, goals, and projects of the indigenous and poor were formally taken into account in diocesan-wide planning through local parish meetings held in advance of the diocesan Assemblies. Yet face-to-face dialogue between pastoral workers and indigenous Catholics did not take place in the assemblies until 1991.

9. It is difficult to describe Pueblo Creyente as having formal members, since by default all diocesan Catholics form part of this community of believers. However, some are clearly more active in Pueblo Creyente meetings and events than others.

10. Like Father Joel Padrón, Santiago was a political prisoner detained as a way to attack the work of the Diocese of San Cristóbal. He was charged with sedition, rioting, rebellion, conspiracy, and terrorism. However, the only witness who apparently had evidence that Santiago was guilty as charged never appeared in court (Fray Bartolomé de Las Casas Center for Human Rights 1995a).

11. Perhaps the Zapatista Army of National Liberation has more members than Pueblo Creyente. Since the EZLN is a clandestine group, it is not possible to know how many Zapatista supporters are in Chiapas.

12. According to folklore and Catholic doctrine, the Virgin of Guadalupe appeared to Juan Diego, an Indian in central Mexico, on December 9, 1531, just ten years after the Aztec capital of Tenochtitlán fell to Hernan Cortés (Taylor 1987). When Juan Diego appealed to the bishop to construct a church on the site of the Virgin's appearance, religious authorities questioned whether the event had taken place. Juan Diego returned to the spot where he had first seen the Virgin. She appeared again, and her image was miraculously imprinted on his cloak. The appearance convinced the bishop, and a church was constructed to commemorate the miracle. The Virgin Mary was also an important symbol in indigenous revitalization movements in Chiapas in the eighteenth and nineteenth centuries (see Bricker 1981 and Wasserstrom 1983). William B. Taylor (1987) notes the paradoxical use of the symbol of the Virgin of Guadalupe in Mexico's history. She was a sign that the Indians were a chosen people, challenged the political

and social order of the privileged, and was associated with the war of independence as well as the Revolution of 1910. At the same time, the Virgin as mediator between God and humans served as a "model of acceptance and legitimation of colonial authority" (Taylor 1987: 20). An individual was expected to approach the Virgin humbly, to give her time to right injustices, and not to take matters into one's own hands. In the pilgrimages of Pueblo Creyente in Chiapas, the image of the Virgin Mary is used as a symbol of the importance of indigenous tradition and is seen as a protector of the indigenous people. However, the symbolism and social history of the Virgin of Guadalupe among the indigenous peoples of Chiapas merits further research.

13. Many Catholics were among the 25,000 indigenous people who attended the march on October 12, 1994, that was organized to demand respect for human rights 502 years after Columbus's landing in the Americas. This political event was not organized by Pueblo Creyente, although many of its members participated.

14. On June 22, 1995, the priests Rodolfo Izal Elorz (of Spanish nationality), Loren Riebe (of U.S. nationality), and Jorge Alberto Barón Guitein (of Argentine nationality) were detained by the Federal Judicial Police in Chiapas. The next day they were expelled from the country. They were accused of being involved in activities not authorized under their visas. The detentions and expulsions were taken to be a political attack on the work of the Diocese of San Cristóbal (Fray Bartolomé de Las Casas Center for Human Rights 1995b).

CHAPTER 9

1. Some of the analysis of this event is included in Eber and Kovic 2003.

2. The community of faith as a Catholic concept is also limiting. It excludes the many indigenous Protestants in Chiapas. Recently, the Catholic Church and its followers have made attempts to incorporate Protestants in mobilizations for indigenous rights, most visibly in the case of Pueblo Creyente.

3. The figure of six deaths comes from an official investigation (Averiguación Previa A 17A/362/995). An article in *La Jornada* of June 30, 1996, reports that people from the hamlet spoke of more than twenty deaths (see Aramoni Calderón and Morquecho Escamilla 1998).

4. Bishop Arizmendi's visit to Chamula is described in Elio Henríquez, 2003, "Pide Arizmendi a Chamula poner fin a pugnas religiosas," *La Jornada*, May 29.

Chronology
Key Events in Chiapas, Chamula, and the Diocese of San Cristóbal de Las Casas

1960 Diocese: Samuel Ruiz García is consecrated bishop of the Diocese of San Cristóbal

1962–1965 Diocese: Bishop Ruiz attends sessions of the Second Vatican Council in Rome

1966 Chamula: Catholic mission is established under leadership of Father Leopoldo Hernández

1968 Diocese: Bishop Ruiz attends the Conference of Latin American Bishops in Medellin, Colombia

1969 Diocese: Catechism program based on the Bible book of Exodus begins in Ocosingo

Chamula: Father Hernández is forced to abandon Chamula mission under death threats

1974 Diocese: Indigenous Congress held in San Cristóbal de Las Casas

Chamula: Municipal elections, first massive expulsion

1975 Diocese: First diocesan assembly, official commitment to work "with and for the poor"

San Cristóbal de Las Casas: First colonia of expelled Chamulas established on the outskirts of the city

1980 Chiapas: Massacre at Golochán, Sitalá, with at least twelve killed

1982 Chiapas: Guatemalan refugees begin to cross border into Chiapas

Diocese: Committee for the Defense of the Threatened, Persecuted, and Expelled of Chamula formed

1983 San Cristóbal de Las Casas: Catholics begin to settle in the colonia Guadalupe

1984 Chiapas: Council of Indigenous Representatives of Highland Chiapas (CRIACH) formed

1989 Diocese: Fray Bartolomé de Las Casas Center for Human Rights founded

1991 Diocese: Pueblo Creyente established; Father Joel Padrón arrested

1992 San Cristóbal de Las Casas: Indigenous March of 500 Years of Resistance

1993 Diocese: On the occasion of Pope John Paul II's visit to Mexico, Bishop Ruiz releases the pastoral letter "In This Hour of Grace"

1994 Chiapas: Uprising of the Zapatista Army of National Liberation (EZLN); Bishop Ruiz named mediator between EZLN and Mexican government

1995 Chiapas: Thousands of federal soldiers enter Lacandon jungle

1997 Chiapas: Massacre at Acteal, Chenalhó, with forty-five indigenous men, women, and children killed

1999 Diocese: Samuel Ruiz García submits resignation to Vatican in accordance with canonical law

2000 Diocese: Ruiz's resignation accepted; Felipe Arizmendi named bishop of the Diocese of San Cristóbal

Glossary

(SP) = Spanish
(TZ) = Tzotzil

agente: a local official who responds to the municipal president and has the power to mediate in community conflicts (SP)

cacique: entrenched local leader within indigenous community (SP)

campesino: a peasant, a person who cultivates land for self-subsistence (SP)

cargo: literally, a burden or duty; work carried out for the benefit of one's community. The term is most commonly used to refer to the work done by the sponsor (cargo holder) of a traditional festival. (SP)

catechist: Catholic lay leader. In the Diocese of San Cristóbal de Las Casas, catechists prepare people for the sacraments and serve as religious leaders in their communities.

Catholic Diocese of San Cristóbal de Las Casas: comprised of forty-two municipalities in eastern Chiapas, under the leadership of a single bishop. From 1960 to 2000, Samuel Ruiz García was bishop of the diocese; Felipe Arizmendi succeeded him as bishop.

caxlan: a non-indigenous person, either Mexican or foreign (TZ)

Coleto: Ladino who resides in San Cristóbal. The term derives from the pigtail worn by Spanish colonists. (SP)

colonia: literally, a colony; neighborhood or unregulated urban settlement, commonly located on the outskirts of a city (SP)

cooperación: a contribution of money, food, work, or another item for a community activity, such as a festival (SP)

costumbre: custom such as the religious and social customs that define traditional Mayan life (SP)

CRIACH: Consejo de Representantes Indígenas de los Altos de Chiapas (Council of Indigenous Representatives of Highland Chiapas), an organization composed primarily of Chamulan exiles residing in San Cristóbal. Most members are Protestant, though Catholics also belong. (SP)

curandero: a traditional healer who cures spiritual and physical ailments (SP)

diocesan Catholics: Catholics who participate in the pastoral project of the Diocese of San Cristóbal de Las Casas

EZLN: Ejército Zapatista de Liberación Nacional (Zapatista Army of National Liberation), insurgent group that publicly emerged in Chiapas on January 1, 1994, with demands for justice, liberty, and democracy (SP)

finca: large farm commonly used for commercial growth of coffee (SP)

Fray Bartolomé de Las Casas Center for Human Rights: nongovernmental organization founded by the Diocese of San Cristóbal in 1989 to promote and defend human rights

hamlet (*paraje* SP): a community within a rural municipality or township

indigenismo: a policy initiated in Mexico after the Revolution of 1910 to integrate indigenous peoples into one unified nation-state through assimilation (SP)

Jovel or Jobel (TZ): *See* San Cristóbal de las Casas

Lacandon jungle: rainforest of eastern Chiapas. Indigenous people from throughout the state established agricultural colonies in the region beginning in the 1930s.

Ladino (SP): See *mestizo*

matz (TZ): See *pozol*

mestizo: people of mixed Spanish and indigenous blood. Tzotzil Mayas use this term interchangeably with *Ladino* to describe non-indigenous Mexicans. (SP)

milpa: cornfield; field cultivated with maize, squash, and beans (SP)

municipio: township or municipality, a legal political unit in Mexico (SP)

Palabra de Dios (SP): *See* Word of God

PAN: Partido Acción Nacional (National Action Party), right-of-center political party in Mexico (SP)

paraje (SP): *See* hamlet

pox: a homemade rum produced from sugar cane juice (TZ)

pozol (SP) (*matz* TZ): a drink of maize mixed with water

PRD: Partido de la Revolución Democrática (Party of the Democratic Revolution), left-of-center political party in Mexico (SP)

PRI: Partido Revolucionario Institucional (Institutional Revolutionary Party), centrist party that governed Mexico from 1929 to 2000 (SP)

Pueblo Creyente: People of Faith, grassroots diocesan group of Word of God
Catholics working to build unity and to resist poverty and oppression
(SP)

San Cristóbal de Las Casas (Jovel or Jobel TZ): mestizo-dominated city in highland Chiapas (SP)

San Juan Chamula: commonly referred to as Chamula, a highland Tzotzil municipality and the place of origin for most of the Catholics of Guadalupe

San Pedro Chenalhó: commonly referred to as Chenalhó, a highland Tzotzil
municipality located north of San Juan Chamula

Sc'op Dios (TZ): See Word of God

tierra caliente: literally, hot lands; lowlands of the Grijalva Valley of central Chiapas. Peasants of highland communities rent lands or practice sharecropping in this region. (SP)

Traditionalists (Tradicionalistas SP): those who worship Mayan deities as well
as Catholic saints and combine Mayan rites with Catholic sacraments

Tuxtla Gutiérrez: state capital of Chiapas

Tzotzil: a Mayan language and the ethnic group that speaks this language

Word of God (Palabra de Dios SP, Sc'op Dios TZ): indigenous participants in
pastoral project of the Diocese of San Cristóbal de Las Casas. The term
refers not only to reading the Bible but also to participation in different
activities of diocesan pastoral work. Mayan Catholics use this term to
refer to their religion.

References

Adams, Walter Randolph. 1991. "Social Structure in Pilgrimage and Prayer: Tzeltales as Lords and Servants." In *Pilgrimage in Latin America*, ed. N. Ross Crumrine and E. Alan Morinis, 109–122. New York: Greenwood Press.

Alvarez, Sonia E., Evelina Dagnino, and Arturo Escobar, eds. 1998. *Cultures of Politics, Politics of Cultures: Revisioning Latin American Social Movements*. Boulder, Colo.: Westview Press.

Álvarez Icaza, José. 1998. "Don Samuel Ruiz García: Un acercamiento." In *Chiapas: El factor religioso*, 117–128. Mexico City: Publicaciones para el Estudio Científico de las Religiones.

American Anthropological Association. 1947. "Statement on Human Rights." *American Anthropologist* 49(4): 539–543.

Aramoni Calderón, Dolores, and Gaspar Morquecho Escamilla. 1998. "El Recurso de las Armas en Manos de los Expulsados de San Juan Chamula." In *Chiapas: El factor religioso*, 235–291. Mexico City: Publicaciones para el Estudio Científico de las Religiones.

Asad, Talal. 1993. *Genealogies of Religion: Discipline and Reasons of Power in Christianity and Islam*. Baltimore: Johns Hopkins University Press.

Ascencio Franco, Gabriel, and Xóchitl Leyva Solano. 1992. "Los municipios de la Selva Chiapaneca. Colonización y dinámica agropecuaria." In *Anuario 1991*. Tuxtla Gutiérrez, Mexico: Instituto Chiapaneco de Cultura.

Azevedo, Marcello de Carvalho. 1987. *Base Ecclesial Communities in Brazil: The Challenge of a New Way of Being Church*. Washington, D.C.: Georgetown University Press.

Balibar, Etienne. 1994. *Masses, Classes, Ideas: Studies on Politics and Philosophy before and after Marx*, trans. James Swenson. New York: Routledge.

Barnes, J. A. 1969. "Networks and Political Process." In *Social Networks in Urban Situations: Analyses of Personal Relationships in Central African*

Towns, ed. J. Clyde Mitchell, 51–76. Manchester, England: Manchester University Press.

Bastian, Jean Pierre. 1983. "Disidencia religiosa en el campo Mexicano." In *Protestantismo y sociedad en México*. Mexico City: Casa Unida de Publicaciones.

Beller Taboada, Walter. 1994. *Las costumbres jurídicas de los indígenas en México*. Mexico City: Comisión Nacional de Derechos Humanos.

Benjamin, Thomas. 1989. *A Rich Land, A Poor People: Politics and Society in Modern Chiapas*. Albuquerque: University of New Mexico Press.

Berryman, Phillip. 1987. *Liberation Theology*. New York: Pantheon Books.

———. 1994. *Stubborn Hope: Religion, Politics, and Revolution in Central America*. Maryknoll, N.Y.: Orbis Books.

Binford, Leigh. 1996. *The El Mozote Massacre: Anthropology and Human Rights*. Tucson: University of Arizona Press.

Boff, Leonardo, and Clodovis Boff. 1986. *Introducing Liberation Theology*, trans. Paul Burns. Maryknoll, N.Y.: Orbis Books.

Bourque, Susan C., and Kay Barbara Warren. 1981. *Women of the Andes: Patriarchy and Social Change in Two Peruvian Towns*. Ann Arbor: University of Michigan Press.

Bouvard, Marguerite Guzmán. 1994. *Revolutionizing Motherhood: The Mothers of the Plaza de Mayo*. Wilmington, Del.: Scholarly Resources.

Bricker, Victoria Reifler. 1981. *The Indian Christ, the Indian King: The Historical Substrate of Maya Myth and Ritual*. Austin: University of Texas Press.

Brusco, Elizabeth E. 1993. "The Reformation of Machismo: Asceticism and Masculinity among Colombian Evangelicals." In *Rethinking Protestantism in Latin America*, ed. Virginia Garrard-Burnett and David Stoll, 143–158. Philadelphia: Temple University Press.

Brysk, Allison. 2000. *From Tribal Village to Global Village: Indian Rights and International Relations in Latin America*. Stanford, Calif.: Stanford University Press.

Burdick, John. 1993. *Looking for God in Brazil: The Progressive Catholic Church in Urban Brazil's Religious Arena*. Berkeley: University of California Press.

Burguete, Araceli. 1987. *Chiapas: Cronología de un etnocidio reciente*. Mexico City: Mexican Academy of Human Rights.

Calvo Sánchez, Angelino. 1990. "Las Colonias Nuevas de Migrantes y Expulsados en San Cristóbal de Las Casas." *Anuario Centro de Estudios Indígenas* 3: 55–64. San Cristóbal de Las Casas, Mexico.

Cancian, Frank. 1965. *Economics and Prestige in a Maya Community: The Religious Cargo System in Zincantán.* Stanford: Stanford University Press.

———. 1992. *The Decline of Community in Zinacantán: Economy, Public Life and Social Stratification, 1960–1987.* Stanford: Stanford University Press.

Cassanova, José. 1997. "Globalizing Catholicism and the Return to a 'Universal' Church." In *Transnational Religion and Fading States,* ed. Susanne Hoeber Rudolph and James Piscatori, 121–143. Boulder: Westview Press.

Castro Apreza, Yolanda. 2003. "J'pas Joloviletik-Jolom Mayetik-Kinal Antzetik: An Organizational Experience of Indigenous and Mestiza Women." In *Women of Chiapas: Making History in Times of Struggle and Hope,* ed. Christine Eber and Christine Kovic, 207–218. New York: Routledge.

Certeau, Michel de. 1984. *The Practice of Everyday Life,* trans. Steven Rendall. Berkeley: University of California Press.

Chenaut, Victoria, and María Teresa Sierra, eds. 1995. *Pueblos indígenas ante el derecho.* Mexico City: Centro de Investigaciones y Estudios Superiores en Antropología Social.

Chesnut, R. Andrew. 1997. *Born Again in Brazil: The Pentecostal Boom and the Pathogens of Poverty.* New Brunswick, N.J.: Rutgers University Press.

Chiapas State Congress (Congreso del Estado de Chiapas). 1992. *Memoria de la audiencia pública sobre las expulsiones indígenas y el respeto a las culturas, costumbres y tradiciones de esos pueblos.* Mexico City: Chiapas State Congress.

Chojnack, Ruth. 2004. "Indigenous Apostles: Maya Catholic Catechists Working the Word in Highland Chiapas." Ph.D. diss., University of Chicago.

Cleary, Edward L. 1985. *Crisis and Change: The Church in Latin America Today.* Maryknoll, N.Y.: Orbis Books.

———. 1990. *Born of the Poor: The Latin American Church since Medellín.* Notre Dame, Ill.: University of Notre Dame Press.

Cleary, Edward L., and Timothy J. Steigenga, eds. 2004. *Resurgent Voices in Latin America: Indigenous Peoples, Political Mobilization, and Religious Change.* New Brunswick, N.J.: Rutgers University Press.

Coello Castro, Reyna Matilde. 1991. "Proceso Catequístico en la Zona Tzeltal y Desarrollo Social." Undergraduate thesis, Department of Sociology and Social Work, Universidad Autónoma de Tlaxcala, Mexico.

Cohen, Abner. 1969. *Custom and Politics in Urban Africa: A Study of Hausa Migrants in a Yoruba Town.* Berkeley: University of California Press.

Cohen, Ronald. 1987. "Human Rights and Cultural Relativism: The Need for a New Approach." *American Anthropologist* 89(4): 939–943.

Collier, George. 1975. *Fields of the Tzotzil: The Ecological Bases of Tradition in Highland Chiapas.* Austin: University of Texas Press.

Collier, George, and Jane Fishburne Collier. 2000. "Chiapas and the Church." Letter in *New York Review of Books* 47(6), April 13.

Collier, George, with Elizabeth Lowery Quaratiello. 1994. *Basta! Land and the Zapatista Rebellion in Chiapas.* Oakland, Calif.: Food First Book, Institute for Food and Development Policy.

Collier, Jane Fishburne. 1973. *Law and Social Change in Zinacantán.* Stanford, Calif.: Stanford University Press.

Comaroff, Jean, and John Comaroff. 1991. *Of Revelation and Revolution: Christianity, Colonialism, and Consciousness in South Africa.* Chicago: University of Chicago Press.

Crumrine, N. Ross, and E. Alan Morinis, eds. 1991. *Pilgrimage in Latin America.* New York: Greenwood Press.

Cruz Burguete, Jorge Luis, and Gabriela Robledo. 1998. "Vivir la diversidad en Betania y Nuevo Zinacantán: Las nuevas identidades comunitarias entre desplazados religiosos." *Gaceta Mensual, Ecosur* 4: 10–13.

Cruz Rueda, Elisa. 1994. "El derecho de los pueblos indios como un derecho alternativo." Undergraduate thesis, Universidad Nacional Autónoma de México, Mexico City.

Denoeux, Guilain. 1993. "Religious Networks and Urban Unrest: Lessons from Iranian and Egyptian Experiences." In *The Violence Within: Culture and Political Opposition in Divided Nations,* ed. Kay B. Warren. Boulder, Colo.: Westview Press.

De Vos, Jan. 1979. "Tierra y libertad: Panorama de cuatro rebeliones indígenas de Chiapas." *El Caminante* 22.

———. 2002. *Un tierra para sembrar sueños: Historia reciente de la Selva Lacandona, 1950–2000.* Mexico City: Centro de Investigaciones y Estudios Superiores en Antropología Social (hereinafter CIESAS).

Dorr, Donal. 1983. *Option for the Poor: A Hundred Years of Vatican Social Teaching.* Maryknoll, N.Y.: Orbis Books.

Duarte, Carlota, coord. 1998. *Camaristas: Fotógrafos mayas de Chiapas.* Mexico City: Centro de la Imagen, CIESAS, and Casa de las Imágenes.

Earle, Duncan. 1990. "Appropriating the Enemy: Highland Maya Religious Organization and Community Survival." In *Class, Politics, and Popular Religion in Mexico and Central America,* ed. Lynn Stephen and James Dow,

115–142. Washington D.C.: Society for Latin American Anthropology and American Anthropological Association.

Eber, Christine. 1995. *Women and Alcohol in a Highland Maya Town: Water of Hope, Water of Sorrow.* Austin: University of Texas Press.

———. 2001a. "'Take my water': Liberation through Prohibition in San Pedro Chenalhó, Chiapas." Special issue on "Alcohol and Drug Studies at the Millennium." *Social Science and Medicine* 53(2): 251–262.

———. 2001b. "Buscando una nueva vida: Liberation through Autonomy in San Pedro Chenalhó." *Latin American Perspectives* 28(2): 45–72.

Eber, Christine, and Brenda Rosenbaum. 1993. "'That we may serve beneath your hands and feet': Women Weavers in Highland Chiapas." In *Crafts in the World Market: The Impact of Global Exchange on Middle American Artisans,* ed. June C. Nash, 155–179. Albany: State University of New York Press.

Eber, Christine, and Christine Kovic, eds. 2003. *Women of Chiapas: Making History in Times of Struggle and Hope.* New York: Routledge Press.

Eckstein, Susan. 1989. *Power and Popular Protest: Latin American Social Movements.* Berkeley: University of California Press.

Edelman, Marc. 2000. "The Persistence of the Peasantry." NACLA 33(5): 14–20.

El grito de la luna. 1994. Document from The Rights of Women in Our Customs and Traditions workshop in San Cristóbal de Las Casas, Mexico, May. *Ojarasca* 35/36: 27–31.

Engler, Mark. 2000. "Toward the 'Rights of the Poor': Human Rights in Liberation Theology." *Journal of Religious Ethics* 28(3): 339–365.

Estrada Martínez, Rosa Isabel. 1995. *El problema de las expulsiones en las comunidades indígenas de los Altos de Chiapas y los derechos humanos, segundo informe.* Mexico City: National Commission of Human Rights.

Estrada Martínez, Rosa Isabel, and Graciela Vega Carrillo. 1992. *Informe sobre el problema de las expulsiones en las comunidades indígenas de los altos de Chiapas y los derechos humanos.* Mexico City: National Commission of Human Rights.

Fabregas Puig, Andrés. 1991. "Entre la religión y la costumbre." *México Indígena* 23: 8–12.

Falla, Ricardo. 2001. *Quiché Rebelde: Religious Conversion, Politics, and Ethnic Identity in Guatemala,* trans. Phillip Berryman. Austin: University of Texas Press.

Farmer, Paul. 2003. *Pathologies of Power: Health, Human Rights, and the New War on the Poor.* Berkeley: University of California Press.

Favre, Henri. 1984. *Cambio y continuidad entre los mayas de México.* Mexico City: Instituto Nacional Indigenista.

Fazio, Carlos. 1994. *Samuel Ruiz, El Caminante.* Mexico City: Espasa Calpe Mexicana.

Felice, William. 1996. *Taking Suffering Seriously: The Importance of Collective Human Rights.* Albany: State University of New York Press.

First Encounter of Latin American Pastoral Workers on Human Rights. 1994. "La espiritualidad cristiana y los derechos humanos: Sus fundamentos doctrinales." *Epéctasis, Revista semestral de espirtualidad* 8: 20–23.

Floyd, J. Charlene. 1997. "The Government Shall Be Upon Their Shoulders: The Catholic Church and Democratization in Chiapas, Mexico." Ph.D. diss., City University of New York.

Forbis, Melissa M. 2003. "Hacia la Autonomía: Zapatista Women Developing a New World." In *Women of Chiapas: Making History in Times of Struggle and Hope,* ed. Christine Eber and Christine Kovic, 231–252. New York: Routledge Press.

Fray Bartolomé de Las Casas Center for Human Rights (Centro de Derechos Humanos Fray Bartolomé de Las Casas). 1994. *En la Ausencia de Justicia: Informe Semestral, July–December 1993.* San Cristóbal de Las Casas, Mexico: Fray Bartolomé de Las Casas Center for Human Rights.

———. 1995a. *Preliminary Report on Human Rights Violations in Chiapas from February 9 to April 9, 1995.* San Cristóbal de Las Casas, Mexico: Fray Bartolomé de Las Casas Center for Human Rights.

———. 1995b. *Detención y expulsión de tres sacerdotes de la Diócesis de San Cristóbal de Las Casas, Chiapas.* San Cristóbal de Las Casas, Mexico: Fray Bartolomé de Las Casas Center for Human Rights.

———. 2001. *Donde muere el agua: Expulsiones y derechos humanos en San Juan Chamula.* San Cristóbal de Las Casas, Mexico: Fray Bartolomé de Las Casas Center for Human Rights.

Freire, Paulo. 1970. *Pedagogy of the Oppressed.* Trans. Mayra Bergman Ramos. New York: Continuum International.

García de León, Antonio. 1985. *Resistencia y utopía: Memorial de agravios y crónica de revueltas y profecías acaecidas en la provincia de Chiapas durante los últimos 500 años de su historia.* Two volumes. Mexico City: Ediciones Era.

Geertz, Clifford. 1984. "Anti Anti-Relativism." *Cultural Anthropology* 86(2): 263–278.

Gil Tébar, Pilar. 2003. "Irene: A Catholic Woman in Oxchuc." In *Women of Chiapas: Making History in Times of Struggle and Hope*, ed. Christine Eber and Christine Kovic, 149–154. New York: Routledge Press.

Giménez, Gilberto. 1988. *Sectas religiosas en el sureste: Aspectos sociográficos y estadísticos*. Mexico City: SEP/CIESAS Sureste.

Gómez Cruz, Patricia, and Christine Kovic. 1994. *Con un pueblo vivo en tierra negada: Un ensayo sobre los derechos humanos y el conflicto agrario en Chiapas, 1989–1993*. San Cristóbal de Las Casas, Mexico: Fray Bartolomé de Las Casas Center for Human Rights.

Gómez Monte, Maruch, and Diane L. Rus. 1990. *Bordando Milpas: Testimonio de una tejedora chamula de los Altos de Chiapas*. Bilingual edition (Tzotzil-Spanish). San Cristóbal de Las Casas, Mexico: Taller Tzotzil, Instituto de Asesoría Antropológica para la Región Maya, A.C. (hereinafter INAREMAC).

Gossen, Gary H. 1974. *Chamulas in the World of the Sun: Time and Space in Maya Oral Tradition*. Cambridge, Mass.: Harvard University Press.

———. 1999. *Telling Maya Tales: Tzotzil Identities in Modern Mexico*. New York: Routlege.

———. 2002. *Four Creations: An Epic Story of the Chiapas Mayas*. Norman: University of Oklahoma Press.

Green, Linda. 1999. *Fear as a Way of Life: Mayan Widows in Rural Guatemala*. New York: Columbia University Press.

Gutiérrez, Gustavo. 1973. *A Theology of Liberation*, trans. Caridad Inda and John Eagleson. Maryknoll, N.Y.: Orbis Books.

———. 1983. *The Power of the Poor in History*. Trans. Robert R. Barr. Maryknoll, N.Y.: Orbis Books.

Gutiérrez Gutiérrez, José Antonio. 1996. *Infundios contra San Cristóbal de Las Casas*. Mexico City: Fundación Chiapaneca Colosio.

Hall, David D. 1997. *Lived Religion in America: Toward a History of Practice*. Princeton, N.J.: Princeton University Press.

Harvey, Neil. 1994. *Rebellion in Chiapas: Rural Reforms, Campesino Radicalism, and the Limits to Salinismo*. Transformation of Rural Mexico No. 5, Ejido Reform Research Project. San Diego: Center for U.S.-Mexican Studies.

———. 1998. *The Chiapas Rebellion: The Struggle for Land and Democracy*. Durham, N.C.: Duke University Press.

Hernández, Leopoldo. 1966–1970. *Circular a los amigos de la Misión Chamula*. Mimeograph. Chamula, Mexico.

Hernández Castillo, Rosalva Aída. 1992. "Entre la victimización y la resistencia étnica: crítica de la bibliografía sobre protestantismo en Chiapas." In *Anuario 1991*, 165–186. Tuxtla Gutiérrez, Mexico: Instituto Chiapaneco de Cultura.

———. 1994. "Dicen su palabra." *Ojarasca* 35–36: 27–31.

———, ed. 2001. *The Other Word: Women and Violence before and after Acteal.* Copenhagen: International Working Group on Indigneous Affairs.

Hernández Castillo, Rosalva Aída, Norma Nava Zamora, José Luis Victoria, and Carlos Flores Arenales. 1993. *La experiencia de refugio: Nuevas relaciones en la frontera sur mexicana.* Mexico City: Academía Mexicana de Derechos Humanos.

Hernández Lampoy, Andres. 1994. "Los pajaritos de Chamula." In *Relatos Tzeltales y Tzotziles,* 33–44. Mexico City: Editorial Diana.

Herskovits, Melville J. 1950. *Man and His Works.* New York: Alfred A. Knopf.

Hewitt, W. E. 1991. *Base Christian Communities and Social Change in Brazil.* Lincoln: University of Nebraska Press.

Hollenbach, David. 1979. *Claims in Conflict: Retrieving and Renewing the Catholic Human Rights Tradition.* New York: Paulist Press.

Indigenous Congress of 1974 (Congreso Indígena de 1974). *Igualdad en la justicia.* Pamphlet from the Indigenous Congress at San Cristóbal de Las Casas, Mexico, October 13–15.

Instituto Nacional de Estadística, Geografía e Informática. 1990. *Chiapas: Perfil Sociodemográfico: XI Censo General de Población y Vivienda.* Aguascalientes, Mexico: Instituto Nacional de Estadística, Geografía e Informática.

Iribarren, Pablo. 1980. "Misión Chamula: Experiencia de trabajo pastoral de los años 1966–1977 en Chamula." Mimeograph. San Cristóbal de Las Casas, Mexico: Diocese of San Cristóbal de Las Casas.

———. 1985. "Experiencia: Proceso de la Diócesis de San Cristóbal de Las Casas, Mexico." Mimeograph. San Cristóbal de Las Casas, Mexico: Diocese of San Cristóbal de Las Casas.

———. 1991. *Los Domínicos en la pastoral indígena.* Mexico City: Imprentei.

Kearney, Michael. 1995. "The Local and the Global: The Anthropology of Globalization and Transnationalism." *Annual Review of Anthropology* 24: 547–565.

Kleinman, Arthur, and Joan Kleinman. 1997. "The Appeal of Experience, the Dismay of Images: Cultural Appropriations of Suffering in Our Times." In *Social Suffering,* ed. Arthur Kleinman, Veena Das, and Margaret Lock, 1–23. Berkeley: University of California Press.

Kovic, Christine. 2003a. "Demanding Their Dignity as Daughters of God: Catholic Women and Human Rights." In *Women of Chiapas: Making History in Times of Struggle and Hope*, ed. Christine Eber and Christine Kovic, 131–146. New York: Routledge Press.

———. 2003b. "The Struggle for Liberation and Reconciliation in Chiapas, Mexico: Las Abejas and the Path of Non-Violent Resistance." *Latin American Perspectives* 30(3): 58–79.

———. 2004. "Mayan Catholics in Chiapas, Mexico: Practicing Faith on Their Own Terms." In *Resurgent Voices in Latin America: Indigenous Peoples, Political Mobilization, and Religious Change*, ed. Edward L. Cleary and Timothy J. Steigenga, 187–209. New Brunswick, N.J.: Rutgers University Press.

Krauze, Enrique. 1999. "Chiapas: The Indians' Prophet." *New York Review of Books* 4(20), December 16.

———. 2000. Letter in *New York Review of Books* 47(6), April 13.

Lancaster, Roger. 1989. *Thanks to God and the Revolution: Popular Religion and Class Consciousness in the New Nicaragua*. Berkeley: University of California Press.

Lernoux, Penny. 1982. *Cry of the People: The Struggle for Human Rights in Latin America—the Catholic Church in Conflict with U.S. Policy*. New York: Penguin Books.

Levine, Daniel H. 1992. *Popular Voices in Latin American Catholicism*. Princeton, N.J.: Princeton University Press.

Levine, Daniel H., and David Stoll. 1997. "Bridging the Gap between Empowerment and Power in Latin America." In *Transnational Religion and Fading States*, ed. Susanne Hoeber Rudolph and James Piscatori, 63–103. Boulder, Colo.: Westview Press.

Leyva Solano, Xóchitl. 1995. "Militancia político-religiosa e identidad en la Lacandona." *Espiral, Estudios sobre Estado y Sociedad* 1(2): 59–88.

Lomnitz, Larissa Alder de. 1977. *Networks and Marginality: Life in a Mexican Shantytown*, Cinna Lomnitz, trans. New York: Academic Press.

López Díaz, Xunka'. 2000. *Li jmuk Ristinae—Mi hermanita Cristina: Una niña chamula*. San Cristóbal de Las Casas, Mexico: Archivo Fotográfico Indígeno, CIESAS, Consejo Estatal para la Cultura y las Artes de Chiapas.

MacLeod, Murdo J. 1973. *Spanish Central America: A Socioeconomic History, 1520–1720*. Berkeley: University of California Press.

———. 1989. "Dominican Explanations for Revolts and Their Suppression in Colonial Chiapas, 1545–1715." In *Indian-Religious Relations in Colonial Spanish America*, ed. Susan E. Ramírez and Murdo MacLeod, 39–53. Syracuse, N.Y.: Maxwell School of Citizenship and Public Affairs, Syracuse University.

Mainwaring, Scott, and Alexander Wilde, eds. 1989. *The Progressive Church in Latin America.* Notre Dame, Ill.: University Notre Dame Press.

Malkki, Liisa H. 1995. "Refugees and Exile: From 'Refugee Studies' to the National Order of Things." *Annual Review of Anthropology* 24: 495–523.

Martin, David. 1990. *Tongues of Fire: The Explosion of Protestantism in Latin America.* Oxford, England: Blackwell Publishers.

McGovern, Arthur F. 1989. *Liberation Theology and Its Critics: Toward an Assessment.* Maryknoll, N.Y.: Orbis Books.

Meyer, Jean. 2000. *Samuel Ruiz en San Cristóbal.* Mexico City: Tusquets Editores.

Merry, Sally Engle. 1997. "Legal Pluralism and Transnational Culture: The *Ka Ho'okolokolonui Kanaka Maoli* Tribunal in Hawaii, 1993." In *Human Rights, Culture and Context: Anthropological Perspectives,* ed. Richard A. Wilson, 28–48. London: Pluto Press.

Messer, Ellen. 1993. "Anthropology and Human Rights." *Annual Review of Anthropology* 22: 221–49.

Mitchell, J. Clyde. 1969. *Social Networks in Urban Situations: Analyses of Personal Relationships in Central African Towns.* Manchester, England: Manchester University Press.

Moksnes, Heidi. 2003. "Mayan Suffering, Mayan Rights: Faith and Citizenship among Catholic Tzotziles in Highland Chiapas, Mexico." Ph.D. diss., Göteborg University, Sweden.

Morales Bermúdez, Jesús. 1992. "El Congreso Indígena de Chiapas: Un Testimonio." In *Anuario 1991,* 243–370. Tuxtla Gutiérrez, Mexico: Instituto Chiapaneco de Cultura.

Morquecho Escamilla, Gaspar. 1992. *Los indios en un proceso de organización.* Undergraduate thesis, Universidad Autónoma de Chiapas, San Cristóbal de Las Casas, Mexico.

———. 1994. "Expulsiones en los Altos de Chiapas." In *Movimiento Campesino en Chiapas.* San Cristóbal de Las Casas, Mexico: Desarrollo Económico Social de los Mexicanos Indígenas A.C.

Nagengast, Carole. 1994. "Violence, Terror, and the Crisis of the State." *Annual Review of Anthropology* 23: 109–136.

Nash, June C. 1970. *In the Eyes of the Ancestors: Belief and Behavior in a Maya Community.* New Haven, Conn.: Yale University Press.

————. 1973. "The Betrothal: A Study of Ideology and Behavior in a Maya Indian Community." In *Drinking Patterns in Highland Chiapas: A Teamwork Approach to the Study of Semantics through Ethnography*, ed. Henning Siverts. Bergen, Norway: Universitetsforlaget.

————. 1993. "Mayan Household Production and the World Market: The Potters of Amatenango del Valle, Chiapas, Mexico." In *Crafts in the World Market: The Impact of Global Production on Middle American Artisans*, ed. June C. Nash, 127–154. Albany: State University of New York Press.

————. 2001. *Mayan Visions: The Quest for Autonomy in an Age of Globalization*. New York: Routledge.

Nash, June C., and Christine Kovic. 1996. "The Reconstitution of Hegemony: The Free Trade Act and the Transformation of Rural Mexico." In *Globalization: Critical Reflections*, ed. James H. Mittelman, 165–185. Boulder, Colo.: Lynne Rienner.

Nash, June C., and Kathleen Sullivan. 1992. "Return to Porfirismo: The Views from Mexico's Southern Frontier." *Cultural Survival Quarterly* 16(2): 13–17.

O'Gorman, Frances. 1983. *Base Communities in Brazil: Dynamics of a Journey*. Rio de Janeiro, Brazil: FASE-NUCLAR.

Orsi, Robert A. 1997. "Everyday Miracles, The Study of Lived Religion." In *Lived Religion in America: Toward a History of Practice*, ed. David D. Hall, 3–21. Princeton, N.J.: Princeton University Press.

Paré, Luisa. 1979. "Caciquismo y estructura de poder en la Sierra Norte de Puebla." In *Caciquismo y poder político en México rural*, ed. Roger Bartra and Eugenia Huerta. Mexico City: Siglo XXI.

Pazos, Luis. 1994. *¿Por qué Chiapas?* Mexico City: Diana.

Pérez Enríquez, María Isabel. 1994. *Expulsiones Indígenas: Religión y migración en tres municipios de los Altos de Chiapas: Chenalhó, Larrainzar y Chamula*. Mexico City: Claves Latinoamericanas.

Pérez López, Enrique. 1990. *Chamula: Un pueblo indígena tzotzil*. Tuxtla Gutiérrez, Mexico: Gobierno del Estado de Chiapas.

Peterson, Anna L. 1997. *Martyrdom and the Politics of Religion: Progressive Catholicism in El Salvador's Civil War*. Albany: State University of New York Press.

Peterson, Anna L., Manuel A. Vásquez, and Philip J. Williams, eds. 2001. *Christianity, Social Change, and Globaliztion in the Americas*. New Brunswick, N.J.: Rutgers University Press.

Pineda, Luz Olivia. 1993. *Caciques culturales: El caso de los maestros bilingües en los Altos de Chiapas.* Puebla, Mexico: Altres Costa-Amic.

Pitarch, Pedro, and Julián López Garcia, eds. 2001. *Los derechos humanos en tierras mayas: Política, representaciones y moralidad.* Madrid: Sociedad Española de Estúdios Mayas.

Pollis, Adamantia. 2000. "A New Universalism." In *Human Rights: New Perspectives, New Realities,* ed. Adamantia Pollis and Peter Schwab, 9–30. Boulder, Colo.: Lynne Rienner.

Pozas, Ricardo. 1952. *Juan Perez Jolote.* Mexico City: Fondo de Cultura Económica.

Procuraduría General de la República. 1998. *Libro blanco sobre Acteal, Chiapas.* Mexico City: Talleres Gráficos de México.

Ricard, Pablo. 1987. *Death of Christendoms and Birth of the Church.* Maryknoll, N.Y.: Orbis Books.

Rivera Farfán, Carolina. 1998. "La diaspora religiosa en Chiapas, notas para su estudio." In *Chiapas: El factor religioso.* Mexico City: Publicaciones para el Estudio de las Religiones.

Robledo Hernández, Gabriela Patricia. 2003. "Protestantism and Family Dynamics in an Indigenous Community of Highland Chiapas." In *Women of Chiapas: Making History in Times of Struggle and Hope,* ed. Christine Eber and Christine Kovic, 161–170. New York: Routledge Press.

Robledo Hernández, Gabriela Patricia. 1987. "Disidencia y religión: Los expulsados de San Juan Chamula." Undergraduate thesis, Escuela Nacional de Antropología e Historia, Mexico City.

Rolland, Miguel. 2000. "On Maya War Captives, Blood Sacrifices, Decapitations, and Other Contemporary Catholic Conundrums in San Juan Chamula." Paper presented at the Annual Meeting of the American Anthropological Association in San Francisco, Calif., November 18.

Rosenbaum, Brenda. 1993. *With Our Heads Bowed: The Dynamics of Gender in a Maya Community.* Albany: State University of New York Press.

Rostas, Susanna. 1999. "A Grass Roots View of Religious Change amongst Women in an Indigenous Community in Chiapas, Mexico." *Bulletin of Latin American Research* 18(3): 327–41.

———. 2003. "Women's Empowerment through Religious Change in Tenejapa." In *Women of Chiapas: Making History in Times of Struggle and Hope,* ed. Christine Eber and Christine Kovic, 171–187. New York: Routledge.

Ruiz García, Samuel. 1978. "Conferencia ecuménica sobre derechos humanos y anuncio misionero en medio indígena." *Christus* 43(51): 33–36.

———. 1993. *En esta hora de gracia: Carta pastoral.* Mexico City: Ediciones Dabar.

———. 1999. *En búsqueda de la libertad.* Interview by Jorge Santiago Santiago. San Cristóbal de Las Casas, Mexico: Editorial Fray Bartolomé de Las Casas.

Ruiz García, Samuel, and Javier Vargas. 1972. "Pasión y resurreción del indio." *Estudios Indígenas* 2(1): 35–48.

Rus, Diane. 1990. *La crisis económica y la mujer indígena: El caso de Chamula, Chiapas.* San Cristóbal de Las Casas, Mexico: INAREMAC.

Rus, Jan. 1983. "Whose Caste War? Indians, Ladinos, and the 'Caste War' of 1869." In *Spaniards and Indians in Southeastern Mesoamerica: Essays on the History of Ethnic Relations,* ed. Murdo MacLeod and Robert Wasserstrom, 127–168. Lincoln: University of Nebraska Press.

———. 1994. "The Communidad Revolucionaria Institucional: The Subversion of Native Government in Highland Chiapas, 1936–1968." In *Everyday Forms of State Formation and the Negotiation of Rule in Modern Mexico,* ed. Gilbert M. Joseph and Daniel Nugent, 265–300. Durham, N.C.: Duke University Press.

———. 2002a. Afterword to Gary Gossen, *The Four Creations: An Epic Story of the Chiapas Maya,* 1019–1026. Norman: University of Oklahoma Press.

———. 2002b. "The Struggle against Indigenous Caciques in Highland Chiapas: Dissent, Religion, and Exile in Chamula, 1965–1977." Paper presented at Caciques and Caudillos in 20th Century Mexico Conference, Oxford University, September 19–21.

———. 2004. "Revoluciones contenidas: Los indígenas y la lucha por Los Altos de Chiapas, 1910–1925." *Mesoamerica* 46: 57–85.

Rus, Jan, and George A. Collier. 2003. "A Generation of Crisis in the Central Highlands of Chiapas: The Cases of Chamula and Zinacantán, 1974–2000." In *Mayan Lives, Mayan Utopias: The Indigenous Peoples of Chiapas and the Zapatista Rebellion,* ed. Jan Rus, Rosalva Aída Hernández Castillo, and Shannan L. Mattiace, 33–61. Lanham, Md.: Rowman and Littlefield.

Rus, Jan, and Salvador Guzmán López, eds. 1996. *Chamulas en California/ Jchi'iltak ta Slumal Kalifornia.* San Cristóbal de Las Casas, Mexico: INAREMAC.

Rus, Jan, Rosalva Aída Hernández Castillo, and Shannan Mattiace, eds. 2003. *Mayan Lives, Mayan Utopias: The Indigenous Peoples of Chiapas and the Zapatista Rebellion*. Lanham, Md.: Rowman and Littlefield.

Rus, Jan, and Robert Wasserstrom. 1981. "Evangelization and Political Control: The SIL in Mexico." In *Is God an American? An Anthropological Perspective on the Missionary Work of the Summer Institute of Linguistics*, ed. Soren Hvalkof and Peter Aaby, 163–172. Copenhagen: International Working Group on Indigenous Affairs.

Scheper-Hughes, Nancy. 1992. *Death without Weeping: The Violence of Everyday Life in Brazil*. Berkeley: University of California Press.

Schirmer, Jennifer. 1997. "Universal and Sustainable Human Rights? Special Tribunals in Guatemala." In *Human Rights, Culture, and Context: Anthropological Perspectives*, ed. Richard Wilson, 161–186. London: Pluto Press.

Second General Conference of Latin American Bishops. 1979. *The Church in the Present-Day Transformation of Latin America in Light of the Council, II: Conclusions*. Washington, D.C.: Secretariat for Latin America, National Conference of Bishops.

Servicio Paz y Justicia (SERPAJ). 1996. *Amatán y Xi'Nich': La Lucha no violenta Continúa por la paz con justicia*. Mexico City: SERPAJ.

Sider, Gerald. 1993. *Lumbee Indian Histories: Race, Ethnicity, and Indian Identity in the Southern United States*. Cambridge: Cambridge University Press.

Siverts, Henning, ed. 1973. *Drinking Patterns in Highland Chiapas: A Teamwork Approach to the Study of Semantics through Ethnography*. Bergen, Norway: Universitetsforlaget.

Smith, Christian S. 1991. *The Emergence of Liberation Theology: Radical Religion and Social Movement Theory*. Chicago: University of Chicago Press.

Sobrino, Jon. 1978. *Christology at the Crossroads*. Maryknoll, N.Y.: Orbis Books.

Speed, Shannon, and Jane Fishburne Collier. 2000. "Limiting Indigenous Autonomy in Chiapas, Mexico: The State Government's Use of Human Rights." *Human Rights Quarterly* 22(4): 877–905.

Spivak, Gayatri Chakravorty. 1988. "Can the Subaltern Speak?: Speculations on Widow Sacrifice." In *Marxism and the Interpretation of Culture*, ed. Cary Nelson and Lawrence Gossberg, 271–313. Urbana: University of Illinois Press.

Stavenhagen, Rodolfo. 1988. *Derecho indígena y derechos humanos en América Latina*. Mexico City: El Colegio de Mexico, Instituto Interamericano de Derechos Humanos.

Stephen, Lynn. 1991. *Zapotec Women*. Austin: University of Texas Press.

————. 2002. *Zapata Lives! Histories and Cultural Politics in Southern Mexico*. Berkeley: University of California Press.

Sullivan, Kathleen. 1995. "Reestructuración rural-urbana entre los indígenas chamula en los Altos de Chiapas, México." In *La explosión de comunidades en Chiapas*, 69–96. Copenhagen: International Working Group on Indigenous Affairs.

Taylor, William B. 1979. *Drinking, Homicide, and Rebellion in Colonial Mexican Villages*. Stanford, Calif.: Stanford University Press.

————. 1987. "The Virgin of Guadalupe in New Spain: An Inquiry into the Social History of Marian Devotion." *American Ethnologist* 14(1): 9–33.

Tejera, Héctor. 1991. "Vivir para creer." *México Indígena* 19: 18–22.

Tickell, Oliver. 1991. "Indigenous Expulsions in the Highlands of Chiapas." *Newsletter of the International Working Group for Indigenous Affairs*.

Todorov, Tzvetan. 1984. *The Conquest of America: The Question of the Other*, trans. Richard Howard. New York: Harper and Row.

Traer, Robert. 1991. *Faith in Human Rights: Support in Religious Traditions for a Global Struggle*. Washington, D.C.: Georgetown University Press.

Turner, Victor W. 1992. *Blazing the Trail: Way Marks in the Exploration of Symbols*. Tucson: University of Arizona Press.

Vélez-Ibañez, Carlos G. 1983. *Rituals of Marginality: Politics, Process, and Culture Change in Urban Central Mexico, 1969–1974*. Berkeley: University of California Press.

Verrillo, Erica, and Duncan MacLean Earle. 1993. "The Guatemalan Refugee Crafts Project: Artisan Production in Times of Crisis." In *Crafts in the World Market: The Impact of Global Exchange on Middle American Artisans*, ed. June C. Nash, 225–245. Albany: State University of New York Press.

Wasserstrom, Robert. 1977. "Ingreso y trabajo rural en los Altos de Chiapas." San Cristóbal de Las Casas, Mexico: Centro de Investigaciones Ecológicas del Sureste.

————. 1983. *Class and Society in Central Chiapas*. Berkeley: University of California Press.

Watanabe, John M. 1992. *Maya Saints and Souls in a Changing World*. Austin: University of Texas Press.

Wilson, Carter. 1973. "Expression of Personal Relations through Drinking." In *Drinking Patterns in Highland Chiapas: A Teamwork Approach to the*

Study of Semantics through Ethnography, ed. Henning Siverts. Bergen, Norway: Universitetsforlaget.

Wilson, Richard. 1995. *Maya Resurgence in Guatemala: Q'eqchi' Experiences.* Norman: University of Oklahoma Press.

————, ed. 1997. *Human Rights, Culture, and Context: Anthropological Perspectives.* London: Pluto Press.

Wolf, Eric R. 1955. "Types of Latin American Peasantry: A Preliminary Discussion." *American Anthropologist* 57(3): 452–471.

————. 1982. "The Vicissitudes of the Closed Corporate Peasant Community." *American Anthropologist* 14: 325–329.

Womack, John Jr. 1999. *Rebellion in Chiapas: A Historical Reader.* New York: New Press.

Index

elders and, 80, 198n.10; courses for, 8, 40–41, 49, 79–80; of Diaconías, 165–167; in Diocese of San Cristóbal de Las Casas, 8, 15, 33, 40–43, 49, 70, 138, 186; number of, 8, 40, 49, 186; and peasant organizations, 60–61; role of, 40; and social networks, 154–160

Catholic Church: in Chenalhó, 26, 149–150, 154–161; conversion to, 22–29, 45, 69–70, 72, 79–80, 117–118, 147, 162, 184; and equality and justice, 123–126; and human rights, 1, 2, 8, 10–13, 15–16, 45–66, 70, 100–113, 116–120, 128–129, 182, 184–186, 190–191, 195n.9; progressive Catholicism, 10–13, 100–102, 153; sacraments of, 23, 41, 51, 72, 80, 82, 88, 89, 90, 117, 139; as universal institution, 168, 175, 185; women in, 26–27, 65; Word of God Catholics, 8, 9, 10, 15, 25–26, 33–34, 69–70, 133–135, 185, 186. *See also* Conversion; Diocese of San Cristóbal de Las Casas; Liberation theology; Vatican II (Second Vatican Council)

Caxlan (non-indigenous people), 15, 21, 23, 193n.9. *See also* Ladinos; Mestizos

CEBs. *See* Christian Base Communities (CEBs)

CELAM. *See* Conference of Latin American Bishops (CELAM)

Center for Human Rights. *See* Fray Bartolomé de Las Casas Center for Human Rights

Chamula: *caciques* in, 36, 39, 47, 69, 75–77, 94; cargo system in, 136, 137; catechists in, 33, 79–80, 82, 90, 198n.8; Catholic Mission in, 69–70, 76–82, 87–89, 184, 198n.8; chronology of key events in, 207–208; colonial period in, 71, 132–133; community development courses in, 82–83, 198n.13; Cuscat Rebellion in, 71–75, 198n.5; dangers of, 73; and Diocese of San Cristóbal de Las Casas in 1990s, 89–90; and Diocese of Tuxtla Gutiérrez, 89–90; domestic violence in, 142; elections in, 2, 75–76, 83–84; festivals

in, 2, 34, *68*, 78, 137, 138; land ownership in, 4–5, 29–30, 24, 76; municipal government in, 75–76, 82–84; Pajarito Movement in, 73–75; politics in, 9, 56, 75–76, 77, 82–85; poverty in, 4–5, 36, 77, 181, 198n.7; Protestantism in, 86–87, 190; Traditionalists in, 161; travel of Guadalupe Catholics to, 161–162, 190; unity of community members in, 71; violence in, 23, 37, 75, 81, 84, 187–190, 205n.3; work and income in, 198n.7. *See also* Expulsion (from Chamula)

Chenalhó: Acteal massacre in, 161, 189; Catholics in, 149–150, 154–161, 193–194n.10; domestic violence in, 203n.15; festivals in, 202n.9; gender relations in, 140; and peasants' right to land, 120–121; PRI in, 160, 161; Protestantism in, 154, 160, 161; rejection of alcohol in, 132, 136; and respect in families, 121; Traditionalists in, 154, 155, 158, 160; violence in, 161; Zapatistas in, 132, 136, 156, 159, 160–161

Chiapas. *See* Chamula; Chenalhó; Highland Chiapas; San Cristóbal de Las Casas

Children's deaths, 40, 47–48, 81, 126, 127, 163, 183, 201n.7

Ch'ols, 2, 55–56, 64, 80, 124, 150, 164, 169, 185

Christian Base Communities (CEBs), 110, 152, 153

CNDH. *See* National Commission for Human Rights (CNDH)

CODIMUJ (Diocesan Coordination of Women), 65

Collective (community) decision-making, 139–140

Collective (community) rights and responsibilities, 3, 71, 108, 109–110, 120–123, 129, 180–181

Collier, George, 8, 86, 163, 187, 201n.5

Collier, Jane Fishburne, 97, 116, 187, 194n.2

Colonialism, 59, 132–133, 180, 185, 195n.4

Colonias, 3. *See also* San Cristóbal de Las Casas

Community. *See* Collective (community) decision-making; Collective (community) rights and responsibilities

Conference of Latin American Bishops (CELAM), 50, 51

Constitution. *See* Mexican Constitution

Conversion: affiliation versus, 25; to Catholicism, 22–29, 45, 69–70, 72, 79–80, 117–118, 147, 162, 184; jail sentences following, 22, 27, 42, 118, 128, 144; to Protestantism, 8, 10, 27, 56, 86–87, 131, 135, 145, 161, 162; and rejection of alcohol, 24, 25, 27, 28–29, 35, 45, 131–136, 142, 147, 162; of Ruiz García to commitment to the poor, 11–12, 45–53

CRIACH (Council of Indigenous Representatives of the Highlands of Chiapas), 35–36, 89, 104, 174, 188, 200n.6

Cultural relativism, 95–98, 116

Cuscat Rebellion, 71–75, 198n.5

De La Madrid, Miguel, 6, 99, 182, 193n.5

Diaconías, 165–167, 174

Dignity: in Catholic tradition, 3, 10, 18, 100–102, 107–108, 121, 123–124, 129, 181, 200n.3; of farming, 119, 125; peace with justice and, 190–191; pilgrimage by indigenous people for, 1; and respect, 121, 147, 181

Diocese of San Cristóbal de Las Casas: and autochthonous church, 58; catechists in, 8, 15, 33, 40–43, 49, 70, 138, 186; and Chamula mission, 69–70, 76–82, 87–89, 184, 198n.8; and Christian Base Communities (CEBs), 152; chronology of key events in, 207–208; and *colonias,* 34, 35, 39–43; diocesan assemblies of, 58, 61, 196n.16, 204n.8; ecumenical work by, 163–164, 190; and Guatemalan refugees, 62–63; history of, 69–70; and human rights, 1, 2, 8, 45–66, 70, 102–113, 129, 184–186, 190–191; and liberation theology, 51–53, 58; Mass in, 33, 41–42, 158, 194n.8; ordination of indigenous deacons in, 58, 196n.17; organizational structure of, 50, 165–168, 185; Pastoral

Plan (1986) of, 61–62; pastoral project of, in 1960s, 47–53, 184; and peasant organizations, 59–62; and Política Popular (PP), 196n.18; and Pueblo Creyente (People of Faith), 1, 2, 3, 10, 64–65, 150, 164–176, 185, 204n.9, 205n.2, 205n.12; relationship between Chamula and, in 1990s, 89–90; and Zapatista uprising (1994), 65–66. *See also* Fray Bartolomé de Las Casas Center for Human Rights; Ruiz García, Samuel

Discrimination, 18, 38–39, 116, 123–124, 160

Diseases. *See* Health care and health problems

Divorce, 139. *See also* Marriage

Domestic violence, 27, 29, 37, 45, 132–136, 142–143, 147, 203n.15

Domestic work, 15, 16, 21, 22, 31, 92, 114, 118, 140, 141

Drunkenness. *See* Alcohol and alcohol abuse

Eber, Christine, 121, 132, 136, 140, 202n.9, 203n.15

Economic and social rights, 3, 61, 108, 109–110, 115, 116, 120–121, 180, 181–182, 191. *See also* Human rights

Economic conditions and economic crisis, 4–7, 15, 181–182. *See also* Poverty

Education, 14, 24, 40, 55, 75, 77, 79–80, 98, 106, 116, 141, 181, 203n.14

Ejército Zapatista de Liberación Nacional (EZLN). *See* Zapatista Army of National Liberation (EZLN)

Elections in Chamula, 2, 75–76, 83–84

Emiliano, Don, 41–42, 128, 134–135

Employment. *See* Wage labor; Work

Equality, 3, 10, 12, 101, 107–110, 123–126, 146, 150, 151, 168, 169–170, 175, 179, 180, 185, 191

Ethnic identity or ethnicity, 160, 185. *See also* Indigenous people; Interethnic relations; and specific groups of indigenous people

Evangelicals, 10, 33, 36, 39–40, 104, 119, 145, 155, 162, 194n.6, 202n.4

Exile, 15, 29, 85, 141. *See also* Expulsion (from Chamula)

Expulsion (from Chamula): Agustín's story of, 126–128, 201n.7; and Bishop Ruiz, 88; by *caciques*, 28, 69, 75, 84–85, 94, 105, 129, 194n.6; defense of, by Chamulan authorities, 85, 93, 129; denunciation of and protests against, 87–88, 124–125, 180–181, 188, 202–203n.10; events leading up to, 4, 82–85; Fernando's story of, 118; and human rights, 3, 9–10, 13–15, 84–85, 126–129; Las Ollas expulsion case, 103–107, 201n.7; Lucas and Micaela's story of, 22–25; Mariano's story of, 131; and Mateo, 35–36, 38; and Office of Indigenous Affairs, 36, 198n.15, 202–203n.3; public hearing on, 93–94; recommendation on, by National Commission of Human Rights (CNDH), 107; statistics on, 4, 85, 88, 193n.7; suffering of, 17–18, 42; violence of, 9–10, 15, 23, 27–28, 75, 84–85, 126–127, 199n.1, 200n.8, 201n.7

EZLN. *See* Zapatista Army of National Liberation (EZLN)

Farming. *See* Agriculture; *Fincas* (plantations)

Fernando, 115, 116–120, 124–125, 138

Festivals, 2, 34, 68, 78, 111–112, 136–139, 202–203nn.7-12

Fieldwork in highland Chiapas, 13–16, 180

Fincas (plantations), 4, 6, 11, 23, 26, 30, 37, 53, 63–64, 75, 118, 133, 142

Fox, Vicente, 99, 182, 183, 184

Fray Bartolomé de Las Casas Center for Human Rights: documentation and denunciation of human rights violations by, 14, 103–107, 199–200n.5, 200nn.7-8, 202n.8; founding of, 13, 54, 63; and Las Ollas expulsion case, 103–107, 201n.7; legal work of, 38–39, 103–107, 112, 113; and Mateo case, 38–39; purpose of, 63; workshops by, 107–113, 136

Freire, Paulo, 45, 48, 195nn.3-4

Gender discrimination, 111, 146

Gender relations, 28–29, 121, 132, 139–147. *See also* Domestic violence; Women; Women's rights

Globalization, 6, 9, 99, 181–182

Golochán, massacre in, 59–60, 61, 88–89, 102

González Garrido, Patrocinio, 63, 93–94, 199n.1

Gossen, Gary, 74–75, 87, 201n.7

Guadalupe *colonia. See* San Cristóbal de Las Casas

Guatemala, 6, 25, 62, 63, 96–97, 152, 153, 189

Guatemalan refugees, 6, 54, 62–63, 197n.22

Health care and health problems, 38, 39, 40, 47–48, 53, 55, 62, 77, 109, 116, 146, 183

Hernández, Father Leopoldo, 69, 70, 75, 76–83, 88

Hernández López, Agustín, 83–85, 199n.21

Highland Chiapas: chronology of key events in, 207–208; fieldwork in, 13–16, 180; map of, 5; political and economic transformations in, 4–10; progressive Catholicism in, 10–13; travel and roads in, 161–162. *See also* Chamula; Chenalhó; San Cristóbal de Las Casas

Housing, 22, 36, 37, 42, 183

Human rights: anthropological perspective on, 94–98, 116–117; Biblical readings on, 101, 110; and Catholic Church, 1, 2, 8, 10–13, 15–16, 45–66, 70, 100–102, 103–113, 116–120, 128–129, 182, 184–186, 190–191, 195n.9; and community, 108, 109–110, 185; conceptualization of, by indigenous people, 3, 107–113, 116, 180–184; and cultural relativism, 95–98, 116; defense of own rights by indigenous people, 111, 112, 113, 124–125, 150, 168–171, 179–181, 190–191; and dignity, 10, 18, 100–102, 107–108, 200n.3; and economic and social rights, 3, 61, 108, 109–110, 115, 116, 120–121, 180, 191; and equality, 108–109, 123–126; and ethnography, 3, 95, 180; and expulsion

Las Ollas expulsion, 103–107, 201n.7
Latin American Bishops Conference: of
  Medellin, 10–11, 49, 50–51, 58, 101, 184;
  of Puebla, 58–59
Leo XIII, Pope, 100, 195n.9
Levine, Daniel, 153, 165, 175–176, 185
Liberation theology, 11, 51–53, 58, 101–102,
  110, 186
López Angel, Domingo, 104, 119, 174, 188,
  200n.6
Lucas, Don, 22–29, 37, 118, 138

Marriage: and community controls on
  abandonment, 139–140, 145; and conversion to Catholicism, 27, 29, 142; and
  divorce, 139; and domestic violence,
  27, 29, 37, 45, 132–136, 142–143, 147,
  203n.15; and husband's taking multiple
  wives, 29, 34–35, 143–145; respect in, 27,
  29, 121, 142, 143, 144, 147; and Traditionalists, 35; and weddings, 41–42
Mateo, 33–39, 119, 145
Mayan languages, 2, 3, 21, 25, 33, 41, 58, 86,
  158, 185
Medellin Latin American Bishops Conference, 10–11, 49, 50–51, 58, 101, 184
Medical care. See Health care and health
  problems
Mestizos: and assimilation of indigenous
  people, 48, 70, 184; Chamula closed to,
  71, 75; and Christian Base Communities (CEBs), 152; and Cuscat Rebellion,
  73; inequalities between indigenous
  people and, 18, 108, 111, 123–124, 160,
  182, 189; Marxist critique of relationship
  between peasants and, 125–126; political and economic power of, 10, 109;
  racism of, 116; rejection of alcohol by,
  136; unity of indigenous people with,
  64, 169, 185; work by, 30, 125, 126; and
  Zapatistas, 66
Mexican Constitution: Article 27 of, 6–7,
  98, 182, 199n.3; and churches as property of state, 198n.11; classes on, for
  indigenous people, 83; and expulsion

of indigenous people from Chamula,
  88; and human rights, 93, 96, 98–100,
  105, 111, 112, 113, 128; and land, 6, 98, 182,
  199n.3; and religious freedom, 128
Micaela, 22–29, 37, 42
Migration, 6, 8, 193n.6. See also Expulsion
  (from Chamula)

NAFTA (North American Free Trade Agree-
  ment), 6, 9, 99, 181
Nash, June, 200–201nn.4-5, 201n.2,
  203n.15
National Action Party (PAN), 84, 87, 183
National Commission for Human Rights
  (CNDH), 107, 188
Neoliberal reforms, 132, 176, 181–182
Networks. See Social networks
Nonviolence, 64–65

Padrón, Father Joel, 63–64, 102–103, 165,
  197n.24
Pajarito Movement, 73–75
PAN (National Action Party), 84, 87, 183
Paramilitaries, 161, 199n.18
Paternalism, 12, 59, 78–79, 82, 88–89,
  185–186
Peasant organizations, 59–62, 182, 187, 190
Peasants: identity of indigenous people as,
  30, 119, 120–121, 125, 201n.6; Marx-
  ist critique of relationship between
  mestizos and, 125. See also Agriculture;
  Indigenous people; Land
Peones (day laborers), 30–31
Pilgrimages, 1, 10, 64, 72, 160, 165, 168–169,
  171–175, 205n.13. See also Walking
Plantations (fincas), 4, 6, 11, 23, 26, 30, 37,
  53, 63–64, 75, 118, 133, 142
Police, 14, 38–39, 63, 120. See also Jail
  sentences
Política Popular (PP), 196n.18
Political mobilization: and artisan cooperatives, 7, 190; and Catholic Church, 11;
  and pilgrimages, 1, 10, 64, 72, 160, 165,
  168–169, 171–175, 205n.13; and Pueblo
  Creyente (People of Faith), 1, 2, 3, 10,

labor by males, 4–5, 30–31, 118–119, 125–126, 140–141, 194n.3; women's work, 7, 13, 15, 16, 21, 22, 28, 31, 92, *114*, 194n.5

Xi' Nich' (The Ant), 64–65

Zapata, Emiliano, 195n.13
Zapatista Army of National Liberation (EZLN): and Catholic Church, 65–66, 161, 163–164, 197n.30; and Chenalhó, 159, 160–161, 204n.6; and Comandanta Esther, 182–184; and demand for justice before Mexico's National Congress in 2001, 182–184; and human rights, 115, 182–184, 197n.28; members of, 2, 204n.11; negotiation between government and, 100, 160, 164; and rejection of alcohol, 132, 135, 136, 146; and San Andrés Accords, 100, 183; and Subcomandante Marcos, 66, 182, 197n.28; uprising of, in 1994, 9, 15, 54, 99–100, 107, 115; women in, 146–147, 203n.11
Zedillo, Ernesto, 2, 99
Zinacantán, 4, 5, 194n.2, 202n.7